The
Family
Tree

Carole Cadwalladr

The
Family
Tree

DUTTON

DUTTON

Published by Penguin Group (USA) Inc.
375 Hudson Street, New York, New York, 10014, U.S.A.
Penguin Group (Canada), 10 Alcorn Avenue, Toronto, Ontario, Canada M4V 3B2 (a division
of Pearson Penguin Canada Inc.); Penguin Books Ltd, 80 Strand, London WC2R 0RL,
England; Penguin Ireland, 25 St Stephen's Green, Dublin 2, Ireland (a division of Penguin
Books Ltd); Penguin Group (Australia), 250 Camberwell Road, Camberwell, Victoria 3124,
Australia (a division of Pearson Australia Group Pty Ltd); Penguin Books India Pvt Ltd, 11
Community Centre, Panchsheel Park, New Delhi – 110 017, India; Penguin Group (NZ), Cnr
Airborne and Rosedale Roads, Albany, Auckland, New Zealand (a division of Pearson New
Zealand Ltd); Penguin Books (South Africa) (Pty) Ltd, 24 Sturdee Avenue, Rosebank,
Johannesburg 2196, South Africa

Penguin Books Ltd, Registered Offices: 80 Strand, London WC2R 0RL, England

Published by Dutton, a member of Penguin Group (USA) Inc.

First printing, January 2005
1 3 5 7 9 10 8 6 4 2

 REGISTERED TRADEMARK—MARCA REGISTRADA

LIBRARY OF CONGRESS CATALOGING-IN-PUBLICATION DATA
Cadwalladr, Carole.
The family tree / by Carole Cadwalladr.
p. cm.
ISBN 0-525-94842-2 (hardcover : alk. paper)
1. Pregnant women—Fiction.   2. Mothers and daughters—Fiction.   3. Human genetics—
Fiction.   4. Married women—Fiction.   5. Grandmothers—Fiction.   6. Scientists—Fiction.
7. Secrecy—Fiction.   I. Title.
PS3603.A+F+
813'.6—dc22   2004052756

Printed in the United States of America
Set in Adobe Garamond
Designed by Francesca Belanger
Figures 1, 3, and 8 by Mark Stein Studios

*To my family. For everything. But especially
for not being Monroes.*

Part One

beginning *n* **1** : time at which anything begins; source; origin

1.1 **fate** *n* **1** : power predetermining events unalterably from eternity **2** : what is destined to happen **3** : doomed to destruction

THE CARAVAN entered our lives like Fate. Although from the outside, it looked like a Winnebago.

It appeared one morning in our driveway, an alien spaceship from a planet more exciting than our own. Inside, there was a miniature stove with an eye-level grill, and a fridge that was pretending to be a cupboard. Tiffany and I, experienced sniffers of nail-polish remover, stood on the threshold and inhaled the slightly toxic smell of new upholstery and expectation. I was eight years old and susceptible to the idea that technology could change your life. They said so in the TV ads.

I have a photograph from that day. We're standing in the driveway, smiling, certain, shoulders locked together in a single row. It reminds me of one of those Soviet posters from the thirties: the Family Monroe, brave pioneers of a new type of holiday, proudly facing the future together. The sun is making me squint, and my mother must have blinked, because her eyes are shut, but otherwise I'd say we looked happy.

The caravan itself is blurred in the picture. A hazy beige outline that befits its semi-mystical presence in our midst. As a family, we'd never been that keen on the outdoors, generally preferring indoor activities such as playing cards or bickering. But we stood in thrall to the brave new world it represented. We'd all read the accompanying brochure and knew that the caravan allied the power of progress with the concept of free will: we would Travel in the Modern Way and Go

As We Pleased. Although we never did. We went where our mother told us, which turned out to be Norfolk.

There she is now, breaking free from the frame of the photo and walking back inside. There is a joint of pork that requires her attention, a hall carpet that must be vacuumed, a freezer compartment that needs defrosting. She tip-taps her way back up the driveway, her hair-sprayed curls bouncing up and down, a small, contented smile playing at the corners of her lips. I've never been much good at divining what goes on beyond the net curtains of her eyes, but my guess is that she is thinking about the new fitted kitchen that will one day be hers. I can sense beige Formica units and a built-in oven hovering just beyond the field of my perception.

Am I exaggerating the role of the caravan in our family history? Or embellishing it? I'm not sure. Alistair's the one who believes in fate, although he calls it "genetic predisposition." But then he has his reasons for this. I'm more skeptical, I'll admit. But then, as you'll see, I have my reasons for this too.

Alistair's my husband. But perhaps you've heard of him already. Alistair Betterton? The author of *Destiny's Child: Nature Versus Nurture in the Age of the Genome*? If you look on page seven of the first edition, you'll find me. "To my darling wife," it says. I didn't make the second edition, but apparently this was due to lack of space.

If I wasn't married to Alistair, I suspect that I'd tell this story differently. But I know what I know. He showed me a gene map once. It was like a temperature chart or a rainfall map, with Europe portrayed as colored contours. It showed how populations have merged and blended, how you can track the passage of people across continents by the DNA left behind in the cells of their descendants. That's you, Alistair said, and me. We are a sum of the past. Don't you mean we are the sum of *our* past? I said. No, he said, we're the sum of other people's pasts. We're made up of other people's genes. We're the bits they leave behind.

And it's true, I have my grandmother's skin (sallow) and my mother's hair (mouse). But I can't blame them for what happened. I can't blame anybody. Or at least I can't blame anyone other than myself. I, Re-

Figure 1. **Patterns of Genetic Inheritance**

becca Monroe, take full responsibility for most of what happened. And the rest? I put it down to chance. Poor timing. Bad luck. It's not a fashionable theory, but then this was the seventies. It's probably best to try and leave fashion out of it.

1.2　　**family** *n* **1** : a fundamental social group in society typically consisting of one or two parents and their children

"Missionary position," said Lucy. "Name given by amused Polynesians, who preferred squatting to the European matrimonial. Libel on one of the most rewarding sex positions."

We were lying on her parents' bed, leafing through the pages of our latest discovery.

"Who's Polly Neezhuns?"

Lucy looked up, her dark hair swinging around her face, and shrugged.

"Croupade. Any position in which he takes her squarely from behind; i.e., all rear-entry positions except those where she has one leg between his or is half turned on her side. See Cuissade."

There was a pause as we both tried to configure this in our minds.

"What does it say under Cuissade?"

We both pronounced it Cue-is-aid. They didn't teach French at Middleton Primary School.

"Cue-is-aid," said Lucy, enunciating the words carefully. She was using her newsreader-announcing-the-unemployment-figures voice. "The half-rear entry position, where she turns her back to him and he enters with one of her legs between his and the other more or less drawn up: in some versions she lies half turned on her side for him, still facing away."

We stared at the picture accompanying this particular passage in the book. The illustration was smudgy and drawn by hand, but there was definitely a man with no clothes on. He seemed to be holding some sort of broom pole. It was rude, that much was sure. Possibly very rude. Poor Lucy. I felt a pang of pity for my cousin, for it was in her parents' bedroom, specifically her father's, Uncle Kenneth's, sock drawer, that we had found the book. She didn't seem to mind though. She was already flicking to the next section on "Coitus à la Florentine."

"Looooooooooooooooooooooocy!" Aunty Suzanne had a good pair of lungs on her, and although we were two flights up and separated by several doors, we jumped up, covered our find with Argyle wool socks and sprinted downstairs, arriving breathless in the kitchen.

"Yes!" We appeared under Aunty Suzanne's elbow.

"Ooh, you startled me. Do you want some milk and cookies?"

"Yes please!"

Aunty Suzanne arranged a liberal quantity of chocolate-chip cookies on a plate and poured us a glass of milk. I couldn't help thinking that America was probably a lot like this. At our house they were called "biscuits" and kept in a tin that was strictly off-limits.

"So?" said Aunty Suzanne, who was always trying to take an interest in her daughter's development. "What have you girls been up to?"

We looked at each other.

"Nothing."

"Oh! Nothing at all?"

Aunty Suzanne looked at us expectantly through a pair of large round glasses. She had the same long dark hair as Lucy, although she covered hers with an orange silk scarf, tasseled at the edges. Of all the different kinds of mothers who waited at the school gates, Aunty Suzanne was by far the most exotic.

"Just playing," said Lucy. "Ripping stuff!"

Aunty Suzanne narrowed her eyes.

"I hope you haven't been reading those books again, have you?"

We looked at each other guiltily. How did she know?

"You know I don't approve of all those old-fashioned boarding school tales. They're terribly reactionary."

"No," said Lucy, although of course she was lying. Aunty Suzanne had a blacklist of authors that included Rudyard Kipling, Enid Blyton and Ivy Compton-Burnett. Lucy, naturally, had made it a point of honor to read them all, acquiring a devotion of the kind that I suspected only samizdat literature could inspire. I had been weaned on *The Jungle Book* and *The Secret Seven* and had never once been tempted to say "ripping."

When we'd finished our milk, we played our new favorite game: studying the dictionary.

"**Missionary** *n* **1** : one who is sent on a mission, especially one sent to do religious or charitable work in a territory or foreign country **2** : one who attempts to persuade or convert others to a particular program, doctrine or set of principles; a propagandist."

We looked at each other blankly. What did that have to do with anything? We returned, again, to the well-thumbed entry for "sex."

"**Sex** *n* **1** : the property or quality by which organisms are classified as female or male on the basis of their reproductive organs and functions **2** : females or males considered as a group **3** : the condition or character of being female or male **4** : the sexual urge or instinct as it manifests itself in behavior **5** : sexual intercourse."

Lucy cross-referenced to "**intercourse** *n*" although we'd done this before and knew it wasn't going to get us anywhere. "**1** : dealings or communications between persons or groups **2** : sexual intercourse."

What a ridiculous concept a dictionary was! It was a wonder we knew the meaning of anything. We spent hours cross-referencing between entries but, somehow, the truth always eluded us. It was six o'clock and time to go home.

"Bye-bye, Lucy! Bye-bye, Aunty Suzanne!"

"Just a minute, Rebecca." My aunt caught me by the door and licked shut an envelope. "Give your mother this, would you? And say we'd be delighted if she and your dad could make it."

"Yes, Aunty Suzanne. Bye, Aunty Suzanne."

"You can just call me Suzanne you know."

"Yes A— *Suzanne*."

I turned and ran off down the driveway.

"Bye, Aunty Suzanne. Bye, Lucy."

When I arrived home, Tiffany was hanging around the kitchen looking moody. Her sulk, now in its second full day, was showing no sign of diminishing. We'd been getting ready to go to school the day before when our mother called us excitedly. I had my toothbrush in my mouth and Tiffany was combing her hair, but we followed her into the lounge, where the television set was switched on. This was in the days before breakfast TV, so we knew immediately that something was up.

"Look, girls!" Our mother was waving excitedly at the television. "It's an Historic Occasion!"

A woman in a peacock blue jacket was talking to the camera. Her blouse was tied into a big bow at the neck, and she spoke very slowly, a bit like the way Mrs. Price at school talked to Steven German, who came from what our mother called a "broken home" and had once wet his pants in PE.

"It's Britain's first ever lady prime minister!"

We both gazed solemnly at the television.

Tiffany stamped her foot. Her Clarks sandals sank silently into the pile, her protest thwarted by the orange and brown swirls of our lounge carpet.

"But I wanted to be Britain's first lady prime minister!"

I looked at her, impressed. I hadn't even realized that Britain had lacked a lady prime minister.

"A lady prime minister!" said our mother. "Who ever would have thought it?" She sniffed. "Of course, it's the children I feel sorry for."

Tiffany marched out of the room and slammed the door. She was tall for her age and had a habit of throwing her head back that made her seem taller still. I followed her up the stairs and onto the landing.

"You could be the second lady prime minister," I pointed out. She glared at me.

"Shut up, Rebecca! Who'd want to be second?"

She stomped into the bathroom. I shrugged my shoulders and went back to my room. But then, I was a youngest child. I was used to coming second.

My mother was toiling over her frying pan when I handed her Aunty Suzanne's envelope and we opened it together.

> *Dr. and Mrs. Kenneth Edwards*
> *At Home*
> *Saturday June 16, 1979, 1pm*
> *The Old Parsonage*
> *Middleton*
> *RSVP*

It was printed on thick cardboard, and the words were engraved in golden ink with curlicues and baroque squiggles, the A in "At Home" its finest swirl. At the top, in brilliant blue ink, it said, "Mr. & Mrs. James Monroe & family."

"Well! It's all right for some!"

But she hummed and smiled and tried to pin it to the cork notice board (ousting a timetable for upcoming PTA meetings). She struggled for a moment trying to pierce the card with a pin, but it was simply too thick and had to stand on the breakfast bar instead, propped up against the sugar bowl. There was a sudden hiatus in the preparation of our dinner (frozen beef burgers and chips, it was a bit of an off night for my mother, and she wouldn't be happy if she knew this particular menu was being recorded for posterity).

"Whatever am I going to *wear?*" she exclaimed.

I looked around but there was only me in the room. It was hard to imagine that my mother was really soliciting my advice. Nevertheless I gave the matter careful consideration before replying.

"Why don't you wear your red dress with the silver buckle?" My mother had what Granny Monroe called a "tidy" figure, and in her red dress with her hair up, she looked like one of the efficient secretary types they had on ITV sitcoms. She narrowed her eyes at me.

"I don't *think* so, Rebecca."

"Mum?"

"Hmm."

"Mum? Do we have to send out cards when we stay at home?" I stood waiting but she'd turned her attention back to her frying pan. The reply never came. But then when did they ever?

"Coitus à la Florentine," said Lucy. We were sprawled across the genuine New England patchwork quilt of her parents' bed and I was seeing how long I could hold my legs in the air. Lucy stumbled over the words, but there was no mistaking that at least half of them were rude.

"Intercourse with the woman holding the man's penile skin forcibly back with finger and thumb at the root of the penis and keeping it stretched all the time," said Lucy. "Excellent way of speeding up ejaculation, and greatly boosts intensity of male sensation if you get the tension right."

She paused for breath and I swallowed hard. I understood only one word in ten, but it was enough to remind me of my only previous encounter of a sexual nature: when I'd watched *Love Story* on the television and Ryan O'Neal's woollen hat had rubbed against Ali MacGraw's in a provocative manner.

Lucy, because her father was a doctor, but mostly because she liked to be right, claimed to have superior knowledge in all matters pertaining to everything. "Kenneth told me," she'd say if I tried to dispute one of her more unlikely claims, such as the assertion that if you swallowed chewing gum it stuck to your heart or that the sun could give you cancer. Lucy didn't call her parents Mum and Dad. She called them "Kenneth" and "Suzanne," which I found bizarre and unnatural. Lucy did know a lot, though; this was undisputable. She'd garnered certain information from her cousin Elsa, on the other side of the family. Elsa had told Lucy that if you hit her in the chest, her breasts felt like two sharp stones; that there was no such thing as Santa Claus; and that Suzanne and Kenneth enjoyed the benefit of an open marriage.

"Open?"

"Elsa says Suzanne says she doesn't want to succumb to the constraints of petit-bourgeois morality."

"Oh." I looked at Lucy, impressed.

Naturally we studied our reference materials, poring over the pages of the dictionary together. We looked carefully at all the entries under "open" but it didn't make any sense.

"Open to suggestions?" said Lucy.

"Open all hours?"

"Open or shut?"

"Open sesame!"

In the end we gave up and played Connect 4 instead.

"Mum?"

It was a Saturday morning and we were sitting around the breakfast bar. My mother seemed to be trying to ignore me. She was reading *Woman's Own* and I jiggled up and down in my seat in front of her, but she turned her head the other way.

"Mum?"

"Mum?"

Finally, she turned a page in her book and said, "Hmm?"

"What's an open marriage?"

My father rustled the paper. My mother hesitated then lifted her head.

"I *beg* your pardon?"

"What's an *open* marriage? Is it different from a *closed* marriage?"

She was wearing her Reactolites, and as she turned her head, her face moved from shadow to sunlight. The glasses darkened. Her eyes vanished.

"*Who* on earth has been putting such ideas into your head?"

"Nobody. I was just wondering." I was beginning to suspect this wasn't such a good idea after all. In our house there was a general rule that questions weren't given a direct answer if an indirect one would suffice.

"Aunty Suzanne and Uncle Kenneth have an open marriage."

My father dropped the *Daily Mail*.

"Well!" said my mother.

I hesitated.

"Aunty Suzanne doesn't want to succor petty morality."

Was that right? I was suddenly unsure.

"Doesn't she now? Well that wouldn't surprise me! A leopard doesn't change its spots!"

My mother liked her proverbs, trusty family heirlooms handed from one generation to the next, made shiny with use. She took off her Reactolites and started cleaning them with a piece of paper towel.

"She's got a nerve. I'll say that for her."

My father coughed, picked his newspaper back up, and from behind her copy of *Woman's Own*, I saw my mother raise her eyebrows at him. What neither of them realized was that this exchange of information cut both ways. Lucy, at that moment, was informing her own mother that Aunty Doreen wore a Playtex twenty-four-hour girdle in bed.

1.3 annotate *vt* : furnish with notes

I WATCHED *Love Story** again the other day. I wanted to remember how we thought falling in love was meant to be. The sex, I have to say, was disappointing: all soft lighting and cut-away camera work. I'm an academic now (of sorts), so footnoting is what I do. To understand my story, you need the cultural references—the historical circumstances— you need to remember what the late seventies were like.

It wasn't all wearing moon boots down to the disco and driving Ford Capris. But people tend to forget that. They forget the silent Sundays, the early closing hours, the fat unfunny comedians cracking racist jokes while your dad sharpened the knife to cut the Sunday roast.

Maybe that wasn't the seventies. Maybe that was childhood. Or the suburbs. I can't say. I've never been back. My seventies—The Long Seventies, I think I'll call them—ended on July 29, 1981. The day my mother died.

Do I need to annotate Alistair and me? Probably. We're one of those couples you meet and think, Well I'd never have put them together. I don't think there's much of a resemblance to Erich Segal's *Love Story,*

**Love Story (1)*

"Told in flashback, this is an uncompromisingly sentimental love story between two star-crossed lover-students—Oliver Barrett IV (Ryan O'Neal) and Jenny Cavalleri (Ali MacGraw).

"The box-office smash hit of 1970 begins with Oliver reflecting on his past: 'What can you say about a twenty-five-year-old girl who died? That she was beautiful and brilliant? That she loved Mozart and Bach, the Beatles, and me?'

"Their love triumphs despite their very different backgrounds. He is a 'preppie' and heir to the Barrett millions. She is the daughter of a poor but loving family of Catholic immigrants.

"The film's most memorable moments are the scenes in which they frolic in a wintry-looking Harvard—kissing and playfully tossing snowballs at one another.

"After overcoming many obstacles, Jenny goes for a pregnancy test only to be diagnosed as terminally ill with a terrible but unspecified disease. She dies in Oliver's arms in a tear-inducing finale as the award-winning musical score builds in the background."

all things told, but I'm going to borrow the structure anyway. Love stories, after all, follow certain conventions. Boy meets girl, boy marries girl, boy and girl live happily ever after. You know the kind of thing.

Love Story (2) Part 1

What would the award-winning musical score be? The Happy Mondays, perhaps? Or Jimi Hendrix? It was a student party, so it could have been anything really. For we were star-crossed lover-students too. And Alistair was drunk.

The party was being thrown by Alistair's friend John, in a student house with posters of James Dean on the wall and Indian bedspreads across the ceiling. I'd brought a bottle of Bulgarian Cabernet Sauvignon and was drinking it out of a plastic cup, clenching my teeth and trying not to notice the metallic edge.

Alistair was standing in the corner of the room. I noticed him because he seemed to be staring at me. I saw him take a swig of his wine and then he walked over.

"I could smell you from the other side of the room," he said. I looked at him. I'd vaguely seen him around before but we had never actually met. He was doing some sort of science, I knew that. The party was full of them. Scientists. The type that got up early to cycle off to their labs.

"That's not the greatest of lines, you know."

"It's your pheromones. They're saying that you want to have sex with me."

I changed my mind. It was quite a good line.

"You must have mistranslated. They actually said, 'Oh God. I can't believe you've brought me to a party full of scientists.'"

He came closer, swaying slightly, and looked down my top.

"You're ovulating."

His face was only inches away and I could see his freckles, the pores of his skin, his eyelashes, the flashes of yellow in the pupils of his eyes.

"Your body is saying you want to have sex with me; it just hasn't communicated that fact to your mind yet."

Actually, it had. Alistair was tall, with rumpled sandy-colored hair. When he smiled, his lips actually turned up at the corners. More importantly, he appeared to fancy me.

"Man is the only mammal who conceals ovulation," he said. He sounded so sure of himself. That was attractive too.

"I thought it was women who ovulated generally."

Alistair wouldn't be put off. He had a point to make.

"Chimps, baboons, apes, they all advertise it. They show that they're ready for sex. Their vulvas swell up or their bottoms go red. In man, ovulation is concealed. Paternity is therefore always in doubt. It's a way of making men stick around just in case the child is theirs."

"And I thought scientists were boring," I said. "When actually they're such good conversationalists."

He'd laughed at that. Although he'd laughed even more when I'd told him I was doing Cultural Studies.

The funny thing was that he was right. I must have been ovulating. Otherwise how would I have got pregnant?

1.4 Theories of Relativity (1)

WE'RE ALL LINKED. Connected in some way, although sometimes it's hard to know exactly how. Take me and Tiffany.

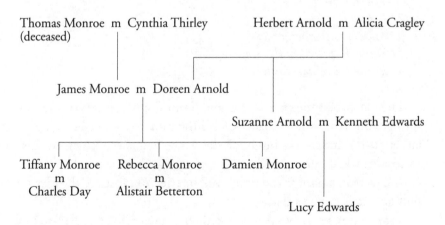

Figure 2. **The Monroe Family Tree**

There, right next to each other. I'm not sure how you'd account for that.

Tiffany is my sister. My *older* sister. I've always considered that significant, although Alistair says it makes no difference. He says that the idea that birth order influences personality is pseudo-scientific hogwash, so perhaps it makes no difference. Apart from the fact that she always gets her own way and always has.

I've been married to Alistair for nearly a decade, so I've absorbed certain information over the years. He's a behavioral geneticist. Deoxyribonucleic acid, DNA, that's his thing, but also alleles, exons, introns, ribosomes, eukaryotes, transgenic mice, dyzgotic twins, nematopoietic stem cells and recombinant clones. It's his secret language. LUCA—the Last Universal Common Ancestor—Jansky's nomenclature, homologous chromosomes, the Kruppel gene, the huckebein gene, the Wolf-Hirschhorn gene. Find a gene and you can name it. Unravel a fragment of life and it's yours forever.

There are people who spend their whole lives looking for genes. They're the big-game hunters of our times, although they use microscopes rather than double-barreled shotguns. Alistair has a tendency to sneer at them, but I suspect that's a professional thing.

How to Find a Gene for a Trait

1. *Take a fruit fly.*
2. *Expose it to an X ray.*
3. *Mate it with another fly.*
4. *Study the defects of the progeny.*
5. *Isolate the mutated gene.*

He's described the process for me. From the mutations of the offspring, you have to track back to find the mutated gene. The child is father to the man. You hunt for the gene that's been changed, distorted, knocked out.

We were in a park at the time. And he tried to illustrate the idea by pulling petals out of a daisy.

"Say that is a gene you've knocked out." He pulled out a cluster of petals to leave a hole.

"I know that game," I said. "'He loves me, he loves me not.' Lucy and I used to play it when we were children."

He frowned at me and placed another daisy over the top of the first. "And pretend this is the progeny of the daisy with a hole." He began to pull out petals at random. I was trying hard to follow.

"Can you see?"

"I think so," I said.

"You see this other flower, the 'child,' has a mutation. But you can work out what's missing, what should be there, from the 'parent.' It's not really like that, but do you get the idea?"

I nodded although I didn't, not really.

"It's not a very good example," he said. "But you have to work in reverse. It's the science of the missing gap. You can see a thing clearly only by the shape it leaves behind. From the effect that is produced by it not being there."

"Like my mother?"

I watched him pulling petals out of the daisy and waited for a reply.

"That's different," he said eventually. I caught the edge of exasperation in his voice. "It's science, not emotion."

I shrugged my shoulders and watched him pull out the last remaining petal. He loves me not. Although possibly I'd miscounted.

1.5   **family** *n* **2** : two or more people who share the same goals and values

MY MOTHER NEEDED a party outfit and had spent days planning a solo shopping expedition before deciding, at the last minute, that it would be "fun" if Tiffany and I came too. It was uncertain, at this point, what form the "fun" would take. Her preparations were as thorough as ever. She was wearing her comfort-fit Scholl's with the bobbles on the sole, and the same grimly determined expression she used for bleaching the toilet bowl after Grandpa Arnold had been to visit.

We followed her through five boutiques and one department store, were told off for loitering, and reprimanded for fiddling with the hangers, all before we'd even entered our first changing room. My mother was carrying a stack of different clothes and had started to look agitated. It was already 2.30 P.M. The first outfit she tried on was an Indian print cotton dress, with two tassels at the neck, and a thin floaty skirt that came almost to the ankle. Tiffany and I exchanged uncertain glances. It was hard to imagine its existence in Beech Drive. She was making strange expressions with her lips in the mirror and checking out her reflection from several angles.

"Is that . . . 'hippie'?"

It was a new word and I used it hesitantly because my mother had a habit of saying, "That's a long word, what does it mean?" and if you couldn't answer precisely and immediately, you were scorned and mocked and thrown to the family wolverines (Tiffany and, if she was around, Granny Monroe). There was no interrogation, however. She shrugged off the dress, glared at me, then decided to let it go.

The next outfit was a long-sleeved purple dress, belted tightly at the waist and buttoned to the neck.

"It's very with-it, of course," she said, twirling in front of the mirror and making pouty faces at her reflection. She had a small, pert nose that wrinkled uncertainly as she scrutinized herself. "I don't know. It's not very sexy, is it?"

I may have been only eight years old but I wasn't born yesterday. It was the sort of question that only a fool, or possibly my father, would have attempted to answer. I took refuge in the communal changing area instead, poking my head under the heavy gray curtain that separated the cubicles.

I'd stumbled into Hell. It was an inferno of heaving, quivering humanity that smelled of armpits and hormones and fear. I regarded the body parts with horror: there were legs and arms and bottoms and bosoms in every corner. Everywhere there were women struggling into clothes, struggling out of clothes, pinching stray pieces of flesh, sucking in their breath to make their stomachs disappear, sighing in disappointment as zips failed to zip and buttons pinged. Portions of dimpled flesh were pinioned into strange and unnatural positions by a multitude of straps and elastic. There were a bewildering variety of undergarments on display. One woman was wearing a belt that looked like a medieval torturing device I'd once seen on a visit to Warwick

Castle. And there was a smell of something in the air that I recognized from Beech Drive but couldn't place at first. It was anxiety, I think. Or, possibly, Cacharel's Anaïs Anaïs. As I turned my head, a woman in a petticoat grimaced at the mirror, her face hollowed out by the fluorescent strip lighting. It was an expression I'd not see again until much later in my educational career when Mrs. Howarth put a transparency of *The Scream* by Munch on the overhead projector.

I ducked back into the cubicle and lay on the carpet and stared at the ceiling tiles while my mother struggled into a two-piece beige safari suit that she teamed with a sheer viscose orange shirt that had long rounded collars.

"Ta-da!"

She swirled for Tiffany (I suspected I was being boycotted on account of the hippie remark).

"You look lovely!" said Tiffany, who had already computed that the likelihood of her acquiring a new dress was in some way related to what passed behind the curtain of the cubicle.

"It is rather marvelous, isn't it?" said my mother, sucking in her stomach and standing on tiptoe. "Of course, I'll have to think very carefully about accessories."

"Of course," said Tiffany, flashing her most winning smile, a near-clone of the one my mother would use later on my father as she deposited her shopping bags on top of the breakfast bar.

After a flurry of activity at the cash register, it was off to the children's department, where in an ecstasy of indecision, Tiffany eventually chose a long maroon skirt that came with a matching sleeveless jacket (that my mother called a "gilet") and hung down to the floor, giving her a commanding air, as if she was about to host a television show or throw a dinner party. I, on the other hand, headed straight for a floor-length purple polyester dress with smocking and light pink frill that cost £9.99 and refused to countenance any alternatives. The dress was placed between layers of tissue paper.

We were on a roll now and my mother was starting to pick up speed. She bought a pair of sunglasses that made her look like an owl, an orange hat with a large floppy brim, and in a last sprint through Stead & Simpson ("Quick! They're closing!"), she made a lunge for a pair of tan open-toed high-heeled sandals without trying them on. We returned home, triumphant, buying fish and chips en route because my mother said she was too tired to cook, and besides, the day had a celebratory feel that no one wanted to end. Even my father looked happy to see his wife flushed and excited and talking him through the trials of our day in town: the exigencies of the new multistoried car park, the desperate hunt for a matching orange lipstick and the panic when she thought she'd run out of checks.

"But we didn't buy Dad anything!"

I looked up at my father.

"Don't be silly!" said my mother, rounding up sauce bottles and pieces of cutlery. "He's got plenty of things he hasn't got the wear out of yet."

We ate our fish and chips off warmed-up plates (I preferred them straight from the newspaper but my mother claimed this was common), and as a special treat, we were allowed to eat it in front of the television.

It was a repeat of *Man About the House*,* which Tiffany and I thought was rather risqué on account of the fact that Chrissy, the blond woman, liked to wander around in a towel for much of the pro-

---

* *Man About the House*

"First aired on ITV in 1973, *Man About the House* (and its American remake, *Three's Company*) was perceived as groundbreaking in its treatment of what has come to be called the 'alternative family.'

"The first episode featured Chrissy and Jo cleaning up the morning after a farewell party for their ex roommate and finding a drunken man asleep in the bathtub. Robin is a handsome bachelor who is studying catering at the local technical college, and once the girls discover that he is looking for somewhere to live, they offer him the vacant bedroom.

"In the seventies, however, two single women living alone with a single man was unacceptable to the vast majority of society, here represented by the Ropers, the girls' landlords who live downstairs. In an inversion of the closet principle, Chrissy, therefore, informs the Ropers that Robin is gay.

"It was the first time mainstream television had grappled with the new social structures created by the so-called 'permissive society'; the comedy is a by-product of the clash between the ideologies of the right and those of the new generation of 'swingers.' However, by doing so within the constraints and parameters of the situation comedy, the 'threat' is effectively neutralized and rendered titillating but ultimately nonsexual."

gram owing to the fact that she was always on the point of getting into, or out of, the bath, and the man was always trying to look up it. I laughed along at the jokes although I wasn't always sure I got them. The man was allowed to live with the two girls because they pretended he was "not that way inclined."

"What way inclined?" I asked my mother.

"What?"

She was flicking through a copy of *Woman* and looked up briefly.

"Which way is he not inclined?"

She hesitated for a moment and looked at my father. He frowned and then burrowed his head into the newspaper.

"I've really got no idea what you're talking about," she said eventually.

"Mum?" said Tiffany, turning away from the television.

"Hnn?"

"Who's the oldest? You or Suzanne?"

"I am."

"So you're like me, and she's like Rebecca?"

"Well, I've never really thought of it like that," she said, looking up. "But yes, I suppose you're right."

"What was Aunty Suzanne like when she was younger?"

"Pushy!"

"Doreen!" Our father looked up from his paper.

"Well she was! She still is. Pushy and affected. She wasn't always Lady Muck, you know. Not until she went off and married Kenneth. I don't know where she gets all those airs and graces from. She's got ideas above her station, has Suzanne."

She'd started clearing the plates, scraping off the remains of the tartar sauce with vicious little swipes, dissipating the mood of family contentment to the far corners of the room.

"Right! You two can wash up before you go to bed. And make sure you rinse them properly." She slammed the living room door shut, in case we were still in any doubt that she was in a bad mood.

1.6 The Scientific Method

ON THE FIRST TUESDAY of every month, I go to Alistair's department. I am weighed and measured, a sample of my blood is taken, and a series of carefully worded questions is addressed to me.

It was Alistair's idea and, in the end, I agreed.

"It's for a good cause," he said. "We *have* to have volunteers; it's the only way we can test our theories. It's not my study if that's what you're worried about. It's a different branch of genetics."

I looked at him doubtfully. "Yes, but why me?"

He stared at me, surprised. "You're *perfect* for it!"

And for a moment, I'll admit, I felt flattered.

"Particularly with *your* family history!"

He said it with a certain excited fervor. I should have known there'd be a catch. I turned my back so he couldn't see my face and twisted on the hot tap. Steam rose from the sink. I could feel it warming my face, turning my cheeks red, condensing as drops on my eyelashes. I stood quite still waiting for the sink to fill.

If you ask Alistair about his childhood, he'll say it was happy. If you ask him about his genes, he can point to the fact that his father is a professor and his mother is the ladies' captain of the local tennis club. They take evening classes together and go on self-improving holidays. Alistair believes we're vehicles of our genes. He believes that our environment plays almost no role in how we turn out. But I can't help thinking it was an intellectual choice. That it was arbitrary. That it could have gone either way.

I washed the dishes, methodically scouring them and rinsing them under the tap.

"You've gone very quiet," he said eventually.

I took a plate from the foam and let the hot water run over it. "Busy day."

"Oh," he said, turning his attention back to the papers stacked high on the kitchen table. "For a moment there, I thought you were upset about something."

·   ·   ·

On the first Tuesday of every month, I go and drink tea from a plastic cup and read ancient issues of *Woman* and *Cosmopolitan* and wait to be calibrated by a team of researchers. I'm not sure what they're investigating. Alistair didn't tell me, and I didn't ask. Sometimes, I think it's easier that way.

I have become a subject of scientific inquiry. I know about the "scientific method." It's one of the very few things I remember of my schoolgirl science.

The Scientific Method

1. *Observe. Examine the details. Note the facts. Detail. Scrutinize.*
2. *Hypothesize. What theory could account for the facts?*
3. *Experiment. Test your hypothesis.*
4. *Evaluate the results.*

He believes that by this method you can arrive at the truth. It's a tempting theory, although I'm not convinced that it works. Or at least, it didn't for me. You never know what piece of information is missing, until it's found.

The scientific method relies upon empirical evidence. I still like to consult the dictionary so I looked it up. (**empirical** *a* **1** : based or acting on observation or experiment **2** : regarding sense data as fact **3** : deriving knowledge from experience alone) Alistair uses it in the first sense. Based or acting on observation or experiment. Whereas strictly speaking, I think the third meaning is the truest. You derive knowledge from experience alone. Or, at least, I did. I derived knowledge from experience alone.

1.7   **dream** *vi* **1** : to have visions of, believe possible

MY FATHER TRIPPED over the ironing board for the second time in five minutes.

"It's like backstage at the London Palladium in here," he said, although nobody took any notice of him. There was more important business in hand. Billows of perfume and hair spray clung to the air, and items of clothing had been strewn around the lounge. ("It's a sitting room! How many times must I tell you that?") My mother was wearing curlers and a slip and had started berating inanimate objects ("Call yourself a hairdryer!" "Where does the sewing basket think it's got to?") until she spotted my father wearing an old pair of corduroy trousers. "For God's sake, James! Try and smarten yourself up!"

He looked down at himself in bewilderment. My mother always managed to look neat and composed no matter what. She said that there was never a good excuse for not wearing a properly ironed blouse. But creases collected around my father like hairs around the bathroom drain; his shirts had a habit of crumpling or sticking out the back of his trousers or being buttoned up the wrong way. He stood unsure what to do until my mother marched him upstairs into the bedroom and picked him out a pale blue V-neck sweater and a pair of beige slacks.

"Look at your hair!" she said, grabbing a comb from the bathroom shelf. He stood miserably in front of her like a dog who'd just been told it was bathtime. She tugged at the comb and tutted loudly. His hair had grown longer recently and curled over his collar. "I really can't think what's wrong with a good old-fashioned short back and sides," she said. "Everybody will think you're becoming some sort of beatnik."

I went to watch Tiffany getting ready, to see if I could pick up any beauty tips. She had inherited my mother's way with clothes and looked almost regal in her skirt and matching vest. She was fussing with her hair, having spent all morning trying to straighten her curls. She had washed it, and then blow-dried it with our mother's hairdryer. She had even stolen some of her hairspray. "Is she?" they said on the ads. "Or isn't she?" Tiffany was. You could tell. Her hair had gone sticky and the strands were all clogged together. It didn't stop the curls from reappearing though. Tiffany's hair was her only flaw. She had creamy, perfect skin, long black curly lashes and lips that were much redder and fuller than mine. But her hair let her down. It was black. It frizzed. Half an hour after being dried, it had curled back into itself. Nobody else in the family had her problem. Our hair encompassed every shade of mousey brown, from light mouse (me) to dark mouse (my father) taking in mid-mouse (my mother—although she called it "ash blond").

Mine was newly washed too and slippery to the touch. I'd combed my fringe over my forehead, trying my best to cover it. It was too high. My hair started too far back; it made my face look moony. I looked in the mirror and sighed, cheering up only when I put on my magnificent new dress and began to track my mother from room to room wondering when we would be ready to go. In the hallway, we came across Tiffany wearing lipstick and eye shadow. My mother stopped in her tracks.

"You'd better clean that muck off your face right now, young lady," she said through a thick haze of foundation, powder and bronzer.

Tiffany skulked back to her room. I trailed in her wake.

"You'll all be sorry one day," she said and threw herself onto her bed.

"Sorry for what?"

"When my true identity is discovered."

Tiffany was an avid reader of mildewed Edwardian hardbacks that had been hoarded by our mother from her own childhood and was modeling her current personality on *A Little Princess*. She had been forced to live in the attic of Miss Minchin's Select Seminary for Girls because of some mix-up over her true identity.

"I'm probably a princess. And when I'm discovered, I'll live in a castle."

I rarely doubted Tiffany, but even I tended to think this was an unlikely scenario.

"But, if you're a princess, then I would be a princess too! I'm your sister!"

She hesitated. She could always trump me with the power of her logic and the fluency of her rhetoric.

"Shut up, Rebecca," she said.

The doorbell rang. *Ding Dong!*

"Who on earth?" said my mother. She was applying a third layer of hair spray to her curls, a task that required her fullest concentration. "Make yourself useful and get that will you, James?"

Reluctantly, he went to the door and opened it.

"It's Gloria from next door."

My mother threw down the canister in exasperation. "Gloria? We're awfully busy. We're just off to a party at the Old Parsonage."

"Ooh, I say!"

"It's going to be quite a do. *Apparently*, they've got outside caterers in."

"The Kennedys did that at their party last month at the Old Barn. Were you invited to that one? I don't believe I remember seeing you there."

My mother glared at her. A false smile played at the edges of her mouth. "Is there anything I can help you with, Gloria?"

"Not to worry, it can wait. Just you have a lovely time now, won't you?" And she walked back out the door, leaving my mother muttering under her breath and stabbing at her eyes with her mascara wand.

I had recently become aware that some sort of caste system operated in Middleton, but its rules were complex, its codes unfathomable.

There were some simple rules of thumb: the bigger your house, the better you were. Oak Avenue was more exclusive than Beech Drive; Beech Drive more than Sycamore Close.

And then there were the Old houses. The Old Parsonage, the Old Schoolhouse, the Old Vicarage, the Old Rectory. The past was a religious time. Although now the buildings were filled with ruffled curtains and thick-pile carpets and the vicar lived in a semi down the road from us and made desperate appeals for the Heating Fund from his pulpit.

I understood this much. It was the exceptions that confused matters. There were anomalies. Us, for example. As a rule, people with trees in their address didn't mix with people with Old in their address. And most people's aunts and uncles lived in Barnstaple or Chesterfield, while ours were just down the road.

There were other exceptions too. Mrs. Browning, who was married to Mr. Browning (he was something big in British Petroleum), made a point of being nicer to Lucy than she was to me, inquiring after her parents, soliciting information about her well-being (they were both Olds). Whereas the Grahams treated us all the same. And, according to my mother, they were as "rich as Croesus." They didn't mind whom their daughter Theresa brought home.

"The more the merrier," they said, which threw my mother into high sniffery. "Nouveau," she said. "You can tell it a mile off."

We were almost ready. There were some last-minute adjustments in the hall mirror and I stamped my feet impatiently. My mother tilted her hat and placed her owl glasses on her head. I looked at her afresh.

"You look like Deirdre Barlow!" I said. "In *Coronation Street.**"

"Do I?" said my mother and gave me a small, simpering smile. "Well, then. Let's go!"

We walked down the road, self-consciously parading our finery through the streets of Middleton. Down Beech Drive, into Sycamore Close, up Oak Avenue, until we left behind the streets of modern, white semidetached houses with their patches of front lawns and family cars parked in the driveways. We reached the point where the road became suddenly more rural as we passed the pub and the church and turned into a road sheltered by tall trees and guarded by a wrought-iron fence.

There were dozens of cars parked in the driveway. We pressed the bell. It was a deeper, more sonorous chime than our own. We listened to the sounds of the party coming from deep within the house. I hopped from foot to foot until, finally, Uncle Kenneth came to the door. He looked very dapper. His hair was black and graying at the temples in a manner that my mother called "distinguished." At his throat he wore a burgundy silk cravat.

---

*Coronation Street

  "First shown in 1960, *Coronation Street* is the longest-running soap opera on British TV, regularly watched by almost one third of the British population. Its audience is predominantly female, older, and generally from lower socio-economic groups (Sonia Livingstone, *Making Sense of Television*, 1990).

  "In common with other soaps, relationships are more important than plot and female characters more important than male. It is this, in part, that has contributed to the genre's lack of prestige within the critical establishment.

  "While characters act according to the limits of their knowledge, viewers are omniscient. They know more than any single character can. Viewers can thereby engage in informed speculation about possible turn of events. Tania Modleski (*Loving with a Vengeance: Mass-Produced Fantasies for Women*, 1982) argues that the structural openness of soaps is an essentially 'feminine' narrative form."

"Ah Doh-Reen!"

"Kenneth!"

My mother gave him her full simper, and they kissed each other twice on the cheek as if they were foreign, or dying.

"And James! Do come in."

"Frightfully good of you to invite us," said my mother to Uncle Kenneth.

"Hello, Doreen," said Aunty Suzanne.

"Suzanne," said my mother briskly as she walked past her sister and into the house.

I ran into the back garden to find Lucy. She was feeding sausage rolls to the neighbor's dog, Charlie, a wire-haired Jack Russell.

We both loved animals. I tickled Charlie under the chin while he swallowed his fifth sausage roll. My mother wouldn't allow dogs in our house on account of the fact they were unhygienic, shed hair on the furniture and couldn't be relied upon not to embarrass you in front of the neighbors. She always averted her eyes in the street when we saw one doing its business. Particularly if it was a he-dog.

Lucy tossed Charlie a sixth sausage roll. She was wearing wide-legged trousers and a stripy top. I was beginning to think that perhaps my purple-frilled dress hadn't hit quite the right note. My mother was evidently having a similar pang. She was eyeing Aunty Suzanne's outfit: a long Indian-print dress not dissimilar to the one she had tried on during our shopping expedition.

"What an *interesting* dress."

Aunty Suzanne looked surprised and gave it a disdainful tug. "This old thing? I've had it for years."

"Really? I do think ethnic is such a *tricky* look to pull off effectively."

Aunty Suzanne looked as if she was going to say something but then changed her mind and turned away. As she did, a shaft of sunlight shone through the Indian print. It illuminated the unmistakable contour of a braless breast. I held my breath. My mother had not not-worn a bra since she was thirteen, and had decided opinions on women who "let it all hang out." "Trollops," she usually called them, although sometimes they were "sluts." I'd looked up both words in the dictionary and had cross-referenced to "**prostitute** *n* : woman who sells her body."

"Does your mother sell her body?" I asked Lucy. She was still stroking Charlie but had moved on to a tray of anchovy toasts.

"She's too old. Kenneth says she's passed her sell-by date."

Charlie seemed to hiccup. Then, in one swift movement, he deposited a yellowish stream of undigested sausage rolls and anchovy toasts over the patio tiles. I couldn't say I blamed him. Anchovy was one of those things adults pretended to enjoy, like Stilton, or coffee or Sundays. He looked at us for a moment, wagged his tail, and then started to lick it up.

"Oh well," said Lucy, walking quickly away. "Let's get a Coke."

We went over to the drinks table, where she expertly wielded the ice tongs and filled our glasses. Carrying them carefully, we went inside.

Tiffany was in the kitchen looking imperious. Her new outfit had effected some sort of change in her personality. Ever since she'd put it on, she'd begun to behave as if she was in a breakfast cereal commercial or auditioning for a part in *Jesus Christ Superstar*.

"Look," she said, pointing to an object on the counter. "It's a Deluxe Kenwood Soda Stream. Recommended retail price, £10.99."

Tiffany made a point of studying the Argos catalogue and sometimes got me to test her. In years to come, she would beat us all hands down on *The Price Is Right*.

Aunty Suzanne appeared at the door. "Would you girls like to help with the vol-au-vents?"

Tiffany swept forward. "I would, Aunty Suzanne!"

She was using the voice she reserved for when she was especially trying to ingratiate herself with a grown-up.

"You can call me Suzanne, you know."

"I would, Suzanne!"

"Super!" said Aunty Suzanne.

"Super!" said Tiffany.

Aunty Suzanne turned to pick up a plate. Tiffany turned and picked up a plate. Aunty Suzanne spun on her heel. Tiffany spun on her heel.

"Suzanne? Were you and Mum alike when you were young?"

Aunty Suzanne looked up from her vol-au-vents and seemed to consider her reply.

"Alike? Well, I think you could say that we've always been *different*."

"Mum says that you've changed."

Aunty Suzanne put down the plate and pursed her lips.

"Well she would say that, wouldn't she?"

We all stood and wondered what this meant. Aunty Suzanne was looking beyond us at a point in the middle distance, although possibly it was her cork-lined notice board.

"Your mother wasn't interested in a career. She wanted to find a rich man to marry."

"But Dad isn't rich!"

Tiffany looked almost hurt by the suggestion.

"We'd live in a detached house if he was!"

Aunty Suzanne shrugged and gave a small almost-smile. "No. But your mother thought he was going to be."

Tiffany cast her eye around my aunt's impressive array of up-to-the-minute gadgets and built-in appliances.

"So, did you marry for money, Suzanne?"

Aunty Suzanne exhaled heavily and put down her plate. "No, Tiffany. I fell in love with a hippie. And ended up married to a man who plays golf." She shrugged her shoulders. "Life doesn't always work out like you think it will, you know."

How did it turn out then? It was one of those things no one would tell you. When I'd say to my mother, "Will I look like Farrah Fawcett-Majors when I grow up?" she'd just snort and say, "In your dreams."

Outside, there was a throng of people on the terrace. The party had divided into unmistakable camps. By the buffet, my father was talking to Mr. Sullivan from the Old Schoolhouse about the merits and demerits of the Ford Cortina, while Uncle Kenneth's medical colleagues from work had gathered by the drinks table. Their wives congregated at the side and swapped notes on their outfits. They wore pretty floral dresses, and when Aunty Suzanne swept past, she said "Drones" under her breath. She had joined the ladies from her women's group underneath the oak tree. They had a coffee morning once a month at the

Old Parsonage, from which men were banned, although it didn't stop Uncle Kenneth from referring to them as "Hags United."

There he was now, circling with a bottle of white wine, his silk burgundy cravat flopping dejectedly to one side.

"Hello, Rebecca."

"Hello, Uncle Kenneth!"

He hesitated, as if another question was required but he wasn't quite sure what it might be.

"Are you having a nice time?"

He looked at me expectantly, as if I was going to leap over the goldfish pond or turn into a toadstool. But then, like most fathers, Uncle Kenneth didn't seem to know what you were supposed to do with children. We didn't play golf or bridge. This left him without obvious conversational gambits.

"Yes, thank you!"

Lucy appeared at my elbow. "Kenneth?"

"Yes, Lucy."

"What's sexual intercourse?"

I gasped and cast my eyes to the ground. But Lucy just stood and stared at her father, daring him to answer.

"Well, it's . . . it's something. It's when a man and a woman love each other very much."

"What? Like marriage?"

"Well, yes, sort of, that's right."

"So if you're not married you can't do sexual intercourse?"

"Lucy, I don't really think this . . ."

"Or you can do sexual intercourse but only with a married person?"

She'd done it. Lucy always managed to push things too far.

"Why don't you ask your mother? She's the expert."

A roar of laughter erupted from underneath the oak tree. Uncle Kenneth shifted his weight onto a different foot.

"Better push off," he said, exiting patio left. "Don't want to be accused of being an oppressor again."

Lucy and I turned our attention back to the party, watching the adults for clues. We did as they did and stood in our best clothes, sipping our Cokes. Was this it? We waited for the moment when the fun would kick in, but nothing happened. We hovered for a moment or two longer, then gave up, sprinting toward the oak tree and scrabbling for our familiar handholds. For the second time that day, I considered that my purple dress might have been a mistake. It kept on riding up, and when I hung off the second branch up, it flipped over my head.

I somersaulted back around and checked to see if anybody noticed. The chatter continued undiminished. I was walking discreetly away when Mr. Sullivan appeared at my elbow.

"Pink ones, eh?"

My cheeks flushed with embarrassment. Although luckily Mr. Sullivan didn't seem to mind.

"Jolly good. Jolly good," he said, patting me on the bottom. "Why don't you try that tree over there?"

I ran off, my face burning, taking the path past the fishpond and along the side of the house. The noise of the party was louder now. Somebody had put on the record player and dragged it onto a windowsill. A few of the women had kicked off their shoes and started dancing. The sun was hotter, the shadows longer. I sat down on a bench and considered my shame. Was I a trollop? A slut? A prostitute?

Tiffany appeared next to me. I wondered if she had heard about the underpants incident. There'd be hell to pay if my mother found out. She always put on a dressing gown over her nightie when the doctor came to visit, and said that no one had ever accused her of putting her prime cuts on display. Tiffany had other matters on her mind, however. She just put her fingers to her lips and said, "Sssshhh!"

I followed her gaze and there was my mother, so perhaps I was safe after all. She was having some sort of heated conversation with Kenneth, although she didn't play golf or bridge either. Her hair seemed to have slipped over to one side of her head. I felt a pang of pity for her because she must have spilled something on her shirt too, as Kenneth was patting it clean.

I turned to Tiffany. "What are they doing?"

Tiffany rolled her eyes. "You're such a baby. You never understand anything."

She was right enough about that. I'd never understood why Tiffany seemed to reserve her most virulent displays of hatred for me. We were sisters! She was supposed to love me. I knew this for a fact. I'd seen it on the television.

"Why don't you just go and play with your dolls?" she said, saying "dolls" as if it was "cow pat" or "dog-sick." "Why don't you just go and play with your *dog-sick?*"

We didn't arrive home until it was dark, after the summer light had finally leached from the sky and been replaced by stars that winked as we walked back down the long, twisting drive, along the road, and down Oak Avenue. Pools of orange from the streetlights guided us now as we turned in to Sycamore Close and up Beech Drive. It took us almost twice as long to reach home as it had to walk to the party. My mother was giggling, although, as she wasted no time in telling us, her feet were killing her, the fault of the impulsively purchased tan open-toed sandals that had left red angry welts across her ankles. Back at home, we gathered in the kitchen and switched on the electric kettle.

"I'm ready for a cup of tea, I can tell you that." She sighed contentedly. "Thinks she's lady of the manor, she does. All those airs and graces."

"Hmm," said my father.

"Just because she lives in a big house, she thinks she's the bee's knees, she really does. Poor Kenneth! He has to sew his own buttons on, you know."

"Mum?" asked Tiffany. "Did you like Suzanne's dress?"

"*Ugh!* Wasn't it awful? She's really let herself go. But then, I never could see what he saw in her."

"Mum?" I said.

She was sitting at the table massaging her toes.

"Mum?"

"Hmm?"

"Why don't you like Aunty Suzanne?"

She stopped massaging and looked up. "Whatever gave you that idea?"

"Well, you always . . . I thought . . ."

"Of course I *like* her, Rebecca. She's my sister."

I studied her carefully, trying to follow her logic. Tiffany was my sister after all. It was hardly what you'd call incontrovertible evidence.

"We just have . . . different values, that's all."

My father made a noise that sounded like a grunt. Or possibly a snort. My mother's head spun in his direction.

"Sorry, James. What was that?"

"Nothing, my dear."

She looked at him suspiciously for a moment and then said, "My God, is that the time?"

According to the kitchen clock, it was eleven o'clock.

"*Bed! Now!*"

Although it was a different sort of "*Bed! Now!*" from usual. Mock, as opposed to actual, horror.

That night, I wrapped my continental quilt around me, relishing its novelty. (My mother had held out against them longer than anyone else on Beech Drive on the grounds you couldn't get a proper hospital corner with them.) I fell asleep and dreamed of owning a dog called Charlie who fetched sticks and cleaned up after himself.

The next day, Tiffany told me she'd had a dream too.

"So did I! It was abou—"

But she didn't give me a chance.

"I was Cinderella!" She looked triumphant. "And my father came back to claim me!"

I thought about telling her about Charlie and the sticks but realized it wouldn't be any good. Tiffany always had to trump me. Even in her dreams.

1.8 The Fruit Fly

THE FAVORED OBJECT of study for geneticists is the humble fruit fly. *Drosophila melanogaster.* They like roundworms too, but for gene hunters, the fruit fly is king. You can knock out a fruit fly gene, mate it with another fruit fly and see the resulting offspring all within a two-week cycle.

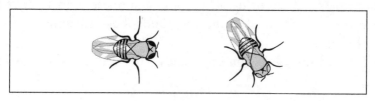

Figure 3.

Scientists know far more about fruit fly genes than they do about human genes because you can't use humans as laboratory animals.

Alistair told me this with a completely straight face. We were walking through the streets of London on the way to a party being thrown by one of his colleagues. I knew already what it would be like. Overloud conversation. A lot of references I wouldn't get. And the wives and a couple of husbands standing around and trying to make small talk about anything that didn't require a degree in science to understand.

It was late summer and still light. Alistair was talking but I couldn't concentrate. The black shirt I was wearing was too tight under the sleeves. It felt clammy against my skin. My shoes pinched.

"You can't breed a tall human with a short human," said Alistair. "Or a small-earlobed human with a large one. You can't mate them together, and you can't wait twenty years to see what offspring they produce."

"You can," I said. My thighs chafed against each other as I walked. "It's called life." Perspiration trickled down my legs. "They're called children."

Alistair, cool in a pair of chinos and a thin cotton shirt, was walking slightly ahead of me.

"But there's no control experiment. In science, you always need a control to check your observations against. In life, there's no control."

The strap on my shoes was digging into my ankle. "So, is that what you're afraid of?"

"What?"

"Losing control?"

Under his breath, I heard the faintest sigh. We'd reached the house where the party was being held. Voices and music drifted out of the open window. We stood by the steps, both of us hesitating.

"Rebecca?"

I turned to look at him expectantly. He reached out to touch my face.

"Yes?"

"You've got lipstick on your teeth."

Part Two

chance *adj & n* **1** : way things happen of themselves; fortune

2.1 Theories of Relativity (2)

I'M MARRIED to Alistair so I know what I know. Half of your genes come from your parents; another half will go to your children. One quarter came from your grandparents; another quarter will live on in your grandchildren. You, right now, are the axis that balances everything in the past against everything in the future. There's a strange but beautiful symmetry to the workings of genetics.

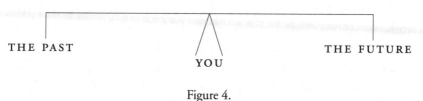

THE PAST   YOU   THE FUTURE

Figure 4.

I, Rebecca Monroe, am the hinge between my mother and my daughter; between my father and my son. I don't have any children, it's true, but a theory is a theory.

There's more though. Take this: Alistair told me about a French study that examined the genealogy of a sample of married couples. On average, it found that they shared a common ancestor, within seven generations.

Or to put it another way, if I search back through my family tree, and you search back through yours, the chances are we'll find we have a relative in common. Your great, great, great, great, great, great, great, great grandfather? He's probably mine.

This is the story of my family. But maybe I should point out that it could be the story of yours too.

Alistair would never let me get away with that, of course. He's such a stickler. I know what he'd say. We might share some of the same genes but then, we share genes with chimpanzees. And fruit flies. And yeast fungi. I'm not a scientist, though, so I shall choose to ignore this. Families, I think, are not so different.

2.2 caravan *n* & *vi* 1 : a large covered recreational vehicle; a van

WE'D SPENT MONTHS preparing for our first caravanning holiday. Every weekend my father buffed the bodywork and my mother pored over her copy of *The Good Housekeeping Guide to a Successful Caravanning Holiday* writing notes and lists and underlining certain key sections.

The vehicle itself had already caused quite a stir in Beech Drive, drawing admiring glances from the neighbors and a steady stream of visitors. Mr. Huxley from next door came round to kick the tires and ask my father complicated questions about fuel/towing ratios, while Mrs. Huxley admired the eye-level grill and apricot-soft furnishings.

We were going to Norfolk.

"It's next to the sea," my mother said. "The North Sea."

Tiffany and I absorbed this information in our own ways. Tiffany looked it up in an atlas and memorized its prime geographical details. I assumed it was next to the North Pole and wondered if I'd make friends with a little Eskimo girl.

The packing took a week. Every day, my mother drove off to the supermarket and came home with a new gadget or specialist item of clothing. There were four matching sleeping bags in royal blue with a vermillion lining, new shatterproof dishes, a kettle with a whistle on top, waterproof jackets that folded up into little sacks, and boxes of food they evidently didn't sell in Norfolk. Tins of beans, Smith's crisps, Heinz tomato ketchup—all of which were carefully packed into boxes and placed by the door.

I trailed my mother from the kitchen to the caravan and back to the kitchen again, anxious that I might be left behind. All week, the excitement mounted, reaching a thrilling crescendo the night before our departure day. I couldn't sleep. I'd never before Gone As I Pleased, and the idea filled me with strange, new desires. At some point in the night, it started raining. I smiled with satisfaction. I'd be able to wear my new waterproof jacket.

It was still dark when we got up. It was also still raining. My mother stood in the driveway waving her arms in the air as if she was marshaling 747s out onto the runway, although it was only my father laden down with suitcases and boxes and stray cans of Heinz spaghetti. Tiffany and I stood under the porch and watched. Rain dripped down our necks.

We ate a full cooked breakfast, while my mother undertook a frantic last-minute clean of the bathroom, hall and kitchen, and after some last-minute fiddling with the tow hitch, we were finally off. It was like the launch of the *QEII*. We rolled down the driveway and splashed out onto the street, waving furiously at the Huxleys next door. Our father handled the steering wheel as if it was a particularly frisky stallion, although five miles down the road we were forced to turn back to check that my mother had pulled the toaster plug out of the wall (she had).

"Right!" said my father. "Next stop Norfolk." Norfolk! Even its name sounded redolent of exotic possibilities.

As it was our first ever caravanning holiday and therefore a Historic Occasion, I had dressed festively in my blue and white sailor dress. Tiffany was wearing her Brownie uniform for reasons nobody had quite worked out.

To celebrate our successful departure, I opened my two holiday treats: a family pack of Fox's Glacier Mints and *The Waltons Big Picture Book*. Tiffany adjusted the angle of her Brownie bobble hat and dreamed contentedly of the day she would be Queen.

I became aware of a certain amount of agitation from the Front Seats.

"James! Slow down! You know I don't like it when you go over sixty!"

I buried my head in my Waltons annual and blocked my ears. I knew each of the Waltons' names plus their individual strengths and weaknesses. My favorite was Elizabeth. She was the youngest and something of a tomboy but always willing to lend a hand.

"*Not* left!" said my mother. "I meant right!"

"Well, you didn't say right, did you?"

Tiffany, who was having some sort of extended coronation fantasy (you could tell from the way she placed her Brownie hat on her head), looked at me. We both focused on the back of the two heads in front of us. My mother's ash-blond curls hair-sprayed into place were quivering slightly. On the whole she made a poor Olivia Walton.* She never wore her hair in a bun, and said that long skirts were old-fashioned.

We watched the muscles in my father's neck tense.

"Well," said my mother eventually. "There's no need to be touchy." There was a communal exhalation of breath. The moment had passed. I breathed a sigh of relief then tasted something else in my mouth. My stomach seemed to upend itself.

"Muuum," I said.

"Oh no," said my father, pulling onto the hard shoulder a split second too late. This was a pity, as it meant that the rest of the journey had to be undertaken with the windows open, and since it had started raining again, our hair went damp and curly, and a mist of drizzle shined our faces.

---

*Olivia Walton

"Olivia is the homemaker in the Walton household, 'Mama' to her tribe; a supportive wife, and a firm but loving mother.

"Broadcast through the seventies, *The Waltons*, a drama serial centered around a rural farming family, nostalgically re-envisioned an America of the not-too-distant past. Set in the 1930s, the Depression serves to bond the family ever tighter. Consumer goods are all but absent, clothes are made by hand, the church is the center of the community.

"Olivia Walton's place is 'naturally' in the kitchen; John's on the farm. By locating the program in the recent past, the show's makers were able to disseminate an ideology wholly at odds with the current political movements sweeping through the country. The program was a means of reassuring viewers of values (family, God, marriage) that outside the confines of the program were steadily being eroded."

"Mum? Is Nanna common?"

"Is that road the A311?"

"Mum, is she?"

"What?"

"Granny Monroe said Nanna is common. Is she?"

"I beg your pardon? Are you talking about my mother, Alicia?"

I hesitated. "I was only asking."

"Yes, well, little girls should be seen and not heard. You ought to remember that."

"Sorry."

"She's my mother, Rebecca, although it's true that she could have tried to make a bit more of herself. But then, she never really cared about getting on. I'm the one who's had to do that."

My father, who had spent most of the journey in silence, concentrating on the steering wheel and the gap in the condensation on the windscreen, coughed and then cleared his throat as if he was about to speak. This was unusual enough for us to stop talking and listen.

"Rebecca, it's not polite to call people common."

"But that's what Granny Monroe said!"

"Well, that doesn't mean it's right."

There was a silence while we thought about this. My mother made a noise that was somewhere between a harrumph and a ha!

"There's nothing wrong in bettering yourself."

There was a silence while our father appeared to think about this.

"There is if it's at the expense of other people."

My mother sniffed. "Well! Hark at him!"

Tiffany didn't say anything. She'd already told me she thought Nanna was common. This was because she was from the North.

"Left! Left!" My mother was holding the map and gesticulating vigorously. I looked up as we rounded a gatepost. A long streak of beige paint trailed in our wake.

It was still raining. What was more, there were no polar bears. Instead, there was a wetland bog crisscrossed with campers in brightly colored waterproof jackets, their bodies folded over against the wind.

"Well!" said my mother, with a cheerfulness that didn't sound wholly convincing. "We're here! What do you think of that, girls?"

It was a long time since anyone had attempted to solicit an opinion from either Tiffany or me. We looked at each other nervously.

"Great!"

"Fantastic!"

Our father turned off the engine. The only sound was the rain pitter-pattering against the roof of the car. Water streamed down the windscreen. The Hathersage End Camping and Caravanning Park disappeared from view. It was hard to consider this a pity. After a couple of minutes, he turned the engine back on. Perhaps so that we could all keep some kind of fix on reality. My mother decided to apply a layer of orange lipstick. If anybody had asked her, she would have described it as "vivacious." No one asked.

"Well," said my father finally. "I suppose I'd better go and find out where our site is."

"Yes, James! That would be a good idea!" My mother's brightness was beginning to unnerve us. Her fingernails, painted pearlized pink in anticipation of our holiday, were performing a complicated drumroll on the dashboard. Our father valiantly struggled with the door, threw his camel-colored car coat over his head and made a dash for the Nissen hut that served as the Reception.

He was waving a scrap of paper when he came back. "Number 58!" he said, getting back into the car, droplets of rain clinging to his hair and neck. "Righty ho!"

The road through the field was Tarmaced and not unlike Beech Drive, with caravans rather than semidetached houses and white picket fences rather than hedges. We drove slowly, scattering multicolored campers before us, pulling up eventually at a tiny sliver of mud in between a VW campervan and the communal rubbish bins.

"Doreen, you'd best get out and direct me in." My mother looked as if she was about to argue with this, but then seemed to think better of it. As daintily as she could, she exited and picked her way through the mud. Our father gripped the wheel and revved the engine. Tiffany and I shuffled forward onto the edge of our seats. The plastic upholstery farted.

My mother stood in the gap and made helicopter motions with her arms, railing at the wind and rain. My father shifted the gears into reverse and turned the wheel. The caravan made straight for the VW campervan.

"The other way," screamed my mother at the unlistening wind, her words already halfway across the North Sea, en route to Denmark. *"Turn the wheel the other way."*

Years later, when Tiffany Monroe had become a successful lifestyle journalist with her own weekly column, it was this particular holiday that would shine through the mists of forgetfulness. It was burnished in the retelling, turned sepia with time. A golden family caravanning holiday from an era when families went on holiday together. Maybe that was what she was thinking about now, her face turned away from the window, her eyes averted.

And me? I'd returned to Walton Mountain.

It might have been a holiday, but the strict gender zoning laws of life still applied. My father, naturally, was in charge of the technical side. He was the one who had toured the showrooms collecting brochures and testing foam mattresses, while my mother's area of operational command was, of course, the kitchen.

"Feet!" she yelled as our father attempted to come in from the rain and remove his shoes. He balanced on a corner of the doorway. Tiffany and I watched in silence. It was a delicate operation and although he managed to pull one shoe off and flick it underneath the caravan, the other fell limply to the floor. We watched as the nylon fibers of the carpet sucked the mud and rain into its apricot maw. An hour into our stay and my mother was on her hands and knees muttering imprecations under her breath and swearing to avenge the Hathersage End Camping and Caravanning Park on behalf of her carpet. She couldn't help herself. She Pledged, she Ajaxed, she Flashed with both efficiency and a certain panache. There was no shortage of house-proud housewives in Beech Drive but my mother was, arguably, the proudest of them all. Her kitchen floor really was clean enough to eat your dinner off.

("Mum?"

"Rebecca?"

"Can I eat my dinner off the floor?"

"I've had quite enough of you for one day, young lady!")

Later that night, when we'd finished our first celebratory meal (Chicken Surprise followed by Pineapple Chunks and Evaporated Milk), when the curtains had been drawn, the washing up had been done, and the Monopoly board had been laid across the foldout table, there was an unfamiliar sense of peace. The stove had warmed the air; the kettle whistled and the rain thrummed against the roof. It was a comforting sound. The weather was outside. And we were inside. It seemed impossible that a thin piece of steel was all that lay between us and the outside world.

I fell asleep dreaming of the Waltons, zipped into my sleeping bag as if I was a pencil in a pencil case. We stole each other's breath like cats. My family, my world, encompassed in a small metal container. I listened to the drumming of the rain. And, looking back now, I can't shake the idea that it was the beginning of the end.

2.3   **academic** *adj* 1 : of, relating to, or characteristic of a school, especially one of higher learning

THERE'S A NEW government initiative to get children interested in science, and once a month, a class of children from a local school troop into Alistair's department to see Science in Action.

He moans about it, but I know he enjoys it. I saw him once. The Scientist in Action. He was flailing his hands at them and showing off in front of the teacher.

She was young, with chestnut brown hair that fell over her face and, at intervals, had to be flicked away. We watched Alistair together, her eyes shining with admiration.

"It must be very interesting to live with someone like that," she said, turning toward me. I nodded, although I can't remember now what I replied.

. . .

He sowed a row of pea plants in terra-cotta pots on our patio the other week. It was for the schoolchildren: he was trying to repeat Mendel's classic experiment.

I watched him carefully pinning the plants onto their bamboo stakes and then drenching them with the watering can. I sat and drank a cup of too-hot coffee, enjoying the last of the day's sun.

"Poor Mendel," he said. "Nobody got it."

I stared at the sky, watching the clouds collide and blend and separate again.

"Got what?" I said eventually. He looked pleased and tapped his trowel on the pot as if he was clearing a space to speak.

"Mendel crossed yellow pea plants with green ones, tall ones with short ones, round-seeded ones with wrinkled ones. But the results were *either* yellow *or* green, tall *or* short, round-seeded *or* wrinkled."

He looked up to see if I was listening. I nodded my head.

"One characteristic simply vanished. Except it didn't. When he left them to self-fertilize, the missing parts returned in the next generation."

I wondered what I should cook for dinner.

"They thought he was talking about pea plants, and he was, but he was also talking about something else too."

I looked up.

"Isn't that a metaphor, then?" I asked hopefully. Alistair doesn't believe in metaphors. Or similes. Nothing is exactly like another thing, he says.

He hesitated.

"No, it's a perceptive failure. Mendel was the first person to discover that at the heart of inheritance, there is something hard, indivisible, nonchanging, particulate. These are things that we call genes."

He sounded like a voiceover on a BBC2 documentary. Alistair's the only person I know who speaks in complete sentences.

I watched him for a few seconds more.

"Do you ever wish you'd married a scientist?"

He emptied the last of the water from the can.

"Of course not," he said. The sun was coming from directly behind him. I put a hand to my face to shade it from the glare, but I still couldn't quite make out his eyes.

I tipped my coffee into the nearest pot and walked into the kitchen. The next day I sat and watched the leaves turn brown.

One person's fact. Another person's metaphor. Someone else's perceptive failure. Take your pick. Yesterday, some workmen came to cut down two trees in our back garden. When we moved into this flat, Matthew, the previous owner, told me about the trees. His Great Aunt Aggie and his Great Aunt Hilda had planted them.

They weren't really aunts. But it was what you called adults you knew back then. Aunties. They were maiden aunts, another forgotten concept.

This is what Matthew told me: Aggie and Hilda were sisters. In 1914, they became engaged, Aggie to Thomas, Hilda to Horace. Thomas and Horace enlisted and went to France. Aggie and Hilda waited for them. They were young, expectant, in love. For two years, every Sunday, they would walk up to Hampstead Heath. It was said that on a clear day, you could hear the guns of France from there.

In July 1916, Thomas was killed in the Battle of the Somme. A month later, Horace was blown up by a shell in the Ypres Salient.

Aggie and Hilda planted two trees. Oak trees to represent two men killed on the fields of France and Belgium, the lives they'd never lead, the children they'd never have.

I forgot to ask Matthew what happened to Aggie and Hilda, and yesterday two workmen from the council came and cut down the trees. Now there's nothing. No sign that the trees were there. No sign that Aggie and Hilda lived in our flat. Nothing left of the two men who died. What's the old adage? If a tree falls in a forest and nobody hears it . . . ?

I'm not sure but I suspect that the trees are metaphors for something, I just can't figure out what. They have no material basis in fact anymore. The only place they exist is in my head.

Memories are not facts. They are not hard, indivisible, nonchanging, particulate. Maybe Matthew made up the story about Aggie and Hilda. Maybe I did. This is my story, but perhaps I should point out that it may not all be true. It has no material basis in fact; it cannot be cross-checked or verified. In this instance the scientific method will not work.

2.4   **caravan** *n & vi* **2** : a company of travelers journeying together, as across a desert or through hostile territory

AT HOME, our family hydra split and divided and silently re-formed, finding refuge in bedrooms or armchairs or garden sheds. But in the caravan we were all together all the time. It was a new concept of space, and we weren't sure of our dimensions. Would there be room to pass? Or would we collide, smash our bumpers, knock out our side mirrors? Time was different too, stretched and compressed into odd, distorted shapes. The car journey lasted forever. The Monopoly game passed in a blur. The previous night's mood of family contentment dissipated into the Norfolk mist. It simply wasn't up to surviving the rigors of breakfast taken in confined quarters with a tide of freshly laid mud lapping at the door.

Tiffany and I squabbled over the Kellogg's Variety Pack of cereals. Our mother and father squabbled over our heads.

"You're the one who invited them."

"Oh, don't start that again."

"Don't start what again?"

"That!"

"What?"

"That!"

When I looked out of the window, I didn't see any little Eskimo girls, or polar bears, only the bleak gray light of a Norfolk summer's day and a procession of elderly family relatives.

Nanna arrived first, chaperoned by Grandpa Arnold. At least afterward everybody assumed that he was there. Sometimes it was difficult to know. There was always an element of doubt (e.g., "All the family was there, Doreen and James, Tiffany and Rebecca, Alicia and Herbert. Herbert was there, wasn't he?")

My father went to welcome them. "Hello, Alicia. And Herbert. Come on in."

"Rebecca! How you've grown! And Tiffany! Look at you!" Nanna smiled and hugged us all. It was hard not to melt under the laser beam of her approval. Even Tiffany relaxed her stiff-backed posture for a moment. (*The Little Princess* had bequeathed a lasting impact on her deportment.) Nanna lunged toward my mother to give her a hug, but my mother was holding a Tupperware box in her hands and used this to fend her off.

"Mother! Good of you to make it. And you too, Dad."

Grandpa Arnold shuffled. "Hello," he said, but his voice didn't carry. It was lost amid the apricot soft furnishings.

Half an hour later, Granny Monroe arrived wearing driving gloves and an orange head scarf. She drove herself, Grandpa Monroe having passed away in his cabbages some years before. She was a great stickler for the Highway Code, indicating and performing elaborate hand signals at startled campers on her approach.

My mother put on a fresh pair of Marigold rubber dish gloves and embarked upon a guided tour of the caravan, pointing out its architectural details (overhead lockers, modern space-saving devices, cushions that matched the curtains). This wasn't without its difficulties; she was forced to herd our visitors in front of her, a sheepdog and three confused sheep.

"Off the bench, Tiffany, I want to show them how it converts into a single divan. Look! You just remove the cushions, pull up the slats, unscrew the table and drop it down, reposition the slats, and eh valla!"

She performed this with a flourish and an imaginary wand.

"But that's not all! It also doubles as a blanket box when not in use!"

She stepped back toward the foldout table and pulled open the door opposite the kitchenette.

"And this," she said, unable to contain the note of triumph that had crept into her commentary, "is the bathroom!"

With the door open, the other end of the caravan disappeared from sight, and the unmistakable aroma of Elsan filled the air. It was a brand-new brand name in our lives, and my mother had spent the morning attempting to master its mysterious blue ways. It resided inside the plastic toilet that *thrummed* when you did your business. Worse, if you peered into the blueness you could see dark, malignant shapes floating past.

"I suppose it's a lot cheaper, isn't it?" said Granny Monroe, casting her eye around the caravan. "Than staying in a hotel."

My mother was busy arranging Dundee cake and shortbread biscuits on plates. She slapped them down onto the table.

"That's not really the point, Cynthia. It's a different sort of holiday!"

"I suppose if James had got that promotion, you'd have gone abroad, would you?"

My mother put the kettle on the stove just a touch too brusquely, and dazzled the kitchenette with her smile.

"It's the modern way. The freedom of the open road! It's not what you're used to, I suppose, is it? It's about being spontaneous."

"Ooh, yes, it's lovely!" said Nanna with a broad smile. My mother turned on her.

"Yes, well I didn't ask for *your* opinion, Mother."

Nanna coughed and looked at the floor. Tiffany and I looked up. Poor Nanna, she was always being upbraided by our mother. I felt a warm surge of solidarity for her and took her hand. We were allies from way back.

"Doreen . . . ?" said my father, looking anxiously at Nanna.

"What?"

"Nothing," he said quietly.

Nobody said anything for a moment or two, and Tiffany, sensing an opportunity, spoke up.

"Mum?"

"What is it, Tiffany?"

"Can I have a flapjack?"

"Tiffany!"

Both Tiffany and I gazed longingly at the laden plates of forbidden cakes. It looked like food! It smelled like food! Neither of us had yet mastered the Byzantine rules that governed our mother's catering arrangements.

"You can have *one* thing each. *One.* Do you hear me? You know what I've told you! A moment on the lips, a lifetime on the hips!"

She stared at her cakes and biscuits as if somebody had replaced them with the dark forms lurking in the Elsan at the bottom of the toilet. I hesitated and eventually decided on the largest slice of flapjack within reach. Tiffany, whose hand had been hovering over the shortbread, followed suit. We placed them on our plates, and guarded them carefully from outside predators. I ate mine, crumb by crumb.

Granny Monroe took ladylike sips of milkless tea and pulled in her perfectly flat stomach at precisely the same moment as my mother. They both crossed their legs, and turned to look out of the window. There was something slightly spooky about this, as if they were meerkats or Mork and Mindy.

When I looked at them together, I always thought that Granny Monroe was my mother's mother, not my father's. They looked so similar; they had the same set of the shoulders, the same trim figure, the same way of brushing imaginary bread crumbs off the tablecloth. Something occurred to me.

"Dad?"

"Hmm?"

"Did you marry Mum because she looks like Granny Monroe?"

My mother turned her eyes on me. "I beg your pardon!"

Her pupils were tiny pinpricks of disapproval. Granny Monroe was looking equally thunderous. My father shifted on his feet.

My mother stepped in to settle the matter, picking up my flapjack and putting it in the bin.

"You'll feel the back of my hand too if you're not careful!"

She glared at me, then stepped over to put the whistling kettle on the stove. We all stood up and shuffled past each other. "Sorry!" "Can I just . . . ?" Apart from me. I was the only one who was built to scale. I slipped though their ankles without them even realizing, rubbing myself catlike against their calves. In the shade of the fold-out table, I sat and thought about my flapjack at the bottom of the bin. I was surrounded by a forest of grannies' legs. Granny Monroe's were straight and thin and covered in American tan tights. Nanna's had a fold over the ankle, three strange scars, and exotic veiny blue branches, as if an elaborate underground watercourse flowed just beneath her skin.

My head bobbed up from under the table. "Nanna? Why do you have scars on your leg?"

She hesitated and folded her hands across her lap. "I was run over and broke my leg," she said, sighing. "And then I married your grandfather."

There was a cough from the other end of the caravan. Grandpa Arnold was drawn abruptly into focus. He was sitting in his hat and coat on the double bed, so absolutely motionless that he didn't appear to be breathing.

"Dad!" said my mother in astonishment. "I'd quite forgotten you were there. Dundee cake? Flapjack?"

I was drawing. It was a picture of two small girls playing ball on a yellow sandy beach with blue waves, and lots of birds. My mother was tidying.

"It's very important in a confined space to try and stay on top of it," she said. "It's why stowage is so crucial . . . !" The end of the sentence was a sharp, inward breath.

"Rebecca!" I looked up from my drawing, a felt-tip poised in my hand, my face caught between the twin emotions of surprise and fear. There, in the middle of the clean, new fabric of her apricot upholstery, was an ink stain; a black hole; something that I would one day learn is the point in the universe in which space and time collapse. She looked at it unbelieving. And then she screamed.

"Oh, Rebecca! How could you!"

It was still raining. Surely there were laws against this sort of thing? I resolved that when I was grown-up, I'd make them. Or maybe Tiffany would when she became Queen. The atmospheric conditions inside the caravan were no better. The pitter-pattering on the roof had changed in tempo and volume from *pit-ter pat-ter* to *pitter-patter, pitter-patter.* Condensation covered the windows. We were fogged in. The outside world was invisible to us. And we were invisible to the outside world.

The grannies had gone. The blue-black permanent marker stain would remain forever. Before I even had the chance to protest my innocence, my mother had slapped me twice across my thighs. The sound of it seemed to resonate in the air of the caravan. My felt-tips had been confiscated, and my pocket money stopped for an indefinite period yet to come. I glared at Tiffany, the real culprit. She looked as if she was wondering if she ought to feel guilty, but had obviously decided against it.

Ker-thwick! My mother was washing up, banging thin aluminum camping pans onto shelves. *Thwap!* She tried to crash a couple of plates together, but they were blue polyurethane picnicware and it was a muffled sort of protest. My father had retreated to the double bed at the far end of the caravan. He was reading *The Greatest Military Blunders of All Time*, and his concentration had undoubtedly been helped by the act of raising the book in front of his line of vision so that he couldn't see my mother at the sink in her new red feathery mules and matching red and white striped apron. Tiffany was practicing her autograph on her sketching pad, pages and pages of Tiffany Monroes, while I, exiled, ostracized, my legs still smarting, my cheeks still burning, was playing a solitary card game of Happy Families. I wasn't doing very well though. The cards all looked the same. I'd united Mr. Bun, the Baker, and Mrs. Bun, the Baker's Wife. But where was Mrs. Plug, the Plumber's Wife? Where was Mr. Monroe, the junior manager, and Mrs. Monroe, the junior manager's wife? Where was Miss Monroe, the junior manager's daughter?

"Mum?"

"Hmm."

"Mum? Are *we* a Happy Family?" I rummaged through the pack again, but I still couldn't find them. There was Mr. Salt, Mrs. Jump, Master Biff, Miss Brick. I lined them all up. And it was only then that I realized that the crashing of shatterproof dishes had stopped and my mother's shoulders were juddering back and forth. She'd buried her face in the tea towel as if it was an oversized hankie, and strange half-moans were emerging from its depths. Her body, which was normally so straight and certain, had crumpled in on itself. Had I missed something? What was happening? Why was I always the last to know?

The rain was a long continuous *rat-a-tat-tat-tat-tat* on the roof now. My father put down *The Greatest Military Blunders of All Time*.

"Doreen?"

But there was no reply, and before anybody had a chance to move, she flung open the door and ran out into the dark and rain. I wiped the window clear of condensation and shielded my hand around my eyes to block out the light. I could see my mother jogging in the dark, flip-flopping her way down the field, her red feathery mules, not so feathery now, throwing streaks of mud up the back of her trousers.

She was running, away from us, and toward the toilet block. Although possibly that wasn't her ultimate destination.

The next day we packed up the polyurethane picnicware, flipped down the foldout table and headed for home.

2.5 The Pathetic Fallacy

I STILL LIKE STUDYING the dictionary. Old habits die hard. As my mother would have said.

pathetic *adj* **1** : arousing pity or sadness or contempt

fallacy *n* **1** : a mistaken belief

However, if you put the words together, they mean something different. Their sum is not the equal of their parts. The words remain the same, but yoked together in a single phrase, their meaning changes. This is how genes work too. Think of "pathetic" as a gene from the mother and "fallacy" as a gene from the father. They do not blend. They do not create **a lactic half type** or **a fatal hectic ply**. Together they create the **pathetic fallacy** (*n* : the attribution of human feelings and responses to inanimate things). Or, to put it another way, a technique whereby an external factor, such as the weather, mirrors an inner state, such as the emotions.

But I've checked the weather office records. And I'm not imagining it. It was raining the morning we set off and it was still raining the day we returned. This much I know is true.

Part Three

trifle *n* **1** : thing, fact, circumstance of only slight value or importance

3.1 Theories of Relativity (3)

THIS IS THE PART of my family tree that tends to arouse the interest of the researchers in Alistair's department. If you look carefully, you'll spot the object of their curiosity. There, side by side, are Herbert and Alicia. My grandparents. Related by more than just marriage.

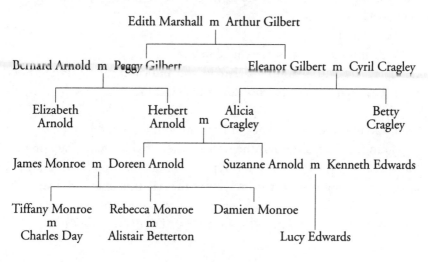

Figure 5.

They've asked me all sorts of questions about my family history. I know that I'm one of their more interesting case studies. My grandmother, Alicia, married her first cousin Herbert. Whenever I have to explain to a new researcher about them, it's always the same reaction:

they raise their eyebrows and say, "Uh-huh" and try not to betray their excitement.

"It's because you're quite rare in Britain," said Alistair.

"Rare?"

"The offspring, or even great-offspring, of consanguineous relationships are relatively unusual."

Alistair was driving, his concentration focused on the road ahead. I turned to look at him.

"There's still a certain taboo about it," he said. "In America, it's illegal in twenty-four states, you know. And in the rest it's still socially unacceptable. They think it's perverse, sexually."

He pushed the gearshift into fourth.

"So what are you saying?"

"You have only three great-great-grandmothers rather than the usual four. Alicia and Herbert share one eighth of the same genes. The opportunity for two recessives to meet is therefore higher than in the rest of the population."

I hesitated.

"I'm inbred, is that what you're saying?"

"No," he said, scanning the road and indicating left. "That's not what I'm saying." But I'm not sure I believe him.

I tell the researchers the story of how my grandfather fell in love with my grandmother, although they're less interested in that. They prefer to take blood tests, ECGs, that type of thing. They prefer to ask me questions. They apply the principles of the scientific method. I sit and read *Cosmopolitan* and drink tea out of plastic cups and keep my mouth shut. It's taken me a long time, but I'm good at that now.

3.2   **odds** *pl n* **2** : the likelihood of the occurrence of one thing rather than the occurrence of another thing

MY GRANDFATHER, Herbert, says that he always knew that he would one day marry my grandmother, Alicia. He fell in love with her over a bowl of sherry trifle. It's part of our family mythology. My grandmother, on the other hand, says she would never have married Herbert if on February 28, 1948, she hadn't been run over by an Austin Atlantic and broken her leg in three places. I'm still not sure whose version is correct. Both? Neither?

The result is, in any case, the same. My grandmother married my grandfather and gave birth to my mother. My mother will meet my father, and on a spring night in a semidetached house in Beech Drive, Middleton, some two decades later, a single spermatozoon bearing twenty-three of my father's chromosomes will encounter an egg bearing twenty-three of my mother's. The odds against this happening, of the accidental joining of one sperm (in millions) and one egg (in hundreds)? Roughly one in 3 billion. My existence is predicated upon a chain of statistically improbable events.

Beneath a pink, flowered acrylic sheet, their nuclei fuse. Twelve hours later the chromosomes mix. Even now, at this stage, I could have been not-me. Every pair of chromosomes, one from my mother and one from my father, line up. I have my father's nose, my mother's hair. But it could have been the other way around. I could be someone else entirely. I have a phantom shadow-self who will stalk my footsteps for years to come.

I am getting ahead of myself though. All this is still in the future. On February 28, 1948, the woman who will one day become my grandmother is walking down Alverthorpe Road, Wakefield, in the West Riding of Yorkshire. She is still Alicia Cragley at this time. And although it's true that she would have never married Herbert if she'd taken a different route home that day, he will not enter her story yet.

As she walks along Alverthorpe Road, her hair, tied in a ribbon, swings from side to side. Her skin does not yet look like it has been put through a boil wash and left to dry in the sun, nor are there lacy skeins of varicose veins across her calves. On the evening of February 28, 1948, her cheekbones have structure, her figure form. Her legs are still intact (although not for long).

"It was lemon yellow, my dress, with a matching ribbon and I was wondering whether I could afford a new pair of shoes—black, they were, with a low court heel."

Alicia's told me the story in quiet asides when Herbert's not around. We've always been alike, Alicia and I. She likes telling stories, and I like listening to them. Some people (i.e., Tiffany) don't have the patience for it. The only family stories she likes hearing are the ones in which she stars as the main protagonist with a well-defined leading role. But I listen. I have a quarter of Alicia's genes, so I think of this as my story too. I'm part of it; only a potentiality at this stage, it's true, but I'm there nonetheless. I picture her tip-tapping her way down Alverthorpe Road. I imagine her eyes are slightly unfocused (she's always been a bit of a daydreamer). Which was probably why she didn't see the car.

Alicia was eighteen years old and waiting for Life to begin. What kind of life it would be was still unknown at this stage, but its possibilities infected everything around her. It was there in the sound her shoes made, tip-tapping along the pavement. It was there in the air, the air that bore the smell of, what was that smell?

There was a top note of something unfamiliar; a thick, viscous layer above the smell of brown coal and the rich stickiness that wafted out of the chimneys of the malt kilns along the canal.

Alicia noticed it without realizing that she had noticed it. Was it chocolate? It was rich and fragrant and not from Yorkshire. No, not chocolate, cocoa-nut. Like the cake Aunty Peggy once made. There was a waft of cocoa-nut on the breeze around her. A sweetness that cut through the spring air, changing it from the known to the unknown, from the expected to the unexpected.

She followed the scent all the way along Denhale Avenue, and when she turned into Thirlmere Road, it was still there, alien amid the privet hedges and carefully netted curtains. What my grandmother didn't realize as she walked along Thirlmere Road, rolling the smell around her nose, expelling it through her mouth, taking it down deep into her lungs, was that it was the smell of a black man. More precisely it was the smell of Cecil Johnston, lately of Kingston, Jamaica, who was leaning against the bus stop, his springy black hair held in place with a slick of solidified cocoa-nut oil from a jar he had carried with him across the Atlantic. He was wearing a too-big jacket and a brown Trilby hat, and whistling a tune that was deep and low.

What was he doing? There was nobody else around, and Alicia could feel herself beginning to panic.

Her eyes tend to open wide at this point in the story, and sometimes she shakes her head.

"I had never seen a black man before. Even if he wasn't *very* black, more honey-colored than black black; the color of a Callard & Bowser toffee, perhaps, or light tan shoe polish."

She cast her eyes to the ground and walked past, feeling, what was that? Hot breath? The sun? A slight shifting in the air around her? She didn't dare look up, but strode purposefully onward, stepping off the curb at the very moment Councillor Donald Anderson, late for his dinner and worried about the row Mrs. Anderson would no doubt give him, accelerated around the corner in his new Austin Atlantic, the steering of which he had not yet quite mastered.

It was as Mr. Anderson told the policeman later: she just stepped out in front of the car. He didn't have a chance. And by the time he'd gathered his senses, applied his brakes, drawn to a stop and gone to help the young lady, he'd found that—and at this Mr. Anderson motioned toward Cecil—the jungle bunny had got there first. He—and Mr. Anderson motioned again at Cecil—the darkie, had picked the young lady up in his arms and ordered him, Donald Anderson, Councillor Anderson, to get in and drive to the hospital. Councillor Anderson drove. "Although I'll be damned if some black fellow thinks he can come over here and bark orders at us," he said, for he had some experience in these matters, having served with Americans during the war. The words helped Councillor Anderson regain some of his swagger. A swagger that had momentarily departed when the girl disappeared under his wheels and he felt something beneath his tires that was hard yet yielding. Like a badger, say, or if he was honest and admitted it to himself, a girl.

My grandmother was in traction for a month. Her mother, Eleanor Cragley, my great-grandmother, worried by her bedside. She couldn't help herself. It was what she did. Where other people had hobbies, collected stamps, did needlepoint, smoked, Eleanor Cragley worried.

It was her defining characteristic. She fretted and pressed cold compresses to Alicia's head and prayed to a God she'd been somewhat remiss in worshipping recently. Betty, Alicia's younger sister, was there too, wearing frills, pigtails and a deep-set frown. Three lines creased her forehead. She was trying to think of ways of re-diverting attention back to her.

"Mum! I came top in maths."

"Did you, Betty? Clever girl, now why don't you go and fetch a vase for these flowers. Are you hurting, my petal? Are you in pain?"

The Cragleys were an unlikely family group, and being thrown together in the small, shiny space beside Alicia's bed pointed up their differences rather than their similarities. Betty was still suspended in the awkward no-man's land of early adolescence. Her arms were angular. Her face, which would fill and change shape, was trapped at a point midway between the soft downiness of a child's and the ripe creaminess of a woman's. It was pasty. She stood apart and fidgeted. Mrs. Cragley flapped. Mr. Cragley, who was, after all, a Yorkshireman, tried to get to the bottom of the matter.

"What on earth were you doing? The policeman says you stepped straight in front of the car. What were you playing at?"

"Cyril, shush. Can't you see she's hurt?"

"I've found a vase! I've found a vase!" Betty's pigtails quivered. Her chin jutted. Alicia had commanded center stage again. Betty thought about what form her retribution would take, but in the interim, she wiped the contents of her left nostril onto the rim of Alicia's drinking glass.

In the end it was the nurses who, with a certain brutal efficiency, shooed Alicia's family from her bed, leaving her to wince and groan and listen to the murmurings of women's bodies that rose and fell around her.

Eighteen years of age and already double-faulted by her body. She was trapped in a world apart, its days marked not by dawn and sunset, but by pills and lights out. She had been wheeled into the cul de sac of life and abandoned. Her Life, the one she was preparing for, was probably going on elsewhere. Without her. She couldn't walk or dress herself or go out into the world. The world had to come to her: cousins and aunts and uncles and a grandmother, and Sylvia from work. And, there, moving quietly through the ward, one hand clutching a crumpled brown paper bag, the other his hat, was a visitor who was neither friend nor family. It was Cecil Johnston.

Cecil's eyes were lowered, his too-big jacket hung limply from his body. His progress through the ward was closely observed by sixteen sets of patients' eyes and one nurse's: Sister Weston, the arch-matriarch of Ward 3. She was a woman who could carry fifteen bedpans at a time, and had once used a Ping-Pong ball to save a man from dying. She had never, however, been confronted by the sight of a black man walking into the scrubbed and disinfected heart of her empire. As she watched Cecil treading softly through her ward, she found herself engaged in an activity that she hadn't indulged in for twenty years or more. She dithered. Her hands rustled. Her feet, normally so sure and decisive, arched up and down inside her shoes.

What should she do? Who was to say? In the end, she had no choice but to shut herself in the ward office and take down her copy of *Rules and Regulations*, a book that governed almost every aspect of her life. She frowned as her finger moved down the Index and then the Contents page. She muttered to herself as she speed-read chapters seven and ten concerning Visitors and Visiting Hours. She scrutinized the text, read sentences aloud, considered the meaning of such words as "precipitately" and "notwithstanding," but in the end, she admitted defeat. There was nothing that formally forbade the presence of a colored gentleman in her ward. Despite the fact that it was quite obviously Upsetting the Patients.

Mrs. Browning, who'd had her womb out, pulled her bedclothes higher. Mrs. Fairchild, who was suffering from a nervous complaint, wondered if she should have accepted the medication the sister had tried to make her take that afternoon. As Cecil walked along the ward, sixteen pairs of eyes watched him. What was he doing? Would he kill them? Or rape them? There was a communal exhalation as he came to a stop.

Cecil sat by the side of Alicia's bed. The insides of his lips were pink. And the whites of his eyes were the whitest thing Alicia had ever seen. She sniffed the air surreptitiously. There it was again. Cocoa-nut. But this time, there was a new fragrance laid over it; a top note of something rich and sweet and foreign. His head was bowed, and instead of attempting to speak, he opened his brown paper bag and pulled out, what? A fruit? Was it a fruit? It was yellow and shiny and Cecil handled it delicately, fishing a knife out of his jacket then carving a sliver of soft, pink flesh.

"Papaya," said Cecil. "From Jamaica." Except that it was more like a song the way that Cecil said it. "Pap-ay-ay-aya from Jiy-make-her." He breathed the word "Jiy-make-her," a soft undulation that hovered above the starched cotton sheets and enamel bedside bowl. "I wahnted a pray-sant for A-leesha Craag-lay," said Cecil. Alee-sha Craag-lay. Her name had a broken rhythm, an afterlife. She had never felt so of the world. He held the papaya to her lips.

Mrs. Browning gasped. Sister Weston, watching from the bedpan sluicing area, felt her dithering fall away. Alicia hesitated. She reached out her tongue, tasted a drop of juice, and then swallowed.

"I'll be having that if you don't mind!" Sister Weston's crisp linen hat bore down upon Alicia and Cecil, swiftly followed by Sister Weston herself. She confiscated them: the unholy trinity of fruit, knife and brown paper bag. But Alicia had tried her first papaya and was too happy to care.

It tasted of yellow. Her favorite color.

After Cecil left, Sister Weston annotated the notes on the clipboard at the end of Alicia's bed. Next to the temperature chart and the medication summary, she made a note for the next day's duty nurse. A series of enemas for the patient, to start forthwith; helpful for a sluggish digestive tract that has recently ingested foreign perturbances. She was particularly pleased with "perturbances."

3.3 Theories of Relativity (4)

THERE ARE SOME PROBLEMS with my story. But you've probably spotted this already. For example, how do I know what Councillor Anderson was thinking? Or who's to say that Sister Weston was pleased with "perturbances"?

Well, you're right. I don't know, not for sure. But I have my primary sources: Alicia's record of events, my grandfather's Bought Ledger files (I'll come to those), the fruit of my own inquiries and investigations. I admit that I may embellish, just a touch, but essentially these are the true facts, as I know them.

Alistair's specialist subject is genetics, but in my corner of academia we believe in historical circumstances, and sociopolitical factors; the interplay between private lives and the dominant culture. The story of how my grandmother came to marry my grandfather is a story specific to its time—the cusp between Britain as it was and Britain as it is. Just as my story, the story of the breakdown of a family, *my* family, is also rooted in a certain period; of Britain in the late 1970s; post sexual revolution, pre Thatcherite reforms.

Which is why I'm using it in my thesis—*Sex and Suburbia: How the Sixties Became the Seventies.* Or something like that. I'm still working on the title. I had *Polyester Pants and Wife-Swapping Circles: Discourses on a Demographic* for a while, but it didn't hit quite the right note. In Cultural Studies circles it's very important to have a catchy title. Usually because the rest of the text is almost entirely unreadable.

Alistair snorts whenever there's something about the seventies on the television. "Nostalgic rubbish," he says. He showed me a book review the other day, a novel set in the period, where the reviewer had taken issue with the "banal catalogue of brand names and petit bourgeois self-referencing."

"I'm doing a Ph.D.," I said. "It's research."

Alistair looked as if he was about to protest but then changed his mind.

"And anyway, that's the point. It's the period when brand names became aspects of our communal memory. When television programs became part of our folk heritage."

But he just shrugged his shoulders and went back to the news section.

.   .   .

Alistair says that there's no such thing as chance. "It's just a word expressing ignorance," he says.

He would never allow for the possibility of yellow dresses or the smell of papaya on a summer evening shortly after the war. Or if he did, he'd also insist upon noting the velocity of the Austin Atlantic and any inconsistencies in the surface of the road. He'd use charts, mathematical formulae, that kind of thing. He'd say that my story lacks precision.

Chance is just another name, he says, for a set of precipitating events that are too numerous or too complex to identify. There is not good luck and bad luck; there is cause and there is effect.

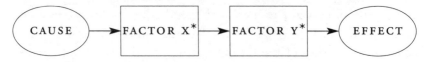

*where Factor X and Factor Y are both unknown and without number

Figure 6.

"Unless Alicia meeting Cecil could be classified as a quantum event, i.e. random at the subatomic level," says Alistair. "Which, on the whole, seems *unlikely*." Coincidences, misfortunes, accidents and random encounters are not what they seem.

My father's sperm and my mother's egg were a billions-to-one union, but this is not chance. According to Alistair's rationale, there's an explanation as to why I am here. I just haven't figured it out yet.

3.4   **trifle** *n* **2** : confection of sponge cake with custard or cream, fruit, jam, jelly, wine, almonds, etc.

HERBERT'S VERSION of events is different. By February 28, 1948, he'd already been in love with my grandmother for six years. His love, therefore, had both constancy and longevity to recommend it. And, if Herbert only knew the word, propinquity. For their blood was closer than most. Whichever way you looked at it, they were linked together forever; adjacent on the family tree; coupled at family gatherings.

Figure 7.

His Alicia. "My cousin." Herbert relished the possessive pronoun. She belonged to him. Even the grammar was on his side. In fact he had been in love with Alicia since 1942, when he had been unmanned by the sight of her holding a bowl of sherry trifle.

Whenever Herbert thought of Alicia, he thought first of sherry trifle, and then of the stirring in the part of his body that Uncle Reginald, a sailor in the merchant navy, called Below Decks. Uncle Reginald, although absent on Christmas Eve 1942, nonetheless played a part in the unfolding of what Herbert thinks of as *Their Story*.

In Herbert's recollection of events, it was snowing, the glass in the window was frosted, and a fire was blazing in the hearth. Alicia was wearing a smocked top and had a ribbon in her hair (although this memory might have been distorted by the fact that Herbert first felt Below Decks activity during a visit to see Walt Disney's *Snow White and the Seven Dwarfs* at the Palace cinema). Alicia's hair was gently waved in the manner of Ingrid Bergman's in the poster for *Casablanca*. And Herbert? Well, in Herbert's imaginings, he was a bit like Bogey and a bit like Cary Grant. A bit smaller, perhaps. A bit paler. Certainly skinnier. But this is Herbert's story, and if he wants to be played by Cary Grant, it is, after all, his choice.

Their Story

(Peggy Arnold, Herbert's mother, enters room, bearing aloft a cake on a silver platter.)

PEGGY ARNOLD
Well I was a bit uncertain about it, but they say it tastes pretty similar.

GRANNY GILBERT
Such a clever girl! It looks just like chocolate cake!

PEGGY ARNOLD
I had to use carrots to sweeten it of course, but then that
makes it nice and moist, doesn't it? And I used three of my
powdered eggs in it, and all of my sugar.

*(The doorbell rings. Aunty Maureen and Uncle Samuel have
arrived bearing a trifle.)*

GRANNY GILBERT
Maureen! How are you, my petal?

AUNTY MAUREEN
Happy Christmas! Happy Christmas, Eleanor! Ooh, it's
cold outside. Now, where should I put this trifle?

*(A silence falls in the room. The fire crackles. The trifle trem-
bles. Everyone stares at the trifle.)*

PEGGY ARNOLD
Goodness. What a trifle! That looks just like real cream.

AUNTY MAUREEN
That's because it most certainly is real cream!

(Beat.)

CARY GRANT
Anybody got a smoke?

GRANDPA CRAGLEY
Herbert, you little bleeder, shut up.

Peggy Arnold started to go pink. She had spent days toiling over her
chocolateless chocolate cake. She had queued and bartered and poured
a thimbleful of her prewar emergency brandy into the mixture. But it
was the icing that had been her tour de force. She had made her own
cream. Ersatz cream, it was called, mock cream. Making it had been a
complicated procedure that involved corn flour and milk and margarine and sugar and more than a smidgeon of culinary expertise.

    It had finished her chocolateless chocolate cake to what she'd thought of as perfection. And then she saw the trifle. It was magnificent. There was no denying the fact. It produced sighs of nostalgia and a wistful longing for normality; for the days when a trifle was not an event in itself, merely a supplement to other events; a guest at a family party, not its star attraction. It was made with proper sponge, made with real eggs. The cream rose in soft peaks, but the pièce de résistance was a storm of multicolored hundreds and thousands, and a whole glacé cherry. Uncle Samuel, Aunty Maureen's husband, a healthy man of twenty-seven not in uniform, said nothing. They'd all heard the rumors about him of course, but it was not a topic of conversation that anyone wanted to pursue.

There was silence. And then the unmistakable sound of a silver spoon plunging into a combination of sponge and custard and real cream. They all visualized the action before they turned their heads and saw Alicia Cragley, twelve years old, with skin that was whiter than snow and lips that were redder than blood. She was sitting on a velvet footstool and, with no regard for the rest of the room, cradling the bowl of trifle in her lap. The glacé cherry had gone. The hundreds and thousands had been scraped away. A criminal white mustache rested on her upper lip.

"Alicia!" said her mother.

"Bloody hell!" said Uncle Samuel.

"It's not fair!" said Betty Cragley and started up a high-pitched whine that made them all wince and cover their ears and think of high-altitude Mosquito bombers.

On board the good ship Cary Grant, there was a lot of activity going on in the engine room, and for reasons that were not clear to anybody, least of all Herbert, trifle, or, more precisely, the thought of trifle would become a mainstay in his nocturnal games of pocket billiards (another of Reginald's Reginaldisms).

Herbert would admit that his recollection of the event has been warped by time, discolored with age, like the curtains in the front room, but this was nonetheless what he thought of as *Their Story*. It was also the moment that my grandfather knew that one day he would marry my grandmother.

My grandfather's right leg was shorter than his left leg, and his left leg wasn't very long at that. He had pale skin and an asymmetrical smile. Out of earshot of Peggy and Bernard, Herbert was known as "the runt." The runt of a litter that had produced Elizabeth, the undisputed beauty of the entire Cragley/Arnold clan. She had inherited all the best features from their father's side of the family (almond-shaped eyes, clear skin, an athletic build), along with the cream of their mother's side (long, tapering fingers, a retroussé nose), as well as a whole new set of attributes that neither family had ever seen before (shapely legs, a twenty-two-inch waist, a beauty spot).

Elizabeth was not present during the unfolding of *Their Story*; she was in Suffolk manning searchlights and receiving extensive tuition in American patois. (Elizabeth had been destined to have a Good War. It was entirely in character that Winston Churchill had chosen to declare hostilities on the day after her eighteenth birthday and that the particular shade of slate blue worn by the Women's Auxiliary Air Force should flatter her complexion. The Japanese assault on Pearl Harbor, she firmly believed, was part of God's Great Plan for her.)

Poor Herbert! He evinced pity at best. At worst, disgust. He was, in point of fact, ugly. Ugly and short with a defective leg, and by the time that Alicia had landed herself in the ladies' ward of Clayton Hospital, he had a light covering of what Reginald referred to as "bum fluff" on his chin, and a battalion of livid acne had started the long march across his face.

Everyone underestimated poor Herbert, but that was all to the good. For Herbert was not stupid, or slow. He knew that success depended upon many factors, and that what could seem like a weakness (a boil on his chin) could in fact be a strength (people averted their gaze, he could act unobserved). Herbert had studied military history. He had analyzed battle strategies and knew about subterfuge and tactical retreats; how to lead on your enemy and draw evasive fire. History was on the side of the army that marched on its intelligence. His enemies' failure to take him seriously would be their own undoing. His spots? His crippled leg? His wonky face? It was his camouflage. It allowed him to pass unnoticed. People would say things in front of poor Herbert that they wouldn't in front of those with balanced features and uncrooked teeth. He was able to pass almost invisibly before them, learning the power of possession as he took hold of their secrets and stored them away. He knew the power of knowledge. Just as he knew that one day, Alicia, his cousin, would be his.

He kept the Alicia Files in a series of hardback notebooks marked "Bought Ledger." They had columns running down the page in which he marked a weekly tally. He had been studying Alicia for the last six years. Ask him a question, any question about Alicia, past or present. The name of her favorite doll? Dolores. The first book that made her cry? *Black Beauty*. The size of her brassiere? 34B. The color of her favorite dress? Yellow. Herbert had balanced on a blossoming cherry tree for hours outside her bedroom window. Even during the blackout, with Mr. Price, the warden, on patrol, he'd had his methods. He possessed Alicia in all ways other than physically. And the thought of Snow White, with Ingrid Bergman's lightly waved hair, sitting down to eat a bowl of cream-topped trifle, was . . .

"Herbert! What the bloody hell do you think you're doing?" Uncle Reginald, who had returned safely from the North Atlantic despite his brother-in-law's black market activities, had caught Herbert with his hands down his trousers.

"You little devil! You'd better not let your mother catch you doing that!" Uncle Reginald had a new profession, selling washing machines to housewives, but he still had a sailor's sense of priorities.

"Tell you what, lad. Would you like to see a couple of pictures?"

Herbert nodded, but the magazine with blurry photos of airbrushed sweethearts printed on scratchy utility paper was not to his taste.

"Bet that's getting you going, eh lad?" Herbert thanked Uncle Reginald politely but gave them back.

"What's the matter with you, boy? Bat on the other side of the wicket? You're not one of those *poofs*, are you?"

It was not pornography that produced the thin, yeasty fluid when Herbert rubbed the part of his body that kinked like his face. And when he discovered Cecil Johnston leaving Alicia's bedside at Clayton Hospital, he began to have troubling dreams. Dreams that involved Happy, Grumpy, Dopey, Sleepy, Sneezy, Bashful and Doc. They stood before him laughing. Bashful turned toward him and from his dwarfish trousers dangled a black penis, the size and girth of an elephant's trunk.

Part Four

revise *vt & n* **1** : read or look over or re-examine or reconsider

4.1 The Science of Happiness (1)

ALISTAIR WAS COOKING when I arrived home.

"Hi," I said, dropping my bags to the floor. He was standing at the stove, his forehead creased in concentration. I reached out and kissed the side of his cheek, feeling the bristle of his twelve-hour stubble on my lips.

"Cooking," he said and shrugged me off with a wave of his wooden spoon. "Do we have any dried basil?"

"We're out, I think. Use the oregano instead."

He frowned and checked his recipe book again.

"It says basil."

I sat down at the kitchen table and rolled my eyes. It was always like this when Alistair cooked. There was always a recipe and he always followed it to the letter, sending me out on urgent errands to find porcini oil or kohlrabi or cinnamon sticks.

"Would you be an angel and go to the corner shop?" He turned to me and used his most wheedling voice. I sighed at him in mock exasperation.

"Why can't you just improvise?"

He frowned and looked back at the recipe book.

I stood up reluctantly, although in truth I didn't mind. Alistair is always so self-sufficient, so capable, that I'm always vaguely flattered when he needs me or wants something from me. I gathered up my purse and keys and went back outside.

The cooking thing was a relatively recent development. I was the one who could cook. It was one of my few areas of marital expertise. Then, two years ago, I gave him a recipe book. It was a joke really, a hint, a wife's present to her undomesticated husband. Alistair, though, being Alistair, spent Christmas studying it and by New Year's Eve he announced that he'd cracked it.

I laughed, but it was true. I spent the following week eating Tuscan bread soup, Indonesian laska, salt-encrusted sea bass, perfectly cooked beef. I put it down to the fact that he's a scientist. That the onions must be diced just so. That the carrots must be cubed into half-centimeter squares, that the lettuce must be torn and never cut. Although he wasn't always so measured, so controlled.

"Got it." I handed him the basil and a bottle of wine. He looked at it, surprised.

"Oh! Expensive stuff. Excellent. Hold on a mo." He opened the bottle, filled the glasses, and took a swig. "Mmmm, nice."

I raised my glass at him. "Happy Anniversary!"

He hesitated just a fraction of a second too long.

"Yes! Happy Anniversary!"

He chinked my glass, then leaned across the table and kissed me on the lips, tasting of garlic and tannin and something else I couldn't put my finger on.

"It was yesterday," I said.

"I knew that."

"Yesterday week."

He lifted his hands in mock surrender.

"Okay, okay. You win."

I didn't answer for a minute or two.

"No," I said eventually. "I don't think so."

Later that night in bed, I reached across him and took hold of his penis. In the warmth of my palm, I could feel the blood flowing, the skin thickening, the capillaries dilating. I felt it grow firm beneath my fingers. Alistair shifted in his sleep. It reminded me of the television sets from the seventies, the ones where after you'd turned the power off, a ghostly image remained for a few seconds more, slowly fading.

4.2 Family Affairs (1)

TIFFANY GOT her column eventually. It's not quite Queen, or Prime Minister, but it makes her feel self-important, so perhaps it's not so different. She writes a slot called *Family Affairs*, which carries a rather flattering picture byline. Her skin is an alabaster white, her hair dark and glossy (she has it ironed at an expensive hairdresser in South Ken). Tiffany loves her column. She pronounces in it. I suspect that she thinks her opinions actually count. She certainly acts like they do. But then, Tiffany has always been convinced of her own unique destiny.

I've never talked to Tiffany about the past; I just read a bowdlerized version of it in the newspaper from time to time. She has a habit of cannibalizing whatever domestic detail she can dredge up. "Material," she calls it. She molds the past to fit her ideas of the present. Although I suppose we all do that; it's just that the rest of us don't get paid £800 a pop for it. That's Tiffany though: one eye on her immortality, the other on her bank balance.

Tiffany and I are siblings. We were raised together, were nurtured in the same womb, experienced the same childhood events. I can't account for the differences; I am merely noting them. I shall include her version, for the record.

Family Affairs
BY TIFFANY MONROE

It is a self-evident fact known to all women that there are certain things a man should never be allowed to do alone. Decide a paint scheme, for one. Shop unaided for a suit, another. And, to that, I'd add a third: in no circumstances should a man be left in sole charge of booking a holiday. The one time I permitted The Husband to "surprise" me resulted in a wet weekend in a two-star hotel without a Michelin-starred restaurant in sight.

I've never quite understood how the presence of a Y chromosome impedes one's ability to operate a washing machine or know where the light bulbs are kept, but I've never doubted the role it plays (or more accurately *doesn't* play) in all matters pertaining to: taste, color, tailored seams, discrimination, and the ability to recognize a good hotel at fifty paces.

This weekend, I spent half a day trying to solve the annual holiday conundrum, whittling down the choices until I'd arrived at a shortlist of Mediterranean villas. Finally, I presented The Husband with my hard-researched results.

"So?" I said. "What do you think?"

"Hmm?" he said, not looking up from his paper.

"Which one do you prefer?"

He glanced at the photographs and said, "Whichever one you want, my darling."

Honestly! If it was left up to him I've no doubt that we'd end up on a last-minute deal to the Costa del Yobbo.

I couldn't decide between a Tuscan palazzo set amid rolling olive groves or an eighteenth-century château on the Loire. And it made me suddenly nostalgic for the days when going on holiday meant a trip to the seaside; when all the world had a brother or sister or both; and when a bucket and spade and the promise of an ice cream was the best of all possible worlds. There were no planes, or airport delays; no agonizing over terra-cotta floor tiles versus hand-finished kitchens. Holidays were simple affairs of perfect contentment. But then these were the days when a "single parent holiday" was an oxymoron not a brochure choice.

"Perhaps we should go to Norfolk?" I suggested, remembering a family holiday from a long time ago. But when I looked up, The Husband had gone. In any case, I knew it was no good. The past is a foreign country, they do things differently there. Although you won't find it in a brochure. And you can't go there by plane.

I thought of the past and sighed. On the plus side, I discovered today that the Tuscan palazzo has Egyptian cotton bed linen.

4.3 **eunuch** *n* : castrated man, esp. one employed in a harem; (fig) person lacking effectiveness

BREAKFAST HAD BEGUN badly and it didn't show any signs of improving. The radio was tuned to the Terry Wogan show and my mother was struggling with the toaster. It had recently started showing signs of temperament, turning the bread the same crispy dark brown color whatever setting it was on.

Ping! Two charred pieces of toast flung themselves out of the slot.

"Right. You're really starting to get on my nerves now!" I looked up from my Sugar Puffs alarmed but relieved to see that she was only talking to the toaster. The toaster appeared to be ignoring her. It obviously hadn't any idea with whom it was dealing. My mother took two more slices of Mother's Pride from the packet.

"Okay, I'm warning you now," she said. "This is your last chance."

"Mum?" I was pushing the last of my Sugar Puffs around the bowl.

"What?"

"Who would you prefer to win the war? Iran or Iraq?"

"For God's sake, Rebecca, can't you see that I'm busy?"

I let out a frustrated sigh. The Iran-Iraq war was always on the news bulletins and *John Craven's News Round*, but it wasn't like Wimbledon or the Olympics, when you knew who should win (us). I didn't know which side I was supposed to support.

"Doreen?" My father looked up from his bills and held out a piece of writing paper.

"What?"

"You'd better have a look at this."

My mother took the letter from him and quickly skimmed its contents.

"All I need!" she said, sighing elaborately. She was wearing her Ali MacGraw–receives-terminal-prognosis expression.

Tiffany and I, dressed in our school uniforms, breakfast eaten, ready for school, waited for somebody to explain. Terry Wogan chatted away. A horn sounded in the street.

"Your uncle Reginald is coming to stay," said my father finally.

"Oh," we said as one. It seemed like the wrong moment to point out that we didn't have an Uncle Reginald.

Ping! Two more pieces of charred toast flung themselves out of the slot. My mother snatched them up and threw them in the bin. She missed and they landed on the floor.

"Dad?"

"Hmm." He had picked up the *Daily Mail* and had started to read the back page.

"We don't have an Uncle Reginald."

"He's your Great-Great-Uncle Reginald."

"Oh."

"He's your mother's great-uncle. Your grandmother's uncle. Well, and your grandfather's too, I suppose, but I'm not sure about that . . ."

I contemplated this but it was too much to take in. My mother had temporarily given up on the toaster. She wasn't used to insubordination on this kind of scale and began on the washing up instead, her scrubbing reaching new heights of vigorousness.

"If *only* . . . ," she began. Tiffany and I braced ourselves. We waited for the line to fall. We knew it was coming. The mother-of-Bambi voice, the down-turned mouth . . .

"If *only* I had a *fitted* kitchen . . ."

My father rustled the paper and began struggling to his feet. "Right. Who wants a lift to school?"

We were almost out of the house, when my mother yelled after us in a tone of voice that would have sent Bambi scurrying through the forest glades searching for cover. *"It's Parents' Evening tonight! Don't forget. I don't want you showing me up!"*

It was being held in the school hall, and all the teachers sat at individual tables while lines of parents formed behind them.

I stood between my mother and father hopping from foot to foot, but when we finally reached the front of the line, all my teacher, Mrs. Graham, had to say was that I ought to pay more attention in class and work on my spelling. It was most unsatisfactory. Tiffany's teacher, Mr. Williams, on the other hand, spent a good ten minutes extolling her conscientious work and creative imagination. She received straight As in all her subjects.

"She's a model pupil," said Mr. Williams. "I think she'll go far."

My mother glowed and smiled at Tiffany, who responded with unusual, not to say unnatural, modesty and bowed her head. She'd recently read *Pollyanna* and had spent long hours practicing her humility on me. I had to give her marks out of ten in various categories, although when I only gave an eight for "Deportment" she'd flounced out of the room.

"Well done!" said my mother. "I suppose we'll have to see about that new bike now, eh?" Tiffany's face broke into a self-satisfied smile but recomposed itself quickly.

"It's not necessary," she said in a small voice. "Hard work is its own reward."

"Rubbish!" said my mother after a moment's hesitation and kissed her on the cheek. "You deserve it."

I sighed. How could I be humble? When I had no dazzling achievements to be humble about?

My father had been left to deal with Mr. Williams and was trying to think of relevant questions to ask but was evidently struggling.

"So, um, how do you think she'll cope when she goes up to the big school?"

My mother shot him a look. "Big school?" she mouthed.

"I'm sure she'll do just fine," said Mr. Williams. "Now if you don't mind . . ."

Abbey Roislin from Oak Avenue was standing with her parents in the line directly behind us. He was something big in the water board and drove a Range Rover. My mother smiled at them as we passed, before adding in an overloud voice, "I suppose brains must run in the family, mustn't they?"

"Hello!" The voice came from behind. We turned around. It was the new deputy head.

"Hello!" said my mother. "How *nice* to meet you!" Although there was something unconvincing about the way she said this. As if "nice" had suddenly changed its meaning and now meant "nasty" or "displeasing" or "undesirable." The new deputy head was a woman. She was also young. Or youngish anyway. You could tell this because her skirt stopped above the knee and her shoes had heels rather than the practical rubber soles favored by the rest of the staff.

My mother shook her hand. "It's Miss Kellaway, isn't it?"

"Mrs. Kellaway actually."

"Oh. I'm terribly sorry. I assumed . . ." She left the sentence hanging. Everybody in Middleton knew the rumors. Mrs. Huxley next door had filled our mother in on the facts. The new deputy head was an "attractive divorcée." They had nodded their heads knowingly.

"And you know what they're like. Morals of an alley cat in all likelihood."

I hovered nervously by my mother's knee.

"No, I decided to keep the name. It seemed easier that way. And so you're Rebecca's mother."

"That's right. And Tiffany's too of course." She smiled the easy smile of someone who has given birth to genius and patted Tiffany on the shoulder. "We can't complain. She had a *very* good report."

"Yes, and Rebecca's doing very well too."

I waited for my mother's reaction, but Mrs. Kellaway had already moved on. There was a long line of people waiting to meet her, including an unusually high number of fathers.

We had frozen pizza and salad for tea, because my mother said she hadn't had a chance to cook.

"Butter wouldn't melt in her mouth, would it?" she said, hacking through the crust to portion it out.

"Whose mouth?"

"That Kellaway woman."

My father gave a noncommittal grunt.

"Taking a job away from a man like that."

"I'm sure she got it on her merits, Doreen."

"Well, *you* would say that, wouldn't you? One glimpse of a stocking top, you're all the same."

This time he didn't bother to respond, but took a mouthful of pizza, attempting to crack through the crust with his jaws.

"It's not right. Imagine taking food out of the mouths of children like that! They should have given it to a breadwinner."

"Mum?"

"You know Mr. Williams? Tiffany's teacher? He applied for it and he's got a family to feed!"

I interjected. "Aunty Suzanne says it's a step in the right direction."

"And what direction would that be?"

That stumped me.

"North?" I said, but quietly in case it was wrong.

"Doreen, do you not think there's a case that men and women should be treated equally in the workplace?" My father had set his knife and fork down and was looking at my mother.

"I'm not saying that. I just think that it's wrong to pay some strumpet more than a married man who's got responsibilities."

"But surely people should be paid according to their ability and the job that they do, regardless of their sex or color or whathaveyou?"

Tiffany and I exchanged a look. Usually our mother and father talked about whether the car needed servicing and when was my father going to get around to mowing the lawn.

"Precisely," said my mother triumphantly. "Which is why she shouldn't have been promoted. They'll have to pay her more than Mr. Williams now, that's what I'm saying.

"I know her type," she continued, delicately spearing a tomato from the salad. "Only after one thing. She'll be the nigger in the woodpile, I'm telling you."

My father opened his mouth to say something and changed his mind. He picked up his newspaper again and started to read.

I toyed with my pizza and decided on a diversionary tactic. "Mum?"

"What?"

"Why can't we live in a council house?"

"*WHAT?*"

"Why can't we live in a council house?"

The council houses were at the other end of Middleton and weren't like our houses. They were where the poor people lived. Although my mother said they weren't really poor, just lazy.

"What on earth are you talking about, Rebecca?"

"Claire Bradley lives in a council house and she goes to Torremolinos for her holidays."

My mother's knife and fork clinked back on her plate. She stood up, took her uneaten pizza to the bin and began to scrape it in. It would have looked like it was some sort of hunger strike. If you hadn't tasted the pizza.

"Oh, that takes the biscuit that does. James, did you hear that?"

"Mum?"

"One more word out of you, young lady, and I shan't be responsible for my actions." She left the kitchen, slamming the door as she went.

We all put down our knives and forks, dry pizza crust sticking to the inside of our mouths.

"And I don't want to see any leftovers either!" she yelled through the door.

After tea, I went over to play at Lucy's, although it appeared a similar argument was being played out at the Old Parsonage.

"For God's sake, woman. I wasn't looking at her legs."

"Don't even think about it, Kenneth, that's all I'm saying. Not on your own doorstep."

"I am not going to hang around here to be slandered." Uncle Kenneth backed into a macramé potholder and made a grab for his golf clubs.

A door slammed. I wondered if all our relatives were door slammers. Maybe that ran in the family too. On *Dallas,** they tended to

---

*Dallas

"*Dallas* was the first of a genre that came to be called 'prime-time soap.' It transcended the normal audience boundaries of traditional soap opera with its evening scheduling, high production values, outside location shooting, and by appealing to men as well as women. It successfully combined 'masculine' interests—power, wealth, success—with 'feminine'—love, families, relationships. Created by David Jacobs, *Dallas*'s first five-episode pilot season aired in April 1978 on CBS, and soon became the top-rated program in the U.S.

"Widely exported, it had arguably the largest range of audiences of any fictional TV program ever. Ien Ang (*Watching Dallas: Soap Opera and the Melodramatic Imagination*, 1985), for example, found a Dutch Marxist and an Israeli feminist who were able to find pleasures in the program by finding in its excess of sexism and capitalism critiques of both those systems.

"Scenes tended to be short and facial expressions were frequently shown in close-up and held for a few seconds before the next scene. As feminist critic Tania Modleski notes, close-ups provide training in the 'feminine' skills of 'reading people'—in understanding the difference between what is said and what is meant."

shoot one another, so at least you knew where you stood. The language of door slamming was infinitely nuanced.

"Ah, there you are, girls," said Aunty Suzanne. "I know you're too young at the moment, but *promise* me one day you'll read this book." She waved a paperback at us. It was called *The Female Eunuch* and had a picture on the cover of what looked like a woman's body drying on a washing line.

"What's a e-un-ooch?" I asked.

"It's a man without a penis!" said Aunty Suzanne triumphantly. "They're better like that sometimes!"

Lucy looked embarrassed and tugged my sleeve to follow her out of the room.

"Your mum just said penis!" I said when we were out of earshot.

"It's a type of flower," said Lucy defensively. "It grows in South America. Kenneth told me."

4.4 Love Story (2), Part 2

ALISTAIR STARTED *ripping off my clothes before we'd even closed the front door of my shared student house. It wasn't like it was in the films. There was no soft lighting or cut-away camera work, only a naked bulb hanging from the hall ceiling and an urgency that created its own obstacles. He kissed me and my hair fell in front of my face and caught in his mouth. He reached for my breasts, cupping them with his hands, and two buttons popped from my shirt. I stood on his toe.*

There was the sour-sweetish smell of whiskey on his breath and his eyes were hooded, his face taut with concentration. He wrestled to remove my tights, his hands warm and clammy. He wrenched them down my legs and his belt caught, and had to be tugged violently, three times, before it came off.

We left a trail of shoes, trousers, a bra, all the way up the stairs, and when we finally reached my room, he hoisted me up and pressed me against the bedroom door, spreading his fingers, wide, like a net, beneath me.

The condom? How did he manage the condom? The mechanics of it are hazy, although I can still remember the cold brass handle digging into the small of my back. I can remember feeling the muscles in his arm flexing just beneath the surface of his skin. He reached down and licked my nipple while his pelvis ground itself against mine. A streetlight outside the window had turned him orange, his eyes catlike, his skin burning. I listened to the noise of the traffic, wet tires slishing around the road and the door rattling in its frame. Rhythmically, at first. Then more urgently. The walls rippled. Three books fell off the sideboard. Dust motes rose from the carpet. And when I came, he came, our eyes wide, locked, astonished.

He gave a last deep thrust, and then, still joined, we collapsed on the floor, a layer of dust settling on our skin like confetti.

4.5   **relative** *n* **1** : one related by kinship, common origin or marriage

THE PREPARATIONS for Great-Great-Uncle Reginald's visit took days. It was always like this when we had visitors. Days of cleaning and baking and listening to complaints about the soft furnishings.

"That three-piece suite is on its last legs, it really is. James? James? Did you hear me?"

In fact, he hadn't. Our father had decided on a tactical retreat and removed himself to the shed.

"Rebecca, get yourself a cloth and you can start on the silver. And you can give her a hand, Tiffany."

It was our favorite chore. Although we kept this a secret from our mother in case she made us scrub the toilet or dust the ornaments instead. Polishing was different. You laid out newspaper and then smothered the brass and silver ornaments in a white fluid, which gave off a high, chemical smell. You let it dry and then rubbed it off. This was the magic part: the white stuff came off but so did the dullness. The metal came up gleaming. The rose vase and the saltcellar and the serviette rings, they all came up brand new, flawless, mirror perfect.

"Why do they get so dirty?"

"They tarnish." My mother was making a bowl of pastry and had a streak of flour through her hair.

"Just from sitting in the house?"

"It's in the air." She added water from a jug without looking up.

I thought about this for a moment. Did everybody's house have tarnish in the air, or was it just ours?

"Mum?"

"Not now, Rebecca. Can't you see I'm busy?"

I checked my wrists and knees instead, looking for evidence of a dulling of the skin.

When Great-Great-Uncle Reginald finally arrived, the house smelled of pine disinfectant and Glade air freshener. The spider plants had been trimmed, the rubber plant had been dusted and polished with a squirt of Pledge, the Tupperware boxes in the kitchen groaned under their load of freshly baked goods, and the metal-framed folding bed had been set up in Tiffany's room. I was relinquishing my bed, and a new duvet cover with a pattern of sprigged flowers had been purchased in honor of this relative we'd never met. We all wondered what he'd be like.

"He's a bit of a card" was all that my father would say on the matter. Still, we were all flattered that Great-Great-Uncle Reg had chosen us over the greater material comforts on offer at the Old Parsonage.

We went out onto the driveway to greet him. He appeared in an ancient Wolseley and a homburg hat, and his natural bonhomie disarmed us all, but mostly my mother.

"Hello, hello, hello!"

He pecked us on the cheek, a whiskery kiss that smelled of tobacco and an unknown soap.

"I say, Doreen, I'd forgotten what a fine-looking filly you are."

My mother rarely blushed, but two minutes into Uncle Reginald's visit and her cheeks were pink and little dimples played at the corners of her mouth.

"Look at that!" he said to her bottom as she walked down the hall into the kitchen. "God bless her and all who sail within her!"

My father coughed. "Come on, Reg. I'll show you your room."

There were flowers for my mother and dolls for both Tiffany and me. Uncle Reginald was turning out better than any of us could have hoped. Only my father seemed immune to his charms, but then Uncle Reginald didn't pinch him on the bottom, just my mother.

"Reg!" she said as a hand hovered over her backside, but you could tell she didn't really mean it.

He was on his way to a sales meeting on the south coast and was staying two nights. Apparently, he had his own chain of electrical goods stores, and even though he was in his seventies, he went into work every single day. "Nothing like a spot of hard work," he said. "Keeps the blood moving." He was going to look at new innovations in kitchen appliance technology at a hotel in Bournemouth. We listened, unbelieving, to his stories.

"There's these new fridges that tell you when they need defrosting, you know. And the ovens, well they're not ovens these days, they've got these new ones that are built-in with ceramic whatsits."

"Suzanne's got one of those," said Tiffany knowingly. My mother positioned herself between her and Uncle Reginald and waved the teapot. She was spinning off into hyper-hostess orbit.

"I don't think Reg wants to hear about Aunty Suzanne's kitchen, does he? More tea, Reg? Another slice of Dundee cake?"

"You're spoiling me, Doreen," he said and tipped her a wink. "I could get you a good discount on a Moulinex mixer, you know. You just have to say the word."

There was Beef Wellington for dinner and Granny Monroe came too. My mother had asked Aunty Suzanne and Uncle Kenneth as well, but Uncle Kenneth was away at a conference, and my mother had promptly rescinded the invitation, claiming that she didn't have a full set of dessert spoons.

"Why don't you invite Nanna?" I asked her. "Isn't Great-Great-Uncle Reginald her uncle too?"

"And your grandpa's," my father interjected looking up from his paper.

"Yes, *thank* you, James," said my mother, fixing him a look. "Why not tell the whole world I'm the product of an incestuous liaison?"

"What's incest?" I asked.

"You're exaggerating," said my father mildly. "It's not *that* unusual."

"What's incest?" I asked again. It was as if my parents deliberately ignored my questions.

"Tell it to the marines," my mother muttered and went off to prove her pastry cases.

Uncle Reginald kissed Granny Monroe's hand when she arrived.

"Another looker!" he said. "How many of you are there in this family?" Granny Monroe, who was wearing a particularly hideous lime green polyester twin set, let out a giggle. Or at least a noise that I would have said was a giggle had it been anyone other than Granny Monroe. Granny Monroe never giggled.

My mother interposed herself between Uncle Reg and Granny Monroe and tried to flick her hair back from her eyes, but it had been Carmen heated-rollered and hair-sprayed into place, on account of the fact that it was a special occasion, and refused to budge.

"Cynthia?" she said. "Perhaps you could help me with the sprouts."

They sashayed together out of the room.

"Uncle Reginald?"

"Yes, Rebecca."

"Why've you never married?" Everybody we knew was married. It was what grown-ups did.

"Never felt the need," he said, settling himself back in the best armchair and taking a sip of his tea. "I've always liked the ladies, but I'm not sure I could live with one."

We had changed before dinner, and my mother had put on her safari suit outfit and left her top button undone. Tiffany and I both wore dresses and had combed our hair until it rose off our heads in crackling static waves.

Uncle Reginald wore a tweed suit and a tie. "Dresses like a gent too," said Granny Monroe, looking pointedly at our father's V-necked sweater.

He told us stories about the War ("Which war?" I hissed at Tiffany but she just shrugged her shoulders) and about our mother when she was young.

"She's always been a right little cracker. A proper little dolly bird from the day she was born. Alicia was over the moon. 'My little angel,' she called her."

"Yes, well," said my mother. "She would say that, wouldn't she?"

"Why?" I asked.

"Oh, for God's sake, Rebecca, don't be so literal." And she swept off to fetch in her lemon syllabub, served, as the photo in the recipe book suggested, in elegant fluted wineglasses.

"Well. Lah-di-dah!" said Granny Monroe, although I noticed it didn't stop her from scraping her glass clean.

After we'd finished it, and my father had opened a second bottle of wine ("Wine, eh?" said Uncle Reginald. "Well tha's come up in the world!"), we got out the photo albums.

"That's me there," said Uncle Reginald, pointing at a blurred photo of a man with slicked back hair. "That was just after the war. Handsome devil, eh?

"And that's your grandmother Alicia. She looks like you, doesn't she, Rebecca?" I peered at the photo. It showed a diffident-looking young woman wearing a blank expression. She didn't look much like the Nanna we knew now. I studied her face. Her eyes were similar, and her hair, although she didn't have my high, moony forehead. Nobody did.

"That was her wedding day. Of course, Herbert wasn't the pick of the crop, but under the circumstances . . ." The sentence petered out as he looked at my mother and seemed to think better of it.

We flipped through the pages. There was a picture of Granny Monroe as a young woman. She didn't look a whole lot different. Black-and-white rather than younger or prettier.

"Who do I look like?" demanded Tiffany.

"Look, there's your Great-Aunt Betty," said Uncle Reginald. "She's a bit of a funny one. And there's Elizabeth, the family beauty."

The photo showed a young woman in a tight uniform with a heavily lipsticked mouth and long blond curls that flowed down her shoulders. Tiffany and I stared at her. Would we look like that when we grew up?

The wedding album came out eventually, in its white cover with the gold writing and its photos secreted between layers of white tissue paper.

We looked at the familiar photos of our mother and father looking young and happy and frozen in time.

"You look a bit like her, I suppose, don't you?" said Uncle Reginald to Tiffany, pointing at a photo. "Isn't that your great-great-aunty Maureen?" The photo wasn't sharp, and the face was at the back of the group portrait outside the church. Great-Great-Aunty Maureen was standing next to Aunty Suzanne.

"A bit, I suppose," said Tiffany unenthusiastically. I couldn't say I blamed her. Great-Great-Aunty Maureen, we all knew, was "not quite all there." Tiffany peered at the photo. "Her hair's a bit like mine."

I was the one who spotted their mistake. "It's Uncle Kenneth!" I said. "When he had long hair!"

Uncle Reginald looked again. "Well, well, well. Can't tell 'em apart these days." We tried to look at the picture again, but my mother snapped it shut.

"Right," she said brightly. "Who's for a nightcap?"

"I tell you what, Doreen, you certainly know the way to a man's heart." Uncle Reginald sat back and allowed her to fill half a tumbler with our father's finest malt.

"James?" she said. He nodded and she poured the smallest trickle into the bottom of a tumbler.

Uncle Reg twirled his glass in his hand. "That should keep the wolf from the door," he said. "You've got a good one there, James." But I had caught sight of my father's eyes and he didn't look quite so sure somehow. Although he may just have been annoyed about the whiskey.

4.6 academic *adj* 2 : having no practical purpose or use

I LIT THE CANDLES on the table and checked on the lamb before calling up the stairs to Alistair.

"They're going to be here in a minute. Do you want to open the wine?"

I went back into the kitchen and made a dressing for the salad and cut up the loaf of bread, checked the lamb again, put the water on to boil for the vegetables and looked at my watch. Alistair still hadn't appeared. I went back to the foot of the stairs.

"Alistair?"

There was no answer. Five minutes later, he appeared, in an obviously bad mood.

"Do I have to?"

"Yes."

"You know I don't like the man."

"He's my supervisor. You don't have to like him. You just have to be polite to him. Here. Have a glass of wine."

I handed him a glass and he took it reluctantly.

"Anyway," I said, "it was your idea that I went back to my Ph.D. It's your own fault."

He didn't say anything and drank a mouthful of wine.

I wiped down the kitchen counter. "What were you doing?"

"I'm writing a paper," he said, taking an olive from a bowl and eating it. "Proper academic work."

They arrived late, which meant that Alistair and I had already finished most of one bottle of wine and he'd slightly forgotten his mood. I, on the other hand, had forgotten the lamb.

"Oh well," he said. "Perhaps they'll push off early when they see the food." I bent over to pick up the oven gloves and he cupped my breasts from behind. I opened the door of the oven, and a wave of heat and a sudden rush of physical memories hit me. The joint looked brown and tough. Overdone.

Alistair went to let them in. Peter was wearing a black polo-neck and a black leather jacket and I knew immediately that there was going to be a fight. Alistair's shoulders had tensed. He looked like a cartoon cat that had just seen a cartoon dog walk into the room.

"Sorry," said Peter. "We went for a drink first and bumped into some friends."

"Let me take your coats," I said.

"I'll leave it on for a bit, if that's okay."

I took Kay's instead. She was the latest in a long line of Peter's girl-friends. Underneath her coat, she was wearing a red miniskirt and knee-length boots, but then Peter likes his girlfriends to be fashionable. He told me once that it showed that they had an ability to tap into contemporary culture.

"Sit," I commanded. "Eat."

We all sat down round the table and I placed dishes and plates and serving spoons and started serving up the meat.

"I'm a vegetarian," said Kay.

"Oh."

Peter looked at her in surprise. "Are you?"

She nodded. "I only eat organic food."

I hesitated, unsure of the logic, but before I could say anything Alistair had erupted.

"Of course, it's mostly anti-scientific poppycock. People have this idea that natural equals good, when one of the most powerful poisons known to man is a green potato. Organic or not."

I turned to Kay. "Would you like the vegetables? I've got some cheese in the fridge if you'd like something else with it. Or an omelette? I could make an omelette."

"The establishment hates it when the masses resist." Peter leaned back in his chair and looked at Alistair. "The forces of global capitalism pump our food full of chemicals for years and then, when we, the people, begin to wise up to their marketing techniques, to deconstruct the misinformation that they feed us, we're denigrated as being illogical. Or childish. Or 'anti-scientific.'"

"So is the 'establishment' the same as 'the forces of global capitalism'?" said Alistair, taking a mouthful of wine. "Or are they something different?"

"I only eat eggs if they've been certified by the Soil Association," said Kay.

I opened the fridge and looked at the box. "They're free-range," I said hopefully. They were also several days out of date. She shook her head anyway.

"Rebecca's making great progress with her research. She's uncovering some really interesting stuff," said Peter.

"Ah yes," said Alistair. "The seventies is the new sixties. Isn't that it?"

"Well, no," I began, but Peter had already moved to interrupt him.

"No. It's a deconstruction of the dominant communal memory of the era. Current popular cultural narratives repeatedly depict the era as a faintly ridiculous suburban pastoral. It's a thoroughgoing analysis of the way the decade has been commodified and sold back to us as nothing but a particularly hilarious period of bad taste."

He paused and took a sip of his wine as if to emphasize his next point. "My theory," he began but then corrected himself. "Well, Rebecca's theory, is that the seventies was when the social revolutions of the 1960s actually began to permeate mainstream British society."

He leaned back in his chair. My hand hovered on the vegetable dish. Kay was looking suspiciously at the *mange-tout*.

"Are they imported?" she said.

"I've never quite understood this 'commodification' business," said Alistair. "Aren't you just trying to cloak some rather banal observations in inflated academic jargon? It doesn't really *mean* anything, does it?"

Peter, riled now, rose to the bait. I tried to impose myself between them, but Peter just leaned around me.

"In terms of how we view the society we live in now, yes, it does mean something. If today's cultural producers recycle the past as retro pastiche, then they are imposing a de-politicized version of history on a period that saw a wholesale fragmentation of ideologies. A breakdown of institutionalized structures—the family, marriage, etc.—the effects of which we are still living with today."

He drank a large mouthful of wine and waited for Alistair's response.

"Let's eat!" I said.

"I've got some photographs of my parents in the seventies," said Kay. "And they look absolutely ridiculous. My dad has sideburns!"

"Quite," said Alistair.

Part Five

memory *n* **1** : faculty by which things are recalled to or kept in the mind

5.1 **evidence** *n* **1** : a thing or things helpful in forming a conclusion or judgment

IT WAS HERBERT who rang me. And Herbert never rings me. In fact I've never known Herbert to use the telephone before. "It's your grandmother," he said. "She's been a bit poorly."

"What's wrong?"

"Come up and visit is the best."

"Is she all right?"

"Aye. But she's poorly." Poorly. Nobody in our family ever gets ill. They're always poorly. A nonspecific state that could mean anything from a cold to cancer.

I caught the train the next day and Herbert met me at the station. I didn't notice him at first, and wandered up and down, looking in the newsstands, the café, the waiting room, but he'd been there the whole time, standing in front of the information board.

"It's her mind," he said once we were in the car. "They think maybe it's Alzheimer's."

He drove me back to the house, where Alicia was sitting in the kitchen looking out the window. She looked smaller somehow than the last time I'd seen her, as if she'd folded in on herself. She was staring out the window in a trance but she looked up when she saw me, a huge smile across her face.

"Rebecca!" she said. "Rebecca! Come and give me a hug!"

She felt as plump and soft as ever. Nanna always had a comfortable, cushiony quality.

"Let me have a look at you! So pretty!"

We sat and drank tea and ate shortbread biscuits.

Herbert sat and drank tea too, which was the only thing I could see that was really unusual. Herbert never sits and drinks tea. He sits in his shed. But there he was perched silently at the end of the table, although he kept his overcoat on.

"Look at you! You look so well!" But so did Alicia, slightly less certain of herself perhaps, but not so very different. I told her about Alistair, and Tiffany, and how my thesis was going.

"Of course it was Betty, I should have realized that."

"Realized what?"

"She couldn't stand the idea that other people could be happy."

"Sorry?"

"Betty, you're just a meddler! A meddler in other people's affairs! How could you? How could you?"

She'd become enraged. Her face was contorted. She slammed her fist on the table and then she burst into tears. I got up from my chair and hugged her. Held her close, and could feel her tears running down my shoulder. Her body was shaking. I found a piece of paper towel and gave it to her.

"What's wrong, Alicia? What is it?"

"What's what?"

"Why are you upset?"

"Upset about what?"

"You. Why are you upset?"

"Me? Upset?"

I felt utterly nonplussed. She just repeated my questions, looking at me with incomprehension. Then she turned to Herbert.

"What's Rebecca upset about?"

Herbert looked resigned. He turned to me.

"See what I mean?"

I stayed the night in my mother's old room. The house she grew up in. The bed that had been hers. It hadn't been redecorated since she was a child, and the flowered wallpaper, faded now, was still covered with the posters of her teenage longings. *Dr. Kildare* featured prominently. I stared at Richard Chamberlain's face and lay awake for a long time, just listening. The house creaked in the night as if it was sighing. In the morning, Alicia pottered around the kitchen making tea and toast.

"They're trying to steal my memories," she said.

"What?"

"The doctors. They ask me all these questions about what I can remember and then they write them down. I know what they're doing."

"They're just trying to help you get better."

"Ha! Well, they're not going to have them. They're mine."

She looked at me, conspiratorially. "I've got something for you."

I waited for her to elaborate.

"Evidence." And she padded off to the front room. I sat at the table and waited. She was holding a large brown box when she returned. I stood up to help her with it, catching a waft of musty paper. I peered inside. There was a bunch of papers, letters and hardback books I recognized as Herbert's Bought Ledger files, the books that detailed and documented his obsession with my grandmother. I didn't have the heart to tell her I'd read most of them years ago. Tiffany and I had found them in the attic when we were teenagers and had spent days poring over them.

"You'll read it, won't you?"

"I'll read it," I said.

"Good."

She sat back down and smiled. It was nearly ten o'clock. I had to go.

"I'll be back soon," I said.

I gave her a hug. She clung to me.

"Don't go."

"I'll be back."

"It was my fault, you know. Your mother's death."

"No, it wasn't."

"I shouldn't have told her."

"Nanna?"

"My fault."

"You can't say that. It wasn't your fault."

It was mine, after all.

"She never forgave me."

"Forgave you for what?"

But she wouldn't say.

. . .

On the train home, I started reading the contents of my grand-mother's box, although I already know most of her secrets. There's a thread of unhappiness that twists down through the generations and links us together. She lost her daughter. I lost my mother. Between us, there's a gaping Doreen-shaped hole.

There are differences too. Alicia lost the love of her life. I married mine. There are differences. But they're not as great as you'd think.

5.2   **fruit** *n* **1** : plant's or tree's edible product of seed with its en-velope

MY GRANDMOTHER Alicia never intended to go into Hosiery. No-body dreams of going into socks. She assumed she would Go Forth and Act, but it didn't happen. Her war never arrived. She was born too late. Her body mapped the Allies' trail of victory across the continent; the passage of hormones through her skin, a blow-by-blow chronol-ogy of the progress of the European front. On the day American troops landed in Anzio, her periods began. As she and her mother went to Cooks in the Bullring to buy her first brassiere, Paris was lib-erated. And as the Red Army marched into Berlin, she discovered a boy in her class blatantly staring at the contents of her sweater. It was historically inevitable that on the day peace broke out, she should find herself in a clinch with a corporal from Wolverhampton who grasped her around the waist and swung her in time to the music being played by what remained of the West Riding Police Band (there were a lot of gaps in the cornet section). Uncle Samuel spotted her and took her back home. She was consigned to Socks.

She accepted her fate with good grace, which is to say, she had no choice. It was the same with her accident. She lay in her narrow hos-pital bed and listened to its hospital noises and smelled its hospital smells. Her automobile accident and subsequent internment in Clay-ton Hospital had driven the pinkness from her cheeks. It had been lost amid the bedpans and saltwater enemas and ministrations of Sister

Weston, whose crisp linen hat seemed to bear down upon her bed more frequently than it did upon the others in Ward 3.

The pinkness, the flush of her adolescence, had gone, but there was no mistaking that it had been replaced by something else. But what? Was it a rash? A pimple? Had Alicia cut her hair? Or reshaped her eyebrows? Nobody was sure, but she looked indefinably different.

"Maybe she's sickening," said Uncle Bernard.

"Well of course she's sickening, you silly man, she's got a leg that's been broken in three places," said Aunty Peggy.

"No but maybe it's affected her insides," said Uncle Bernard. "You know, where we can't see."

Herbert said nothing. He watched Alicia, noticed the way Sister Weston looked at her, observed her hands fidgeting on the sheets and followed her eyes as they cast sideways glances at the entrance to the ward. He catalogued it all. While Mrs. Cragley fluttered around Alicia, pressing flannels to her forehead, and cousins came and went bringing bunches of freesias and white paper bags of Mint Imperials, Herbert had no choice but to withdraw his troops, regroup and undertake detailed and intensive surveillance.

He was the only member of the family who knew about the visitations of the tall, thin brown man whose jacket hung limply from his shoulders. As Cecil came pad pad padding through Ward 3, it was Herbert who slid noiselessly between the beds, slipping between Mrs. Browning, with the missing womb, and Mrs. Fairchild, with the nervous condition, neither of whom noticed the pimply teenager with the lopsided face. They were too preoccupied with the Colored Man.

Herbert was used to watching. He was good at it. He bought a new book, this one marked "Outgoings," and in this he commenced the Cecil Files. It had a column for weekly tallies, in which he tried to evaluate the nuances of Alicia's expressions. Herbert could track Cecil for miles. He trailed him from the hospital to Denmark Street to the dairy where Cecil worked, and on his aimless ramblings around the streets of Wakefield.

It wasn't difficult. Cecil stooped more heavily in the weeks following Alicia's accident. He wore his guilt like his suit; the uncomfortable, new, ill-fitting suit that his mother had bought him on a hot, humid September day in Kingston. It was his fault that Alicia was lying with her leg encased in plaster of paris and suspended in the air via a complicated system of ropes and pulleys. His remorse was absolute. He'd seen it all: her face, Councillor Anderson's face, the sharp, acrid smell of the brakes and the *bump, bump, bump* as she'd disappeared from sight. And all because he'd whistled.

As Cecil lay on the sagging mattress of the boardinghouse on Denmark Street, his nose was filled with the smell of Brussels sprouts and his mind with the image of his mother's face. It was as well that Felicia Johnston was oblivious to what had occurred on Thirlmere Road, February 28, 1948, for had she not predicted on numerous occasions that Cecil's habit of blowing profanities through his lips would bring down the wrath of the Lord and that He would smite his head?

"'Ave I not told you, Cecil Johnston, that whistling is de mouth-music of de devil? Dat it is a kind of satanic flatulence that will be the undoing of you and your everlasting soul?" She emphasized this point with a whack around his ear holes and a swipe across his cheek.

Felicia Johnston was a Seventh Day Adventist, and she knew that actions had consequences. She was an obedient servant of the church. She thought that Easter was a pagan ritual, she abhorred the flesh of swine, and she knew that the Catholic Church was the Great Whore who had committed fornication with the kings of the earth. Just as she knew that the Anglicans, Baptists, Methodists, Anabaptists and Moravians were her harlot Protestant daughters. She did not whistle.

Cecil sniffed the air. The smell of Brussels sprouts was becoming stronger. The boardinghouse was a dank and depressing place and cost two shillings, six pence a week, which Mrs. Armitage, the landlady, pocketed every Monday morning while attempting not to breathe through her nose. Unlike Wakefield's other landladies, she had agreed to rent a room to Cecil, the only black man in Wakefield. Her reasoning was sound (she could charge him more). She just couldn't abide the smell of him.

It was not Cecil's hair oil that was the offending aroma this time. The smell that Mrs. Armitage refused to inhale was a malodorous combination of mold spores and masonry, of plaster that was wet to the touch and wallpaper that appeared to sweat.

Cecil jumped to his feet and whistled as he strode down the road. He walked and he whistled and then he caught himself. What was he to do? He had to stop himself, but how? Had he not caused enough damage already? He had seen the bruises across Alicia's arms, the grazes on her elbows, the pallor of her complexion, and her leg, useless, like a broken wing. He wondered if perhaps his mother had been right. If his actions would have consequences. If he would pay for his sin.

He walked down the street, self-consciously not-whistling. He notwhistled all the way to Westgate. And, not-whistling, he scoured the shops. He searched for the foods that would atone for the sin of causing Alicia Cragley to fall beneath the wheels of an Austin Atlantic and break her leg in three places. He hunted for the foods that would cure her ills and mend her bones, that would restore color to her cheeks and fill her soul with the joy of living and the marvelousness of creation.

Cecil knew about these things, for he was the son of Felicia Johnston, and had absorbed the teachings of the Jamaican conference of the Seventh Day Adventists even as he had deliberately and comprehensively flouted them.

He knew that "Tea and coffee drinking was a sin, an injurious indulgence" (*Counsel on Diet and Foods*, Ellen White). He knew that "cheese should never be introduced into the stomach" (*Testimonies to the Church*, Volume 2, Ellen White), nor should eggs "be placed upon your table" (*Ibid*, Ellen White). And he knew that of all these things, the worst of them was tea. Ellen White, the prophet, was abundantly clear on the subject. "Tea is *poisonous* to the system" (*Counsel on Diet and Foods*). "Hot drinks are debilitating" (*Ibid*). Tea causes "intemperance, and is at war with the laws of life and health" (*Evangelism*).

It is hard to know the nature of the malady from which Cecil was suffering as he stood in line at the greengrocer's shop. Forgetfulness? Delusion? Brain fever? Did he really think he would find the fruits of his island piled in tall luxuriant heaps? Mounds of pink-skinned mangoes? Pineapples that were so ripe their skin had split? Or would he find a handful of bruised apples? Some dirty cabbage? A pile of sorry-looking potatoes?

Cecil was troubled by Sister White's teachings on tea. Poor Alicia! She lay in her bed being brought the Yorkshire cure-all, cup after cup of hot sweet tea. She was being drowned in tea. Was it any wonder that she was pale? Did these people not know that the souls of tea drinkers would not be translated at the time of the Investigative Judgment? He walked purposefully onward, although it is unclear if it was fear for Alicia's soul that propelled him along the pavement. Or the image of her reaching forward for the drop of papaya juice, her tongue outstretched.

Not that it mattered. Whichever way you looked at it, Wakefield, in February 1948, was not the place to find vegetable cures. The emporiums (such a pointlessly optimistic name) of the West Riding were empty. The long-anticipated postwar boom had yet to arrive. Rationing coupons still stalked the nation's consumerist dreams. Cecil abandoned the cabbage and the potatoes and instead bought a pad of paper and a pen. He would write to his mother.

Sitting in her small, neat house in Kingston with the oilcloth on the table and the rocker on the porch, Felicia Johnston fell to her knees and rejoiced.

It was the moment for which she had been praying. The first sign of repentance. He had ignored her pleas and prayers and threats and promises and in 1942, when U-boats were rumored to have penetrated Kingston harbor, and Jamaica was being touted as the Enemy's stepping stone to America, he had left school early and gone to sign up with that idiot friend of his, Glen.

Felicia put on her coat and her bonnet and prepared to go to market. She would find the foods that would show him the kingdom of heaven in all its glory. She knew the power of the smell of a freshly squeezed lime. She would gather up the bloodred oranges that made her neighbors dribble in anticipation, and wrap them in ancient copies of the *Gleaner*. She would send salvation by means of His Majesty's Royal Mail. Packages of wholesomeness and righteousness bound in brown paper would travel by steamer across the Atlantic to Denmark Street, where they would arrive moist and sticky and leaking juices over Mrs. Armitage's disapproving doormat. And by this means, Felicia Johnston knew she would save his soul.

She knew that when he tasted the soft but yielding flesh of the small yellow mangoes that dropped like teeth from her tree, he would forsake the flesh of swine and the drink of the Scots. She would send him papaya. Food from heaven. The breath of angels.

That night as Cecil lay on his mattress, damp flecks of whitewash sitting like dandruff on his black springy hair, he heard the creaking of the roof and the groans of the building as it shifted on its foundations. What he didn't realize was that the creaks were the sound of Herbert's shiny-soled brogues as he rested each foot on the crossbeams of the roof, and the groans were the lintels of the windows suffering under his weight. Nor did he realize that at this moment in time, Herbert was dislodging another tile through which more water would pass, bubbling more whitewash, which would rain down eventually onto Cecil as he lay on this very mattress, leaving a dot-to-dot game on his smooth brown cheek.

Cecil knew none of this. He was dreaming of cream skin and cream hair that left a taste of tapioca and mashed potato in his mouth. For it was not only Alicia who experienced the synaesthetic confusion of taste and color.

5.3   **black hole** *n* : (*astron*) region from which no matter or radiation can escape

I WENT ON the Internet straightaway. "Alzheimer's," I typed. There were 211,000 entries.

"Alzheimer's disease." Named after Dr. Alois Alzheimer, a Viennese physician, who on November 25, 1901, admitted a fifty-one-year-old woman with no personal or family history of mental illness to a psychiatric hospital in Frankfurt. She was suffering from inexplicable outbursts of emotion and a bizarre set of memory problems.

What happens is this: Parts of the cerebral cortex, the thin layer that coats the outside of the brain, become clogged with two different types of cellular matter: brown lumpy plaques that move between the neurons and straggly black tangles that choke them from within.

The neurons begin to die. The brain shrinks. The thousands of synapses, each representing a fragment of a memory, vanish. At the end, there is no trace the neuron itself ever existed, except for one thing. All that is left is a small clump of "ghost tangles" where a neuron once stood. Black holes of the mind.

Recent memories go first, because the act of remembering itself creates a brand-new memory of that memory. Which is why the more you remember something, the more you remember it. It's why sometimes your most powerful memories may not actually be true. They are stories that have solidified into fact.

In the end, the brain forgets everything. Words. How to speak. Or to recognize the face of a husband, a son, a daughter. Or to walk. Or smile. Or breathe.

You forget how to breathe. That was when I started crying, I think, although it might have been later. When I tried to hug Alistair in bed. And he turned the other way.

Part Six

crack *n* : a narrow opening formed by breaking

6.1 Love Story (2), Part 3

WHEN ALI MACGRAW went for a pregnancy test, she discovered she was terminally ill. When I went for a pregnancy test, I discovered I was pregnant. I take this as a sign of my own literalness. It shouldn't have happened. The odds were very much against it. We used two different forms of contraception (efficacy rates: 98 percent and 96 percent respectively). And still I conceived. That first night.

I didn't realize at first. That stuff about how you know immediately, about how your breasts swell and ache, how your body changes—it's all rubbish. I didn't know. I didn't even guess.

Alistair didn't either. Neither of us realized until I had the test and it came back positive. That night we lay together under my duvet. We talked about the future. I wrapped my legs around his, felt his skin next to mine, felt his pulse beating, beat for beat, with mine.

The next day my cervix was stretched open with a dilator. A small metal loop scraped the inside of my uterus and an electrically powered aspirator vacuumed out the contents.

It was too soon, Alistair said. And he was usually right.

6.2   **home** *n* **1** : a place where one lives; a residence

MY MOTHER had decided to redecorate the lounge ("IT'S A SITTING ROOM! DOESN'T ANYBODY HEAR ME? DO I TALK TO MYSELF?"). Actually she did talk to herself. There she was now: "Forheaven'ssakeamItheonlypersoninthisfamilywhoiscapableofholding apaintbrush?" And "SometimesIwonderifanythingatallwouldeverget doneinthishouseifitwasn'tforme!"

She was halfway up a ladder, wearing one of our father's shirts. I suspected that he hadn't realized it had been made redundant until he caught sight of it on her back with a streak of something pink down the sleeve. There was a sloshing of paint onto brush and a gentle murmuring as she provided a running commentary on her activities. She'd been up since five o'clock in the morning stripping wallpaper and consulting color charts, although she'd decided to get in professionals to Artex the ceiling; a repetitive half-moon pattern that would preoccupy my mind's eye for years to come. There were speckles of paint on her Reactolites but she was too focused on the job in hand to notice.

"Right, come on, James, we're going to go and look at suites."

Tiffany looked up expectantly. There was nothing she enjoyed more than the prospect of a shopping expedition.

"Can I come? Please!"

My father stood in the middle of the living room. He shuffled his feet and opened his mouth to say something then changed his mind. Eventually he spoke.

"Doreen, the thing is I'm not sure we can afford it right this month."

Tiffany and my mother both turned to stare at him with the same narrowed eyes.

"And I suppose you don't mind living in a slum, do you?"

"There's the car payments. And the caravan . . ." Our father had managed to flog it through a small ad in the back of the *Advertiser* to a harassed-looking man with dandruff on his collar, but there were still eighteen months of payments left to make.

"And what are we supposed to do in the meantime? Sit on the floor?"

"Well what's wrong with this settee?"

"*It's a sofa*. Only a man could ask that question. You've got no idea, have you? No idea at all."

"It's all right, isn't it? It'll do, won't it?"

"And that's my lot, is it? I have to put up with things that 'will do,' that are 'all right,' do I? That's as much as I can hope for, is it?"

There was a new, high-pitched urgency to our mother's words and she turned and started attacking the wallpaper above the fireplace. "I'msickofalwayshavingsecondbestandofmakingdo . . . Don'tIdeservebetterthanthis? Other people have new sofas *and* foreign holidays."

The *foreign* holiday had lately come to obsess her. She'd started watching the *BBC Holiday* program with an almost religious devotion, sighing over the swimming pools and exclaiming at the fat-bodied jumbo jets.

"REBECCA, WILL YOU GET OFF THAT CHAIR RIGHT NOW? DON'T YOU CHILDREN HAVE ANYTHING BETTER TO DO THAN HANG AROUND HERE AND ANNOY ME?"

Uncharacteristically, our father simply vanished. We heard the sound of the car engine starting up and then nothing. Banished to the upstairs, we attempted to play quietly and listened to the noise of buckets being sloshed and wallpaper being ripped. There were a lot of loud banging noises when the windows shook and the walls rippled and then quiet until the kitchen radio was switched on. The sound of Blondie and Rod Stewart started filling the house. It unnerved us because our mother usually listened to Radio 2, where the only pop music they played was by dead people. By three o'clock we were both hungry and decided to risk a trip downstairs. The hall was covered in what looked like gray volcanic dust. The kitchen was wrong too. One of its walls was missing. Mount Doreen appeared to have blown its top. Her hair, coated with masonry particles, had turned white and stiff; her glasses had almost completely frosted up. She was standing in the middle of the lounge grinning, a pickax in her hands.

"I borrowed it from Kevin Huxley next door. What do you think?"

Where the serving hatch from the lounge to the kitchen used to be, there was now a serving hole, its edges jagged and uncertain. The door frame, shattered and useless, hung like a broken arm.

"Great!"

"Fantastic!"

Carole Cadwalladr

Our words came out just a little too quickly. There were chunks of plaster and brick all over the carpet. Three days earlier, I'd spilled peas on it and had been sent to my room. She didn't seem to mind though—in fact, she didn't even seem to have noticed.

It was Tiffany who spotted the crack. We looked up to see a Zorro-esque zigzag crevasse right across the ceiling. Our mother looked momentarily uncertain.

"Oh well, it's going to be Artexed anyway." She paused. "You won't be able to see it." There was nothing it seemed that could dent her cheeriness. "See how it's opened the place up? It's much lighter, isn't it? Everything's going open-plan these days. It's so much more modern to have one big living area rather than these pokey little rooms."

There was a solidarity between Tiffany and me as we took the Mother's Pride from the bread bin and cut slices of Cheddar. Tiffany switched on the grill and we carefully toasted one side of the bread.

"Mum?"

"Hmm?" She had given up with the pickax and was now trying to untack the nails from the carpet.

"Would you like some cheese on toast?"

"Do you think I've got time to eat? Somebody's got to get this place in order and it won't be your father. Mind you don't make a mess in there now, girls."

We crouched down and pressed our foreheads next to the grill, waiting for the cheese to rise up and bubble. Then we wrapped up the Cheddar, returned the bread to the bread bin, rinsed the knife and carefully transferred our cheese on toast to two plates. Tiffany raised her eyes upward, and with both hands we carried our lunch out of the kitchen and up the stairs.

As a special concession to our confinement, Tiffany had deigned to play with me, and we painted blue eye shadow onto her Girl's World, a plastic head with acrylic hair on which you could practice being a grown-up. We added pink lipstick and powder and eyeliner and spent hours extending the hair and wrapping it in curlers. Downstairs the banging seemed to be slowing. The crashes and rumbles became steadily more intermittent, like thunder in retreat. It was getting dark when we heard the car in the drive, and through the window we watched our father steer it carefully into the garage. Noiselessly we opened Tiffany's door and waited.

"I'm hooo . . . What? On? Earth?"

"Ta-ta!" She sounded like she was introducing the winner on an ITV game show.

"What do you think? I did it all by myself. Stronger than I look, eh?"

We couldn't hear our father's reply distinctly but he sounded suddenly tired.

"Oh Doh!" he said. Or possibly, "Oh no!"

On the landing, peering through the banisters, we could see the dust motes in the hallway falling and rising as if the house were breathing. And then, it seemed to hiccup. The ground shifted almost imperceptibly. There was silence until our father screamed, "Where are the girls? Are they upstairs? Oh God! Doreen, *get out of the house!*" We froze as our father lunged up the stairs two steps at a time, spotted us and yelled, "*Girls!* Come on. Out. Now."

We ran down the stairs after him, down the hall, through the hole in the wall and out the patio windows to where our mother was standing in the middle of the lawn. I didn't have any shoes on.

"I don't have any shoes on," I said. But our father wasn't listening to me. He was listening to the house. There was the far-off sound of *The Six Million Dollar Man* theme tune coming from next door. A car engine turned over. It was quite dark now, and the back of the house was lit by three pools of yellow electric light; the rectangular frame of the patio doors, the largest, brightest pool. Then we heard it. *Crrack!* It sounded like thunder, an enormous, sudden release of days of pent-up energy. The patio windows fogged up. It looked like the bubbly glass in the bathroom window: luminous but opaque. We watched a typhoon of dust and debris swirl and settle. It was as if the weather were inside the house.

"Oh, Doreen!" said our father. It was not the "Oh, Doreen!" of the time she bumped the car on the way to the shops. Or the "Oh, Doreen!" of when she made rude remarks about Granny Monroe. It was a new "Oh, Doreen!" that we hadn't heard before, a mixture of despair and pity and fatigue. "Oh, Doreen!" he said. His shoulders slumped. "It was a supporting wall!"

Through the patio doors, we could see that the air in the lounge was starting to clear. There were bricks and bits of plaster on the floor, on the settee, on the hearth rug. Everywhere. And amid the rubble, a familiar-looking face. It was Tiffany's Girl's World, her eye shadow smeared, her lipstick smudged, pieces of grit clinging to her freshly curled hair.

"You could all have been killed." My father's hands were shaking. We all turned to look at my mother, but her expression was like the bathroom window, luminous but opaque. Blank. The net curtains were drawn.

"Come on," said my father eventually. "We'd better find you some shoes, Rebecca." I'd forgotten about my feet.

Later that night, when Granny Monroe had taken us in, and I had been given dead Grandpa Monroe's socks, my toes were still numb. They were little blocks of ice that shivered in between Granny Monroe's unyielding sheets. We slept in our father's old room. Around our heads flew Spitfires and Tiger Moths and Dakotas, Airfix models suspended on pieces of nylon fishing thread. They drifted in slow, silent circles around my head. I felt as if I'd been pinioned to the bed. I wrestled the blankets and curled up my legs and pressed my toes against my thighs, but they refused to thaw. I wondered if they'd ever be warm again.

In the morning, our mother had already gone by the time we got up for breakfast. Our father was hovering in the kitchen.

"Ah, girls, so you're going to be having a little holiday with your granny, isn't that nice?"

We looked at him dubiously. A holiday? With Granny Monroe? What kind of holiday was that?

"Where's Mum?"

"She's having a little holiday too."

Granny Monroe sat at the table with her arms folded.

"We all make the bed we must lie in," she said, looking pointedly at our father.

We were left to Granny Monroe's devices for what were surely the longest two weeks in history. Her house was foreign and filled with objects that were terrifying in themselves (the vicious ceramic Pekinese dogs on the hearth), in their name ("antimacassars") or in what would happen to us if we broke them (the porcelain crinoline ladies on the mantelpiece).

It didn't smell like home either (an irreducible mixture of Pledge, Ajax, the air from the Hoover, Heinz spaghetti, bubble bath, Vaseline, Mazola cooking oil, spider plants, Elnett hairspray, fitted carpet, Dettol, Avon lipstick, pork chops, Stork margarine, dental floss, Savlon, Birds Eye frozen peas, Aquafresh toothpaste, Bold washing powder, Ski yogurt, Dick Francis paperbacks and Maxwell House). Granny Monroe's house smelled of old age. There were the underlying currents of Ajax and Pledge and Avon lipstick, but there was a thick and heavy smell that reminded me of museums and made me shiver (beeswax), as well as other alien aromas (pickled beetroot, sponge fingers, boiled tongue, coal dust, Heinz Piccalilli, parma violets, Lily of the Valley talcum powder, setting lotion, Nivea cold cream, Reader's Digest hardbacks, Nice biscuits and leaf tea).

It was the furniture though that scared me the most. Tiffany and I were sharing our father's old room, where a dark oak wardrobe and a dark oak set of drawers surrounded the bed. The curtains were lined and there was no Pooh Bear nightlight. In fact, there was no light at all, not even a chink. I could feel the furniture looming around me, ready to pounce. The only way I knew to prevent this happening was to tap a secret code on the wall. I knocked softly twice. And then I felt a rising tide of panic. What if two knocks was the code for awakening the evil wardrobe spirits? I knocked again. Just in case. But what if I'd accidentally entered the password that would bring forth all the demons of the wardrobe underworld? I tapped again, a complicated tap, tap, tappity, tap, tap.

The door flung open. *Aaaagggghhhh!* My breathing stopped. My heart ricocheted against my rib cage. A ghostly white face appeared, too huge to be human.

"What the devil do you think you're playing at, young lady?"

It was only Granny Monroe, a thick layer of cold cream on her face, her head a cloud of curlers. The wardrobe hadn't moved, so perhaps I'd cracked it after all. The light snapped off and I was reduced to contemplating the horrors of the room in silence. I could hear the wardrobe breathing. Although maybe that was Tiffany.

We went shopping every day. "Why don't we just go to the supermarket at the weekend like at home?" I said, but Granny Monroe had our mother's knack of not hearing questions she didn't want to answer. She ritualistically applied two layers of Avon Pink Lady lipstick, knotted a see-through plastic bonnet over her hair and polished our shoes before the daily outing, pulling my hair into a ponytail vise that made my head throb. "Only tidy little girls can come shopping," she said, filling me with an urge to tear the baubles from my hair and roll in the nearest patch of mud. Every day we went to the baker's, the greengrocer's and Dewhurst's family butchers.

We stared at the bloodstains down the butcher's apron and hid in the far corner of the shop. There was a cow without a head or skin, and lurid pieces of flesh from unidentifiable animals (pig? chicken? child?). I vowed never to eat meat again, not even the meat that our mother bought that came in a plastic wrapper.

The assistant, a woman, bustled forward. "So who are these two then?" she asked, smiling at us.

"They're James's little girls."

"Are they now? Hello there."

"Hello!" we chorused from the corner. We both kept our distance.

"How is he? Haven't seen him in a long time."

"Oh, he's doing well enough, although I told him I didn't think he should have taken that job. He's not really progressing, like he should. Doreen, you know, his wife, she's *poorly* at the moment. So I've taken the girls in."

She put special emphasis on the word "poorly," as if our mother had some terrible contagious disease or had lost a limb. I wondered if perhaps she had and nobody had bothered to inform us. It wouldn't be the first time a major news event had occurred in Beech Drive and nobody thought of telling us. The day color television entered our lives, it just appeared, one day, in the corner of the lounge.

The woman smiled at us.

"Well, they're bonny little things, aren't they?"

Bonny? Tiffany and I looked at each other trying to assess if this was a compliment or not. Tiffany shrugged blankly.

Granny Monroe kept on talking.

"Yes well, you cut your coat according to your cloth, that's what I told him. Three lamb chops, please Jill—no, not those ones there, they look a bit gray to my eye. That's right, the ones nearer the back, if you don't mind."

The assistant had put the chops on the weighing scales and was waiting for an approving nod from Granny Monroe. None came. She bent down to examine the meat under the counter and dropped her voice.

"I told him at that time, How do you even know it's yours? But he just said 'Mum' and told me to keep my nose out of it. You know, I think I'm going to change my mind and have pork after all. I'm not very convinced about that lamb."

She put the lamb chops back under the counter with a long-suffering look.

"And look where it's got him! That's it, yes. How much do I owe you? It's a scandal, isn't it, these prices?"

"Is Mum ill?" I asked her when we left the shop, but she'd already started to harangue the greengrocer on the poor quality of his sprouts.

Every night, when the lights went out, I could feel the wardrobe leering at me. I missed my doll's house. I missed my little bed, and my Pooh Bear nightlight. I missed lying on the living room carpet and watching *Dr. Who* and *Charlie's Angels.**

We watched them at Granny Monroe's but it wasn't the same. She

---

*Charlie's Angels

"First broadcast in 1976, *Charlie's Angels* courted immediate controversy, being denounced by both left- and right-wing commentators as 'massage parlor television.'

"The voice-over at the start of each show stated that it was 'the story of three little girls'—actresses Kate Jackson, Jaclyn Smith and Farrah Fawcett-Majors. Trained as policewomen, they are hired to work for Charlie, a male authority figure whom the women unquestioningly obey.

"Although trumpeted as dynamic female role models, the program was structured around not female liberation, but the male gaze. The fetishization of the female body was its guiding principle; in the first season alone, the Angels are seen working undercover as hookers, swimsuit models, prison inmates, student nurses and ersatz Playboy Bunnies."

made us sit in tall wing-backed armchairs instead of lounging over the hearth rug as we did at home, and although we played along as usual (Tiffany, naturally, got to be Farrah Fawcett-Majors *and* Jaclyn Smith; I had to be the ugly one), Granny Monroe told us off when we took off our T-shirts and did somersaults across the floor wearing only our underwear.

"What if the house has fallen down?" I asked Tiffany later when we'd gone up to bed.

"Ssshh," said Tiffany, her mother's daughter, her grandmother's granddaughter.

6.3 The Science of Happiness (2)

I THOUGHT it was just a saying but it's true apparently: opposites do attract. They've proved it. Alistair told me about a study that was carried out at an American university. A professor enlisted six students to wear a T-shirt to bed for two nights in a row. They were not allowed to wear perfume or deodorant, and when they handed them in, the professor enlisted another 121 students to sniff them.

He asked them to rank the T-shirts according to the attractiveness of the smell, then took DNA samples from all the students, analyzing a set of their genes on chromosome 6. His discovery? That we are most attracted to the smell of a member of the opposite sex who is most different from us genetically.

I find it pleasing to think that there's truth behind the cliché. Although Alistair ruined it almost immediately by telling me that it's probably only true at a molecular level. Humans, he said, like songbirds, tend to mate assortatively. [NB. ASSORTATIVELY]

"What do you mean?" I said.

"Like marries like," he said. "Smart people marry smart people. Good-looking people marry good-looking people. Neurotics tend to end up with neurotics."

I thought about this for a moment. "So what are we?"

But he'd already gone.

Sometimes I think that science is like the Bible; it can prove anything you want it to prove. But, of course, in saying so, all I'll prove is that I'm not like Alistair. Ergo, opposites attract.

In any case, sex does things to the brain. That's true as well, you know. Pheromones can actually change the shape of your neural pathways. And besides, it felt like fate. Or some other matter that can't, easily, be explained away. That first night, I got pregnant. What are the chances of that? Even Alistair was stuck for an answer. He just breathed hot, humid breaths in my ear and told me he loved me.

You can test it, empirically, you know. Love. They've done laboratory-controlled trials on it. In the presence of the object of your affection, your heartbeat quickens, your pupils dilate, the temperature on the surface of your skin increases. Love has a material basis in fact. Although only within a two-and-a-half-year time frame. Evolutionarily speaking, that's as long as you need to be attracted to your mate: sufficient time for courtship to take place, bonding rituals to be performed, and the first infant conceived and safely delivered.

There's no test for happiness. No empirical proofs. The most scientific test you can perform is to ask someone whether they're happy. If they say yes, then in all likelihood they are. You are happy if you think you are. With love, it's different.

It was a cold, dank March night when Alistair asked me to marry him. We were standing in the middle of a traffic island waiting to cross the road.

"What?" I was holding plastic carrier bags from the supermarket and they were cutting into my skin. The lights changed and we walked across the road.

"I said 'Will you marry me?'"

I glanced at him sideways on. He hadn't broken stride. He was walking on, as purposefully as ever, his head up, his shoulders back. I hesitated, but only for a second.

"Yes."

"Good," he said and pulled me toward him. I felt his breath on my face, and my heartbeat quickened. My pupils dilated. The temperature of my skin increased. I dropped the shopping bags.

"Careful," he said. "You'll break the eggs."

.   .   .

My father came to the service, and Tiffany, and Alistair's parents, and a couple of friends, and that was it. We almost sprinted into the registry office, and afterward, after a quick drink in the pub opposite, that was it. Man and wife. We sat in the pub and felt each other's skin; our fingers, warm, and newly encircled by slender gold bands, plaited together beneath the beer-sticky table.

6.4   home *n* 3 : an environment offering security and happiness

WHEN ARE WE going home? I asked Granny Monroe every day. Is it soon? When are we going home? But we weren't going home; we were going to Nanna and Grandpa Arnold's, on account of the fact that Granny Monroe had forgotten she had to do the flowers for the Rotary Club luncheon. I was beginning to feel like the tall brass vase my mother had once received as a Christmas present from Nanna and which she had passed on to Granny Monroe the following Christmas. Granny Monroe in turn promptly gave it to Aunty Suzanne, and it had finally made its way back to Beech Drive on the occasion of my mother's last birthday.

"Typical of Suzanne!" she'd said when she removed the wrapping paper. "How cheap!"

Where was it now? I wondered. Still wandering the purgatory of unwanted presents and unloved objects? A desolate limbo of broken toasters and nylon-frilled toilet-brush holders.

Nanna was at least pleased to see us. She gave us our dinner in her little back kitchen. There were no chops or overboiled vegetables or glasses of orange juice. A teapot held center stage on a table that had been laid with a white linen cloth.

"Proper Yorkshire tea," said Nanna. "Strong enough to put hairs on your chest."

"I don't want hairs on my chest," I said. Nanna laughed.

"Don't worry, Rebecca. It's just a saying."

Nanna and Grandpa Arnold had moved down south years ago, before my mother was born, but Nanna still said "bath" to rhyme with

"Cath" and insisted it was "parky" when actually it was cold. She presided over the teapot, a white-haired geisha with a flowered apron tied across her well-upholstered hips.

There were thick slices of bread and strange-tasting jam, chunks of pineapple but in rough irregular cubes, not like the ones from the can we ate at home. The pièce de résistance, though, was a round, perfect flan, under whose gelatine glaze glistened slices of kiwi and strawberry and a fruit that was foreign to Beech Drive.

"It's papaya," said Nanna in a wistful voice. "You won't believe how hard it is to get hold of. Eat up. It's the food of angels, you know."

"Mmmmmm," I said, taking a mouthful.

"Yeuch," said Tiffany, spitting hers out.

Grandpa Arnold coughed and went off to his shed.

In the evening, Tiffany and I played snap on the hearth rug in the front room. Nanna watched us and smiled.

"*SNAP!*" we yelled simultaneously, although Tiffany still won. But in between the rounds, there was always silence. It sat heavily in the front room, in the hallway, in the kitchen. We gave up the game eventually, the effort at jollity too overwhelming for either of us. The silence seeped back in. At night, we slept in our mother's old bedroom, where yellowing pictures of Richard Chamberlain stared down at us from the walls.

After three days, it was Tiffany who noticed why it was so quiet. Grandpa Arnold and Nanna didn't speak to each other. Nanna talked to herself, little asides punctuated by laughter. She hummed too, but not like we did. We hummed TV jingles ("Beanz Meanz Heinz!" or "From the valley of the Jolly—Ho! Ho! Ho!—Green Giant!"), but Nanna hummed fragments of strange melodies that we didn't recognize and that made the house sound sad and lonely. Instead of talking to each other, our grandparents tended to exchange information via a third party or an object. The cat, a fat brindled tabby called Victor, functioned as their telephone.

"Right, we're going out for a walk," Nanna told Victor. He was lying on a kitchen chair washing his paws. "And dinner might be a bit late tonight, but perhaps someone could put out the rubbish." Victor looked up lazily but then went back to his paws.

Nanna took us out on long walks. We went down by the river, along little-used footpaths, through the woods, to the shops, across the park, all over the place. She enjoyed walking, she said.

"I used to bring your mum and Suzanne here when they were little," she said. "Having you two here reminds me of them, I have to say."

"What was Mum like when she was a child?" asked Tiffany.

"Oh, she's always been very independent. Very strong-minded."

"Like me?" said Tiffany.

"Well yes, I suppose she was a bit like you."

"Why doesn't she like you coming to see us then?" demanded Tiffany.

I saw her look at Tiffany and then her mouth seemed to quiver at the corners. Poor Nanna. I took hold of her hand and glared at Tiffany. Not that she noticed; my glares rolled off her like water from my mother's Teflon nonstick frying pan.

"Mum says she's got better things to do than listen to you carp on."

"Oh," said Nanna. "Does she?"

"I like you coming to visit," I said.

She was silent for a while and then said, "It's just that . . . Well. You know. Mothers and daughters. She . . . We had a bit of a falling-out, I suppose you'd call it, when she was younger."

Tiffany and I absorbed this information, storing it away, hamster-like, for later analysis.

"Is that why she gets annoyed with Aunty Suzanne too?"

But Nanna didn't seem to be listening. She was walking along, her eyes fixed at some imaginary point in front of her.

"Hmm?" she said, suddenly focusing again. "Oh no. That was something different."

We played in the park for a bit. Nanna was very patient, pushing me on the swings for ages, until Tiffany demanded she go on the see-saw with her.

"I think I'm a little old for that," she said, although when she got on it she laughed and whooped and made Tiffany bump up and down. We laughed along with her, enjoying the treat. Our mother said that messing around in the park wouldn't get the dishes done or the sitting room dusted. Nanna even came on the carousel, which was perhaps why her sitting room was on the dusty side and her dishes tended to be piled up by the sink. Afterward she had to sit on a bench for five minutes to recover while we did handstands on the grass.

"Who am I like?" I asked her.

Nanna looked down at me and smiled. "You, Rebecca, you're a bit like me."

Tiffany looked annoyed, which pleased me.

"Am I?" I said. "How?"

But she just shrugged her shoulders. "You just are," she said.

We were on our way home and standing on the pavement, about to step out into the road, when a car whizzed past us going well over the speed limit.

"Goodness!" said Nanna. "Gave me quite a turn. I was run over once, you know. February 28, 1948."

We looked at her, impressed. She stood on the side of the road waiting, although the road was clear. "And you wouldn't be standing here now if it wasn't for that."

"What do you mean?" said Tiffany.

"If I hadn't been run over. You two might never have been born."

I felt a sharp, painful stab of pure panic. I could feel myself dematerializing, vanishing into nothing. It was like the moment I'd first understood the nature of death: nothingness for ever and ever and ever. I took hold of my grandmother's hand, feeling the skin and the pulse beating in her thumb.

"It's all right, Rebecca," said Nanna. "That's the thing about the past; you can't change it, however hard you try."

In our second week, Nanna took us to visit Great-Great-Aunty Maureen. We didn't see her often, on account of the fact that she was "doo-lally" and was reputed not to wear any underpants. Her husband, Uncle Samuel, had been the source of some sort of family scandal, although nobody would say what. She'd been in a "home" for a time, which was different, apparently, from a home, although nobody would explain that either. Nanna had made her move down south, because she didn't have any other relatives to look after her. I tried, but I failed to imagine what it would be like not to have any relatives. They were everywhere, popping up unexpectedly, being served cake on china plates, exclaiming over how much you'd grown.

Great-Great-Aunty Maureen's house was dark and quiet when we arrived, the curtains half-drawn, the light filtered by a coating of dust on the windows. She was wearing a floral skirt and what looked like a wig.

"Well, well! My little great-nieces. Come in! Look at the pair of you! Little cherubs!"

I'd never been called a cherub before. Great-Great-Aunty Maureen smiled at us and ushered us into her front room.

There were piles of old newspapers in every corner. Two cats patrolled the doorway, watching us with yellow eyes. Teacups had been laid out on a tray, along with a plate of pink iced biscuits, a saucer of Whiskas and a pair of socks.

"Go on, have a biscuit."

Tiffany boldly went first. After a moment's hesitation, I followed.

"I'd eat them all if I was you. It'll save you from Alicia's cooking. Go on, eat up."

"Maureen?" There was a worried look on Nanna's face. "You've been taking your pills, haven't you?"

Great-Great-Aunty Maureen looked up. We paused mid-mouthful. The cats' tails stopped twitching.

"Just because you made a mistake in your life, Alicia," said Aunty Maureen, standing erect, her wig poised on top of her head, "doesn't give you the right to sit in judgment." She held her head high. "*I* married for love. Even if he did turn out to be a worthless cur."

We left soon after that.

We went home via the bakery, a warm, sweet-smelling heaven.

"So who are these two then?" asked the baker. Did all butchers and bakers and greengrocers have the same line of questioning? I wondered.

"They're Doreen's little girls."

"Are they now? Hello there."

"Hello!" we said with more enthusiasm than we'd used on the butcher. Under the counter were cream cakes and fresh buns and custard slices and chocolate-chip cookies. We gazed at them longingly.

"So. She didn't marry that long-haired hippie who was after her then, I take it."

"No," said Nanna and paused. "Suzanne did. Four iced buns, if that's all right. For our supper."

When we were outside, Tiffany questioned our grandmother.

"Who's the long-haired hippie? Is it Kenneth?"

"Come on, we've still got to get the eggs."

"Does he mean Kenneth?"

"Yes, Tiffany."

"Why did he think that Mum married Kenneth?"

Nanna hesitated.

"Kenneth used to be sweet on your mother," she said. We skipped after her, trying to keep up. "But it was a long time ago."

I reached for her hand and wondered if all shopkeepers knew so much more about Monroe family history than we did.

6.5 Theories of Relativity (5)

ALISTAIR HAS thousands of stories about identical twins. They're his fruit flies. He measures heritability. It sounds like a made-up word to me. But it's there in the dictionary (**heritability** *biol.* : quality of being transmissible from parent to offspring).

Identical twins reared apart used to be his specialist subject. They're the holy grail of behavioral geneticists because they're the closest things there are, in human terms, to a controlled laboratory experiment. They are clones. They share all of the same genes but none of the same environment.

True story:

James Arthur Springer and James Edward Lewis, identical twins, were born in Ohio and separately adopted at five weeks of age. At the age of thirty-nine, they were reunited. Both called themselves Jim, had married a woman called Linda and then divorced her. Both remarried women called Betty. Both chain-smoked Salem cigarettes, enjoyed mechanical drawing and carpentry, drank Miller Lite, watched stock-car racing in their spare time, hated baseball and every year went on vacation to the same resort in Florida.

In all the twin tests ever done into intelligence and personality, the results are roughly the same. There is almost nothing to separate twins brought up together and twins brought up apart; i.e., the environment has almost no effect.

"Don't you get it?" said Alistair when I failed to be overwhelmed by this. We were in the kitchen, and I was cooking. It was Spaghetti Bolognese, an old standby that I had watched my mother cook and now, in turn, was cooking for us.

"It goes against every parenting book ever written. Whatever you do, as a parent, in practical terms, makes no difference."

"How would you know?" I said. I went to get the meat out of the fridge, and started chopping the onions. He hesitated but then seemed to decide to ignore me.

"That's the thing; this isn't a hypothesis. It's empirically proven. As a parent, it doesn't matter what you do, whether you read to your children or don't read to them; take them to the circus, make them listen to Beethoven, whatever. At the end of the day, it makes no difference, not to their personality, not to their intelligence. Not even to their happiness." He poured himself a glass of red wine. "You simply are the way you are."

I put some olive oil in the bottom of a frying pan and turned on the gas.

"Adopted siblings brought up in the same house are no more alike than two strangers pulled off the street."

He took a sip of his wine. I think Alistair enjoys these discussions. My role is to be the uninformed public. I have to say that I play the part quite well. I rarely manage to score a point over him because he can always trump me with scientific knowledge. He knows more than I do. More facts anyway.

"So is that why you don't want to have children?" I said. I put the onions into the pan and began to stir. My back was turned and the oil was spitting and I'd turned on the extractor fan to get rid of the smoke, but I still heard him sigh. My eyes began to water but I expect that was the onions.

6.6 crack *vi* : to break or snap apart

WHEN OUR FATHER finally arrived to pick us up, we leaped into the car before he'd even put on the hand brake.

My heart lurched as we lumbered back down Oak Avenue, turning right into Sycamore Close and left into Beech Drive. "*Helloooo!*" we yelled as soon as we were over the threshold, thankful to see the red carpet in the hall again (hello hall!) and the telephone table (hello telephone table!) and the beige curtains (hello curtains!). But only silence answered us. It felt as if the house had been empty for months, as if it had forgotten us. Could a house forget its inhabitants? In the lounge, where the jagged hole and the pile of rubble had been, there were now neat lines and a steel girder. It smelled of fresh paint and new carpet. I sniffed the air, trying to reconcile it with the old smell of home, but I couldn't. The Monroeness had gone somehow. Along with the sofa and armchairs. There was a brand-new chocolate brown velour three-piece suite in its place. More crucially, the room was motherless.

"Where's Mum?"

"She's resting. She's not been very well. Now, don't go disturbing her." We crept upstairs and peeked around our parents' bedroom door. Our mother was in bed. She was wearing her owl sunglasses. "Hello, girls," she said, but it was weak and indistinct.

"Are you okay?"

"I'm just a bit tired. Now, go and play quietly downstairs."

"The new settee's fantastic!" said Tiffany. "Brown! My favorite color!"

"Mmm," said our mother in a very un-motherlike way. It was almost as if she didn't care, although of course that couldn't be right. She looked so small all by herself in the big double bed. The duvet was pulled up to her chin.

"Mum?" I went up to the side of her bed. Her hand rested on the pillow. I picked it up and squeezed it. "Are you all right?"

"Oh, Rebecca!" she said in a voice I'd never heard before. It quivered. Tears filled the corners of her eyes. Was she *crying*?

Tiffany elbowed me out of the way. "I'm here too, Mum."

"Oh, girls," she said, sighed almost. We crouched by the edge of her bed. She seemed to be on the verge of saying something.

"Mum?"

She bent her head to look at us. "I love you. You know that, don't you?"

I gulped. Next to me, I could hear Tiffany's breathing quicken. I started to panic and shifted uncomfortably. As a family we weren't prone to unsolicited testimonials about our feelings. Perhaps she was dying and no one had bothered to tell us. I felt tears well up in my eyes, and a little sob erupted from my chest.

"You're not . . ."

"Oh, for God's sake, Rebecca, there's no need to snivel."

I looked up, instantly cheered. She couldn't be that ill.

"I'm just a bit . . . tired." And she patted our hands. "Now, go. Go on. I need to be left alone."

We ran down the stairs, newly burdened by our knowledge. In the kitchen, our father was struggling to fill the domestic void.

"So, um, what should we have for tea?" It was a conscious echo of a Doreenism, although when our mother asked, it was nearly always rhetorical. ("Pancakes? Don't be ridiculous. It's either fish fingers or chops.") Our father, on the other hand, was staring quizzically at the contents of the cupboard (three tins pineapple chunks, one Fray Bentos steak and kidney pie, two tins Heinz Baked Beans, one tin Heinz Oxtail Soup, one jar Crosse & Blackwell chutney) and seemed to be actively soliciting suggestions.

Tiffany realized that this was her moment and took our mother's apron off the hook on the back door and steered our father toward the lounge.

"Go and sit down. On the *sofa*." It was a mark of respect. We'd both realized the gravity of our mother's illness when she'd failed to correct Tiffany for saying "settee."

"I'll make dinner." And she looked almost impressive, bustling around the kitchen, peering over the counter, frowning à la Doreen when our father lifted his left buttock and silently blew off. I switched on the TV. Our father opened the paper. It was almost normal, apart from the smell of the carpet, and the swirly patterns across the ceiling. After an abortive fifteen minutes of trying to extract the Fray Bentos steak and kidney pie from the tin, Tiffany gave up and made her specialty, cheese on toast and Heinz Oxtail Soup, which, with a touch of sophistication, she served in mugs.

"Do you think Mum would like some?" I went to see but was waved out of the room by an arm that appeared from a hump under the duvet. Later we watched *Nationwide*,* and although it was okay when the newsreader was talking, during the gap before the reports, we could all hear the sound of muffled sobbing from upstairs.

"Lovely cheese on toast. Well done, Tiffany!" Our father was lavish in his praise, although truth be told it wasn't Tiffany's best effort. She'd cinderized the corners.

Ding dong!

I raced to the door. It was as if nothing was normal. Cheese on toast for dinner. Visitors at the door. Whatever next? It was Mrs. Huxley from next door holding a Pyrex dish covered in a red and white tea towel.

"Daaaad!"

"Oh hello, James. I thought you'd probably not had a chance to cook, so I just made a bit extra for you."

---

*Nationwide

"From 1969 to 1983, up to ten million viewers a night tuned in to *Nationwide*.

"The early evening news program featured not just current affairs but also parachuting clergymen, humorous housewives, and topical songs, becoming a British TV institution during the seventies. The regular stable of presenters formed a *Nationwide* 'family' with frequent in-jokes among themselves. The mask of formality, that traditionally distinguished the broadcasting establishment from the viewing masses, had begun to slip.

"News was no longer a commodity to be disseminated from on high. The vox pop had been born."

"That's very kind of you, Gloria." Our father looked embarrassed as he took the dish.

"It's just a cottage pie. Nothing fancy." Mrs. Huxley was wearing her slippers and an apron, and she was looking over James's shoulder into the hallway. Her voice dropped. "How *is* Doreen?"

"Oh well. She's um, she's just got a bit of mental exhaustion. Needs to rest, that's all."

"If there's anything I can do, you just have to say. How are the poor bairns?" She said this looking at me as if I was an injured dog or one of those babies born without arms. "Anything at all. Liz, across the road, said she's making Cornish pasties for you tomorrow, and Caroline said she'll do Thursday."

"It's really not necessary, thank you." He was tapping his feet now.

"No, no, it's all been arranged. You don't worry about a thing, you poor man."

"Well if that's all . . ."

"Now, remember! Anything at all!"

"Yes. Thank you. Bye-bye now."

My father finally managed to close the door and leaned against the wall.

"James! James!" It was my mother's disembodied voice floating down the stairs. "I CAN'T BELIEVE YOU'VE TOLD THE NEIGHBORS!"

"I haven't told them anything!"

"Then how do they know?"

"I DON'T KNOW."

Tiffany had joined us in the hall. "Know what, Dad?"

"Nothing. It's nothing. Your mother's tired, that's all."

But he refused to catch our eyes and retreated to the shed to smoke his pipe. Tiffany and I washed up together without arguing once.

Our mother was so tired, she didn't get out of bed for a month, and then it was only to watch television and sigh. She refused to wear anything but her pink dressing gown and stopped washing her hair, so it stuck up in strange, inhuman peaks. Even the hairs on her legs had grown long and wiry.

I tried to cheer her up by painting her pictures or bringing her toast and honey to her bed, but she just gave the same sad smile and waved them away. Sometimes she cried.

"Your mother's poorly," said my father after he'd seen me returning my uneaten offerings to the kitchen. He sat me down at the table. "She's a bit sad, that's all." I nodded confidentially at him.

"Like chicken pox?" I said. "That made me sad."

He hesitated.

"Yes," he said finally. "Like chicken pox."

Later, when he was frowning over the washing machine instructions, I had an idea.

"Why don't we invite Nanna over to cheer her up?" I said.

"Do trousers go on a 'boil-wash,' do you think?"

"Dad?"

"What? Oh no. She's part of the problem, Rebecca, not the solution."

"What do you mean?" I asked, but he wouldn't say.

His trousers hung two inches off his ankles for the rest of the week, until Tiffany made him throw them away.

I began to play at Lucy's house more and more, and when Aunty Suzanne said, "How's your mother?" my throat closed up and I started to feel dizzy. She gave up asking eventually and gave me cookies instead, but even those stopped working after a while.

At home, Tiffany had become Doreen. She had seamlessly taken over as mistress of 24 Beech Drive, berating me when I forgot to take off my shoes in the back porch and insisting that our father cut off my pocket money when I failed to tidy up my Lego. Life bent and adapted around the mother-sized space in the house. Every day, we woke up late and burned the toast. We were continually amazed when things ran out (toilet paper, milk, electricity). We'd always thought the house was a concrete, inorganic thing, constant and unchanging, but without our mother, it started to develop wrinkles and spots and strange unidentifiable smells. Mold appeared on the bathroom tiles and we watched it grow in fascinated disgust. The handle fell off the hall cupboard door and it flapped and banged and left a shower of paint across the carpet. The spider plants died.

"Where's the butter?" asked our father, staring at his blackened pieces of toast.

"We finished it yesterday," said Tiffany. I was having cold baked beans for breakfast (because I could) and was eating them straight out of the tin. None of us were expecting to see our mother. She'd had a bath, washed her hair, shaved her legs, sailed downstairs and was pouring herself a bowl of Special K. We watched her much like we watched the mold, wondering what would happen next.

"Well I see that nobody's bothered to do much shopping, have they?" She didn't seem to notice that the Special K had been sitting at the back of the cupboard for two months now, sucking moisture out of the air. It bent rather than crackled. Maybe it was not our real mother. Like in the episode of *The Bionic Woman* where Lindsay Wagner was gagged and tied up in a cupboard, and a Lindsay Wagner–looking robot took her place.

We watched her spooning Special K between her lipsticked lips. "Rebecca? What on earth do you think you're eating?" It was her, all right.

"And, Tiffany, you can wipe that supercilious smile off your face. I've already seen the state of your room." She'd waltzed back into our lives without so much as a by-your-leave. She could have warned us. We would have vacuumed the lounge.

"Mum? Are you not feeling tired anymore?"

"No, Rebecca. And that's the last I want to hear about that for the time being, do you hear me?"

There was homemade cottage pie for dinner (a far superior specimen to Mrs. Huxley's, who put her mashed potato on with a fork not a piping bag), a bottle of wine in a thin brown bottle that our father pronounced "very fruity" and Queen of Puddings for dessert. Normal service had been resumed, although every time I lay back on the floor of the lounge and saw the half-moon swirls on the ceiling, I wondered about the long zigzag crack. Had it been mended? Or was it still there? Underneath the swirls?

6.7 Theories of Relativity (6)

WHAT ABOUT non-adopted siblings then, I asked Alistair later. Biological siblings brought up in the same house together. Brothers, say. Or sisters. How similar are they?

About 50 percent, he said. Or at least, over a large study, the characteristics they share average out at about 50 percent. Of course, he said, in any two individuals, it can be much higher than that. Or much lower.

I thought about this. So is that nature or nurture then? It depends, he said. All of the current studies into identical twins suggest very strongly that it's nature, but, and he hesitated, when it comes to yourself, you will never be able to know. I looked at Alistair. He was always so sure of everything, so definite. But he just shrugged. You will never know why you are the way you are, he said. You just are. The last thing you can know is your self.

Part Seven

like *adj* **1** : having feature(s) in common with something
or each other or the original

7.1 Theories of Relativity (7)

I'VE BEEN THINKING about the trees again. You remember. The trees in the back garden, Aggie and Hilda, Thomas and Horace . . . It's like a family tree, of course. I don't know why I didn't think of that before.

We'd both watched the tree surgeons cutting them down. Alistair and I. We were in the kitchen drinking coffee.

"So that's how they do it," he said. "I've always wondered."

Our back garden is enclosed on all sides, with no outside access. It's one of those London gardens created in the back-to-back space of two terraces. You couldn't just go in with a chain saw and hack the trees down at the trunk: you'd wipe out three houses. They had to be dismantled, branch by branch, until all that was left was the trunk, and then that went too.

There were three men. One climbed as far as he could, wearing a harness and ropes. He attached himself to one branch, fixed a rope to the branch above him, threw the end to his workmate on the ground and then used a chain saw to slice the higher branch off. It was reverse tree chopping: it had to be cut down from the top to the bottom.

There was a knack to it. The trick lay in choosing the right branch. You needed to attach yourself to one that was strong enough to support you, but high enough to be able to reach the topmost bough. You could see how it could go wrong though. By cutting the wrong branch, or harnessing yourself to an offshoot that was too weak or too far away.

Like a family tree then. You look for similarity: the shape of an eye, the cleft of a chin. Genetics is a science, but it's also common sense. You know who you resemble, where the stronger branches are, which ones will bear your weight. At the end of the day, it's a judgment call. I know that Alicia, my grandmother, and I are on the same branch; I'd fix my harness to her and cut from there. And I know that she knows that too. We have the same slightly hooded eyes, the same sallow skin (Alicia thinks it's "fair," but believe me, it has a sallow tinge). We are connected; tied together by family bonds, by DNA; two strands of a double helix twisting onward and upward.

Alistair and I sat by the kitchen window and drank coffee and watched the tree surgeons together. I thought about Aggie and Thomas and Hilda and Horace. Or maybe it was the other way around. Aggie and Horace and Hilda and Thomas. Whatever. Four lives wasted. I listened to the buzzing of the chain saw and watched limb after severed limb fall to the ground.

"That reminds me," said Alistair. "The crankshaft on the car needs servicing."

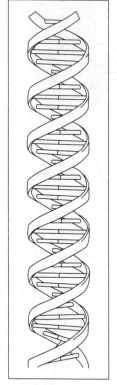

Figure 8.
The Double Helix

Alistair likes to employ visual devices in his work. He especially likes graphs.

It is his opinion, he told me once, that language is faulty. That words are ambiguous.

"But that's the beauty of them," I said.

He paused.

"But in terms of communicating facts, language is an imperfect system. There's always slippage."

Sitting there then, across the table from my husband, the light falling through the window, my hand on my coffee mug, still warm, I realized that he was probably right. At that moment, with the sound of the chain saw buzz-

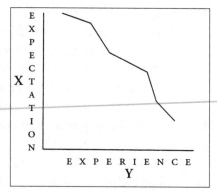

Figure 9. **Example of a Graph**

ing outside and the smell of sawdust filling my nostrils, there was nothing I could think of saying to him.

With graphs, you plot one thing (X) against another thing (Y). The line depicts the relationship between the two. I'm not sure, though, if it works for people. If you can plot a marriage. If you can fix the points between the universal and the particular, between the things you share (a history? a home? a fondness for Italian restaurants?) and the things you don't (the way you look at trees? the way you look at life?).

I don't know what shape it should be. A U-shape? A bell curve? A wavy line?

7.2 **fruit** *n* 2 : produce of action

Figure 10. **Possible Relationship Models**

ALICIA HAD ALWAYS known that Life would happen to her, but who would have thought it would arrive in Councillor Anderson's motor-car? That it would be heralded by the smell of cocoa-nut and attended by Sister Weston and her white-robed henchwomen. As my grand-mother lay in Bed 14 of Ward 3 of Clayton Hospital, learning about the illnesses that beset women's bodies when their husbands have stopped looking at them and their children have stopped needing them, she thought about Callard & Bowser's toffees and light tan shoe polish. She thought about the color black, the nature of blackness, and the in-betweeny shades therein. She used to think it was one mono-lithic shade; the antithesis of the pretty greens and blues and yellows that lifted your spirits and signaled the coming of spring.

But that was before. Now when she peered within its dark heart, she saw an infinite variety of color and texture, of tone and detail. She thought of the burnish of Cecil's arm, when the sun caught the hairs and refracted its beam. She thought of the inky blackness of the pupils of his eyes, the quasi-translucence of his lashes. She thought of how, when he walked into the ward with its clinical white walls and clinical white sheets, he seemed to throw them into relief. They exaggerated each other. She remembered her fear and how the lilting singsong of his voice had calmed her like the sea. Her leg throbbed. It was a dull, slow ache that came and went and beat beneath the plaster. She felt the first feather touches of the itch, the itch she had felt for days and that, with her leg encased in plaster of paris, she could not reach. And then, as she thought of the pink delicacy of the inside of Cecil's lips, it was another part of her body that started pinpricking. At the next bed, Sister Weston and a junior nurse had drawn the curtains and were giv-ing Mrs. Browning a sponge bath.

"Turn over!" Sister Weston was not a woman who was used to hav-ing her orders disobeyed. "Now. Come on, Mrs. Browning! If we can't go to the bathroom ourselves, we're going to have to have the bath come to us, aren't we?" There was a rustle and a pause. "Mrs. Brown-ing! Will you please stop that!"

Alicia could feel Cecil's breath, sweet and honeyed, could hear the modulations of his voice, a rhythmic pulsating in her ear. Under the cover of her sheets, she felt the flesh that reminded her of the mango that Cecil warmed in his hands, before he fed her secretive slices, shielding them from Sister Weston's gaze with a copy of the *Daily Express*. She parted its skin and remembered Cecil's invocation, "A man-go from Ji-make-her." She tried to swallow her breaths, which had become fast and shallow, and reaching down she felt the hairiness of a cocoa-nut shell, and the touch of Cecil's hand stroking her hand, his palm rough like a cat's tongue. Feet away from Sister Weston's back, she could hear Cecil's voice, "A pray-sant for Al-eesha," imagined his hand stroking, exerting pressure now, and without even thinking, concentrating only on the noises of Mrs. Browning's sponge bath, Alicia's hand rocked back and forth.

She shut her eyes and could see only black, a multitude of black-nesses, a spectrum of darkness that shimmered before her eyes. She wasn't expecting the shell to crack. The air quivered and the cocoa-nut's milky fragrant liquid flooded out. She hadn't even known it was there.

Alicia lay motionless on her bed, hearing the sounds of the ward around her. The sponge bath had finished; the tea trolley was beginning its rounds. Furtively, she withdrew a finger from the nest of sheets, and as she turned her head, exhaling heavily, her eyes locked Herbert's. Herbert, her cousin, was by her head. Herbert the runt. Before she had the chance to exclaim, or gasp or object, he'd grasped her finger and sniffed it. And then he vanished. On the adjacent bed, Mrs. Fairchild wondered about the content of the little pink pills the doctor had prescribed her.

Was it because of Elizabeth that Herbert became Herbert? Elizabeth Arnold, Herbert's sister, family beauty and possessor of a twenty-two-inch waist, had already departed to the States; swept off by an American GI, first prize in the sexual lottery that was 1945. But her legacy lived on.

It began on a Sunday night shortly before the war. She hoisted her legs onto the footstool beside Herbert just a touch too fast. Her skirt slipped, exposing the tops of her stockings. And when she was sure that Herbert had seen them, she smiled at him and crossed her legs, taking care that he caught a glimpse of her thighs. Thighs that she knew were milky in color, delicate in texture. Her undergarments started wandering through the house. They found their way into Herbert's bedroom. When he drew the blanket from his bed, or opened his chest of drawers, there was no saying what he would find. There was nowhere to hide. He never knew what would happen next. For Elizabeth, it was sport: harmless, carefree, meaningless.

For Herbert, however, it was the condition of living. He would never be free of the confusion, frustration, longing and repulsion that she made him feel, because it was part of him now. He was marked. Permanently altered. He found that if he sat in a certain way, with his head at a precise angle, and didn't move, people would look straight through him. He could enter a room, and people would see him and say hello, but then he disappeared. They forgot he was there. You had to *need* to be invisible though, not merely want to play at being invisible.

But it had its uses. There he is now, watching Cecil watch Alicia. She was being discharged from the hospital and a gaggle of relatives was crowding around her, fussing over her leg, her suitcase.

She looked up and spotted Cecil, but there was something that made her raise her eyebrows at him and motion him away. He hovered at the end of the ward, loitering by the bedpans, a hairsbreadth away from the forward observation position occupied by Herbert. They both watched as Alicia was borne away in a wheelchair, pushed out of the ward, through the main entrance, and manhandled, stiff-legged, into a waiting taxi.

Cecil watched Alicia's departing back. He could feel the power of the sun as it penetrated the haze of smeary coal dust on the windows and rapidly warmed the air. It was a bright, perfect English spring day as Alicia was borne away by taxicab to a healthier, Cecil-less future. Cecil didn't notice the figure by his elbow scribbling something into a book marked "Outgoings" but stepped outside and wondered what to do next, couldn't think of what he should be doing if he wasn't visiting Alicia.

A sharp, chill breeze caught him beneath his ribs; a breeze that had originated in Siberia, crossed the Russian steppe, the Baltic Sea, the Danish peninsula, the Continental mainland, the North Sea and the Yorkshire coast before whistling through the streets of south Wakefield. It was a bright, perfect English spring day, and Cecil shivered. England was always catching him unawares like that. It looked like one thing, but actually it was another thing altogether.

7.3 sister *n* : the daughter of same parents

I READ THIS in the paper yesterday.

Family Affairs
BY TIFFANY MONROE

Women are not made to put up shelves. The feminists won't thank me for this, but it's true. Husbands are made to put up shelves. That's what they're there for, surely?

The truth of this was demonstrated to me recently, when after weeks of subtle suggestions and polite reminders, The Husband had still failed to put up the new oak shelf and mid-Victorian bathroom cabinet. I decided to do it myself. I got the drill and the toolbox out of the shed. If The Husband can do it, I reasoned, how difficult could it be?

It took me half an hour to assemble the drill bit, before I realized that I didn't have the right kind of screws, and set off to the shops. I came back, realized I didn't have any rawl plugs, and went out again. It was 2.30 P.M. by this time. By 3.30 P.M. I'd turned the drill on. By 3.31 P.M. I'd knocked a large chunk of plaster out of the wall and into the bath. And by 3.45 P.M., the drill bit, which had somehow managed to work its way loose, had embedded itself in the bathroom wall. It was when I dropped the chisel into my original Georgian claw-footed bath, and chipped the enamel, that I finally gave up.

The Husband was not impressed. "That's a £150 drill!" he roared. "That's my brand-new chisel!"

"Well if you'd done it when I asked you," I said, "I wouldn't have had to." My logic stunned him into silence. There's no such thing as a nagging wife, only a husband who doesn't do things the first time he's asked.

The thing that people seem to have forgotten is that men and women are different. The Husband and I are chalk and cheese. I can cook a perfect roast chicken that will make your mouth water and your salivary juices drip. The Husband likes playing with his Black & Decker power tools. Women are not designed to be able to put up shelves. It's a genes thing.

It runs in my family anyway. I remember the time my mother tried her hand at a spot of home improvement. She decided to redecorate the drawing room. The result? The ceiling collapsed. We ran outside and stood on the terrace and watched the roof fall in.

"Women!" roared my father (in a not dissimilar mode to The Husband's reaction upon finding drill bit in aforesaid bathroom wall). And then he took her in his arms and kissed her. "Perhaps you ought to stick to flapjacks," he said. She was good at making flapjacks, baking a batch for us on the day that the ceiling was finally repaired. We sat in the drawing room, our mouths full of warm honey and oats, and admired my father's handiwork.

People understood the division of labor in those days. Last night I made roast chicken, and The Husband, *finally*, got around to putting up the cabinet, although he's still sulking about the drill.

Sometimes I wonder about Tiffany, I really do.

Part Eight

observe *vt* **2** : perceive, mark, watch, take notice of, become conscious of

8.1 The Deductive Fallacy (1)

THE DEDUCTIVE FALLACY goes something like this:

    a. Francis Galton and Charles Darwin were cousins.
    b. Charles Darwin married his cousin.
    c. Charles Darwin married Francis Galton.

The deductive fallacy: when A is true and B is true, but A and B do not necessarily make C, although they could. Or to take another example:

    a. I am unhappy.
    b. I am married.
    c. I am unhappily married.

It's an easy enough mistake to make. You add up two observations to create a hypothesis, rather than treat each observation as a separate occurrence. I tend to think that sometimes it's best not to add things up at all. Not that it ever stopped me. Or Tiffany.

When Alistair explained the concept to me, he used the first of these examples, not the second. Is this because . . .

    a. Alistair is not unhappy?
    b. Alistair is not married?
    c. Alistair is obsessed with Francis Galton?

Answer? You think it's A or C, don't you? Well it's not. Not necessarily. The framing of the question has dictated the nature of the answer.

Because I have presented you with three different possibles, you've assumed that only one of these could be correct. You are wrong. In this instance both A and C are correct. Alistair is not unhappy. He is also obsessed with Francis Galton.

I'd never even heard of Francis Galton before I met Alistair, although he is quite famous in his way. Or infamous. He's the father of behavioral genetics. He also believed humans should be selectively bred for the good of the species. Unfit, unhealthy people, those of lesser intelligence and "lower races" should not breed, at all, if possible.

Ultimately, and I'm skipping a few stages here, it was the philosophy behind the Final Solution; the justification for the death camps.

Alistair's voice has a tendency to become agitated at this stage of the argument. Eugenics is not genetics, he says. He shouts, actually. Particularly if you mention Mengele. That was not science! It was murder! I know all of Alistair's arguments by heart: inside our cells are answers to questions that philosophers and writers have been asking for hundreds of years! What is human nature? What is innate?

"But don't you think that people are formed by the time in which they live?" I argue. And he looks at me as if I'm a particularly thick child.

"Don't be so banal," he says. "Of *course* they are, but increasingly the evidence is that there's something much more fundamental at work."

He's passionate about the subject. There's no other word for it. Which is why he's so good on television.

Have I mentioned Alistair's burgeoning TV career? No? It began by accident. There was a last-minute vacancy in a late-night discussion program, and a desperate producer phoned the secretary of his department. Could they suggest someone? Alistair was a natural. Tall, good-looking scientists with boyish smiles are evidently thin on the ground. The calls kept coming. But then his greatest talent is his ability to communicate complex ideas to unscientific dunderheads. He's married to me, after all.

I'm amused by this latest development, I have to say. You see, television, films, magazines, newspapers, are *my* specialty. Popular culture. I study the ephemeral. There were enough people doing the eternal, I decided. I deal with disposable culture, the trivial, the popular, the throwaway. The flow of ideas from high culture to low, and vice versa; television as sign system; the interplay between the narrative texts of the dominant culture and those of people's lives. When people ask Alistair what I do, he says I watch *Coronation Street.*

But Alistair has become part of my field of study. He has become a television regular, one of those people you see on the screen with the word "Expert" beneath their face. "Alistair Betterton, Expert." I love that. The noun not the adjective. He is *an* expert, not expert *at* something, although he's quite good at evasion and not bad at denial.

Maybe you've seen him? He was on *Newsnight* last week. We did a dry run before he left for the studio. I pretended to be Jeremy Paxman, drumming my fingers on the kitchen table and lobbing him questions.

"But isn't genetic engineering the covert mission of genetic studies?" I said. "Are you trying to tell me that if we know how to improve the human race by doctoring people's genes, we won't use that information?"

"No, that's a total misconception," he said. "What we are doing is seeking information. Information on curing illnesses, identifying diseases, on what it is to be human."

He looked at me to see how he was doing. I nodded. Like I say, he was a natural.

"The idea that some people would be considered more 'fit' than others, that they would be more deserving of life than someone else, is absolutely abhorrent to every right-thinking person. That idea was grotesquely discredited fifty years ago by Nazism."

"What about abortion?"

He paused as if he was about to say something but changed his mind. He looked at me and hesitated.

"That's completely different."

I said nothing, but we both knew that Paxman would never have allowed him to get away with it.

I watched him later. "Alistair Betterton, Expert," it said beneath his face. But Paxo never asked the question. You see. I told you he was good at evasion.

8.2   **abroad** *adv* 1 : in or to foreign lands

"MUM?"

"Hmm."

"Mum?"

"What is it, Rebecca?"

We were in the kitchen, where my mother was trying to read a recipe from volume 15 (Pra-Rhi) of her twenty-two-part *Supercook* cookbook. I was trying to make sense of more than a recipe. I was trying to understand life. I'd stolen a back issue of one of Tiffany's photolove magazines and was attempting to decipher the agony column, although it might as well have been written in hieroglyphics.

"What are periods?"

She looked at me suspiciously. "What are you reading?"

"Nothing. A magazine."

She hesitated.

"Well. They're intervals. Of time."

I tried to fit this explanation into the sentence I was reading: "There's no set age at which girls begin their intervals of time." And the next: "Some girls start as young as ten. Others don't have their first interval of time until they are sixteen years old."

Was it any wonder that secrets ran through our family like underground rivers? Bursting forth at inopportune moments?

My mother sliced open a packet of kidneys. They slithered across the chopping board, leaving a trail of watery blood that seeped onto the work surface. I shuddered and went next door to find Mr. Huxley.

The steak and kidney pie was being prepared in honor of our parents' wedding anniversary, and between us (me, Tiffany, and Mr. Huxley) we'd been plotting. Tiffany had found the old cine film of our parents' marriage, and Mr. Huxley was going to set up his projector in our living room.

My father walked in through the back door, put down his briefcase, loosened his tie and handed my mother a bouquet.

"Happy Anniversary!" he said and kissed her on the cheek. The bouquet was large and expensive-looking, and you could tell she was pleased.

"Oh, James! How wonderful!"

He looked relieved. Last year he'd bought her an electroplated cruet that had elicited a much less favorable response and whose current whereabouts were shrouded in mystery.

"Why don't you go and have a beer in the garden, darling?"

My father looked surprised, then pleased.

"Well, if you're sure . . ."

I followed him out the back door. He loosened his tie and cracked open a can.

"Don't you want a glass, darling?" Her voice wafted through the kitchen window. My father rolled his eyes at me and then put a finger to his lips.

"Got one, thanks!" he shouted back and took a large swig straight from the can.

"Ah," he said, wiping the foam from his lips and sitting back on the bench. "Our little secret," he said, tapping his nose.

I smiled at him, honored to have been drawn into his confidence. We sat for a moment or two in silence and then I felt I ought to offer something back. "Lucy broke one of Aunty Suzanne's sculptures, and she didn't tell her and just threw it away."

My father laughed. "Uh-oh! Was that one of the ones she did on that 'Discover Your Inner Artist' course?"

"I think so."

He laughed again. "Dreadful, weren't they?"

"They weren't *very* good," I conceded, as if I made a habit of critiquing modern art on a daily basis.

"She's always been one for wild enthusiasms, your aunty Suzanne. I remember, years ago, it was rock 'n' roll and then it was jazz and then it was . . ." He took another swig of his beer. "When you're as old as I am, Rebecca, you'll be able to look back at your life and wonder what the hell it's all about."

I looked up, confused. It felt as if the conversation had slipped its moorings. I scoured my brain for a suitable follow-up question.

"What number anniversary is it?" I asked.

He took a swig of his beer. "You've got me there," he said. I tried again.

"So, why did you marry Mum?"

He stopped mid-swig and stared at his can.

"Because. Because she needed me, I suppose."

I waited.

"And you loved her," I prompted him helpfully.

"Yes," he said, taking another mouthful of beer and crumpling the can in his hand. "And I loved her."

"*Dinner's ready!*" My mother's voice rang through the garden.

"Come on," he said. "We'd better look sharp or your mother will serve us both up for dessert."

The best cloth was on the table (green Irish linen), the best china (Eternal Beau rather than our everyday Midwinter), the good cutlery and two glasses apiece. My mother had taken a few sprays of carnations and arranged them for a centerpiece. We chinked glasses and Tiffany and I, co-conspirators, exchanged looks of excitement.

"And now for our surprise!" said Tiffany the moment the last of the lemon meringue pie had been scraped from our plates. We led our parents into the lounge.

"What the devil?"

"How on earth?"

"Sit down," commanded Tiffany and with a flourish she drew the curtains and pressed down the switch as Mr. Huxley had shown her.

Another world flickered onto the screen, a world where people moved jerkily and noiselessly, mouthing to the camera words that would never be heard. Everything was bathed in a yellow light and there was my mother in a tiara and veil, her hair swept off her head, her dress pinched at the waist.

"You look beautiful!" I said.

She looked at the screen and sniffed. "I told your father not to wear that suit. He looks like a pimp."

Granny Monroe was wearing an extraordinary hat, like a bowl with a bow at the front, and then we saw our father, pacing outside the church, clasping and unclasping his hands. The film jumped. And in the next scene we were at the reception, where women in beehives and miniskirts jostled against those who looked like the Queen. Uncle Kenneth was there too, with long hair straggling down his shoulders.

He looked like a girl apart from the fact that he kept on grabbing Aunty Suzanne and kissing her on the lips.

I looked at my parents sitting on the sofa. My mother appeared to have been stunned into silence.

There was a close-up of the cake, a three-tiered affair, and our mother and father clenching a knife and attempting to hack through the icing. The film cut, and then they were standing together, grinning, holding aloft a slice of the cake. Then it stopped abruptly. A *flutter-flutter-flutter* noise came from the projector, and strange triangles and flashes filled the screen.

"Well, well, well," said my father. "That takes me back."

"I told you we should have got a professional to shoot the film. But you wouldn't listen, would you?"

"No," said our father, sounding suddenly tired. "No. You know best, Doreen."

Something had gotten into her again. She was on her feet, flinging open the curtains.

"If I knew then what I know now!" she said. "I could have married Jonathan James, you know. At least he's got some ambition! He goes *skiing*, you know."

My father stood up. His face had gone red; his hands were shaking.

"You were the one who said you were pregnant! But then, we never really did get to the bottom of that, did we?"

He glared at her, his collar tight against his neck, his tie straining at his shirt. He slammed the door on his way out.

The atmospheric conditions inside 24 Beech Drive were unfavorable for days. The anniversary dinner had caused a cold front to sweep in, and it refused to budge. In the end, it was the promise of a foreign holiday that proved to be our domestic Gulf Stream, although Tiffany said that the new see-through black negligee we'd seen in the washing basket had played some part in it.

Abroad! The Continent, to be precise. Although exactly when and where had yet to be decided. On the day after the announcement was made, we arrived home from school to discover a huge pile of glossy brochures on the breakfast bar. They emitted a high, slightly toxic smell of ink, which Tiffany and I breathed in and held in our lungs. Was it that that made my head feel light and my hands tremble? I touched the pages carefully, afraid that I'd soil them, but they were so shiny they slipped through my fingers.

I opened the first brochure and flicked through the pages. The photographs showed an impossible paradise: soft golden sand, happy smiling faces, the bluest sea I'd ever seen (a *lot* bluer than the North Sea, which had been more gray than blue and spouted dirty foam like our kitchen sink when the pipes blocked). The skies were even bluer than the sea. Just looking at the photos hurt my eyes. Everyone in them was a dark brown, like Lucy when she came back from Majorca, and Claire Bradley after she went to Torremolinos.

I flicked through the pages, murmuring the names, foreign and exotic: "Benalmadena, Costa del Sol, the Romanian Riviera, Rhodes, Bulgaria, Benidorm." It sounded like an incantation; a catechism of possibility.

"Listen to this one," commanded my mother. "The Hotel Golden Sun offers our clients a veritable home away from home; its twenty-five stories and three hundred rooms are a landmark of comfort and sophistication. Rooms are decorated to the highest standard and fully equipped for the needs of the modern holidaymaker while the twenty-five-foot-long swimming pool provides a focus for both daytime activities and nighttime entertainment."

We crowded around, peering at the slightly fuzzy photograph, the dazzling white of the hotel offset by the rectangle of blue at its foot. We were going abroad!

Even our father deigned to watch the *BBC Holiday* program with us. We'd always watched it, it was true, but in the same way we watched *Dallas* and *Blake's Seven*. Until now, going abroad had been in the same league as owning an oil well or using a teletransporter. But that had all changed. We hung on Cliff Michelmore's every word, learning the specialist vocabulary required for foreign holidays ("surcharges," "small print," "transfer buses"). Every time there was a shot of a woman in a bikini walking down a beach (which was often), we imagined it was us. Apart, perhaps, from my father, who seemed to be enjoying the program a lot more than he let on. Lucy had already told me all sorts of facts about abroad. About how you drove on the other side of the road, about how the waiters winked at you, how Coke tasted different and crisps came only in plain. And how when you jumped in the sea you didn't run out screaming that your legs were going to fall off because of the cold.

Our foreign holiday was still months away, but it had already had a significant influence on my career plans. Alongside nurse, hairdresser, teacher, secretary and weather girl there was now a sixth possibility: air hostess. I'd seen them appear fleetingly on *Holiday* and had read about them in one of Tiffany's magazines. They were impossibly glamorous, immaculately dressed in little pillbox hats and matching jackets. And they looked so happy, always smiling and helpful. I longed to be an air hostess.

"Well more fool you," said my mother when I confided my plans to her. "Glorified waitresses that's all they are."

I suspected she was jealous. The international jet age had yet to arrive in Beech Drive, and in any case, my mother had shown decided opinions on the subject of "career women," although the only one we knew apart from the deputy head with the morals of an alley cat was Mrs. Bellamy from Oak Avenue. She was also a teacher and, according to my mother, lived in a slum. This seemed to have something to do with the fact that you didn't have to take your shoes off inside her house.

"Those children of hers . . . ," said my mother, shaking her head.

"What about them?"

"Latchkey kids!"

"What's a latchkey kid?"

"They have to let themselves into the house after school."

I thought about this for a moment.

"Can I be a latchkey kid?"

"Don't try and be smart, Rebecca."

It wasn't just my mother, however, who failed to show any interest in my career plans. Nobody was very encouraging. When I told Aunty Suzanne, she dropped her tea towel and turned to face me.

"Why don't you want to be a pilot?"

"Pardon?"

"Why do you want to be an air hostess when you could be a pilot?"

You had to hand it to Aunty Suzanne, she had some funny ideas.

"Because they're *men*." It had never crossed my mind to want to be a pilot. They wore navy blue trouser suits and peaked hats, which would hardly be the most flattering outfit in which to travel the world. And besides, you wouldn't meet rich businessmen and oil tycoons if you were stuck in the cockpit.

"Air hostesses wear pretty dresses and they smile a lot and *marry* the pilot," I said, concluding my argument. I spoke slowly and enunciated my words carefully because sometimes my aunt could be a bit thick about really obvious things.

She sighed. "Right, girls. What do you want to drink? Would you like some milk? Now we're going to sit in the conservatory and we're going to have a little talk."

It sounded ominous. We helped her assemble a tray that included two glasses of milk, a plate of chocolate-chip cookies and a glass of chamomile tea that looked (and smelled) suspiciously like urine. We followed her through to the conservatory at the back of the house, overlooking the lawns and hedges and trees and ornamental pond. The sun was shining weakly, and Aunty Suzanne seemed to be thinking about something.

"Now, Rebecca, why do you think it is that men become pilots and women become air hostesses?"

Blimey. I looked at Lucy for help, but she was swinging her legs underneath the rattan chair and looking at the sky. I wanted to say, *Because they are*, but I suspected it was not the answer Aunty Suzanne was looking for.

"Because men are better at flying planes? Because women aren't allowed to fly planes?" This wouldn't surprise me. My father was always reluctant to let my mother take the wheel of our Ford Cortina and he always said "woman driver" when somebody cut him off. Although not if it was a man.

I racked my brain. A flash of inspiration struck.

"Because air hostesses have to serve the dinner," I said slowly. "And women can cook, and men can't?"

"No, Rebecca. That's not the reason. It's because little girls like you are conditioned to *want* to become air hostesses, and little boys are conditioned to *want* to become pilots, that's why. And until recently, there weren't even any laws to prevent airlines or what-have-you from only recruiting men. You don't really *want* to be an air hostess. It's false consciousness."

My mother had taught us that it was rude to contradict adults, but Aunty Suzanne had got it all wrong. I *really really* wanted to be an air hostess. And I was conscious of it more than anything.

"The thing is that men like to see women in subservient positions. They like to have women waiting on them. It reminds them of being in the infantile state where their mothers looked after them and nurtured them. It's a Freudian hang-up and that's why air hostesses are seen as sex objects. And with nurses too, it's the same thing."

She seemed to have been carried away on a train of thought. She didn't even appear to be directing her comments at me particularly, which was just as well, because I didn't have a clue what she was going on about. Apart from the fact that she had used the word "sex." I squirmed in my seat. My mother had never used the word "sex" in her life. Unless it was concealed inside another word, like "Middlesex," and even then she looked uneasy.

"So, Rebecca, do you understand now? Biology Is Not Destiny." She gave each word its full weight. "You'll remember that, won't you? You could be anything. A pilot. An astronaut. A train driver."

Train driver? I looked at her and wondered if perhaps she'd had some sort of brain spasm.

"So, if I said to you now, 'What would you like to be when you grow up?' what would you say?"

I wanted to say air hostess, of course, but I didn't like to upset Aunty S, so I chose the next best thing.

"Secretary!" I was triumphant because I was pretty sure that this must be the right answer.

Aunty Suzanne groaned.

"Okay, girls, today's lesson is over."

"Jiminy Crickets!" said Lucy, jumping up. Aunty Suzanne looked at her suspiciously.

"Lucy? You haven't been reading those books again, have you?" But it was too late, because we'd been released and had scrambled down from our chairs and raced off down the hallway and up the stairs.

"Kenneth says the best thing is to ignore her," said Lucy once we were safely cloistered in her room. When we heard Aunty Suzanne go into the garden, we tiptoed down the stairs to the study and pulled out the photo albums. Our favorite was the red velvet one, of photos of Aunty Suzanne and Uncle Kenneth's overland trip to India. They were black-and-white and obviously from a *very* long time ago. There were faded handwritten captions: "The market in Herat," "Washer women in Persepolis," "The Taj Mahal at dawn." It wasn't really the land-scapes we were looking at though. It was Aunty Suzanne in droopy cheesecloth blouses with a scarf over her head. She looked very beau-tiful: tanned and lithe and smiling. There was a picture of the camper-van and of Uncle Kenneth changing the wheel by the side of a road where the only other vehicles were skinny cows and clapped-out old trucks. He didn't look anything like he did today. He had a long, straggling beard, little round glasses, and was wearing a necklace.

"Was he a 'sissy'?" I asked Lucy. She ignored me and flicked on through the pages, past the photo of them kissing and on to one where Aunty Suzanne was smoking a long cigarette. The caption said: "Sam-pling the local product!"

"I didn't know your mum smoked," I said, but Lucy just shrugged. "Elsa says it's Mary Yewana." I scrutinized it again. It certainly looked like Suzanne.

"Suzanne says that Kenneth doesn't know how to have fun any-more. And he says she's being juvenile. And she says he's sold out. And he says well one of them's got to keep us in Chablisandshoes."

We abandoned the albums eventually and turned our attention to the bookshelves. There were hundreds of books. At our house there were cookbooks and a few paperbacks with gold lettering on the front, but not many. My mother said they were dust magnets.

We scanned the shelves. There were rows and rows: battered or-ange Penguin paperbacks with cracked spines; fat, glossy gardening books filled with vivid Technicolor flowers; books with titles like *Know Your Child* and *Test Your IQ*; and, my favorite, a medical dic-tionary from 1938 that had many graphic pictures of tapeworms and head lice. I was leafing through the pages, studying symptoms and making a mental note to ask my mother if I might have rickets, when I spotted a yellow paperback called *Fear of Flying*. It immediately de-manded my professional attention. When I was an air hostess, I'd have to know how to deal with nervous passengers. The first few pages were electrifying, if incomprehensible.

"The zipless fuck was more than a fuck. It was a platonic ideal. Zipless because when you came together zippers fell away like rose petals, underwear blew off in one breath like dandelion fluff. Tongues intertwined and turned liquid. Your whole soul flowed out through your tongue and into the mouth of your lover."

I showed it to Lucy. I could tell she was impressed, although she was reluctant to admit it. If there were discoveries to be made, she liked to be the one to make them. We read on together.

"Another condition for the zipless fuck was brevity. And anonymity made it even better."

We paused. I turned it over in my hand. "Is it a *mucky* book?"

I used the word carefully. I'd once heard my mother say it in the same breath as loose morals, divorced women and broken families. Weren't they illegal? I wondered if I should tell Lucy, but she'd already had ideas of her own.

"Do you want to try it?" she said. "We could practice for when we have boyfriends."

I looked at her uncertainly.

"Like in the films?"

"It's easy! Go on. You just have to lie on top of me and then we kiss. You've got to do it with tongues."

"Won't we get into trouble?"

She gave me a scathing look. We lay down on the chaise longue and shifted together uncomfortably.

I wasn't sure where to start, but Lucy's lips came puckering toward me. They closed in over mine; then she sucked in her cheeks. This seemed to create some sort of vacuum between our two mouths. She was sucking out my breath and making strange noises. It was like a cross between someone eating soup and blowing a raspberry.

"They don't do it like that! You've got to put your head to one side, close your lips and breathe in," I said.

Lucy cricked her neck. She was beginning to suffocate me. Maybe that was why it was illegal. She pressed her lips at a ninety-degree angle to mine and this time rubbed them up and down. I was sure it was wrong. All I could feel was her skin chafing against mine and her weight pinioning my arms to the cushion. She was crushing me to death, her mouth attached by suction pads to mine.

I wrestled myself free and jumped up, my cheeks burning.

"I think we should stop it now," I said primly. Lucy never knew when to draw the line. I looked at her, embarrassed. We'd done a zipless fuck. What if my mother found out?

"Suit yourself," said Lucy unconcernedly. "You were rubbish anyway."

When I arrived home, Tiffany was lying in wait for me.

"Do Kenneth and Suzanne have a bidet?"

"A what?"

"A bidet. In the bathroom. It's like a toilet but smaller."

"Yes!"

"A-ha!" she said and went back to her book.

"What's it for?"

"It's for washing your bum," said Tiffany. "It's French. The middle classes began installing them when they discovered adultery."

"What's adultery? Is it what adults do?"

But Tiffany just gave me one of her looks and went back to her book.

When we sat down to tea, there was something bothering her.

"Mum?"

"Hmm?"

"Mum?"

"*What* is it, Tiffany?"

She was apportioning minted new potatoes and wasn't in the mood to be distracted.

"How come Suzanne's upper middle class and we're lower middle class?"

"*What?*"

"In my book, it says that if you have a bidet and live in a house with a name, you're upper middle class. And if you have an avocado bathroom suite and drawers under the bed, you're lower middle class. But you and Suzanne are sisters."

We watched our mother's hand clench the serving spoon. She dol-

loped the potatoes down on the plates, then picked up a spatula to attack the chops under the grill. We waited for her reply. But none
came. She slapped our plates down in front of us, an angry tendril of
hair escaping from behind her ear.

"I've had quite enough of you for one day, young lady! You're not
too old to put over the back of my knee, you know."

8.3   family *n* 4 : a locally independent organized crime unit

LATER, when my mother had gone off to a Rotary Club fête, I was left
alone with my father, who was pacing the house, listening to a football
match on his transistor radio.

"Come on! *Come on! Yes!*"

He was holding the radio to his ear, and it was emitting a loud
crackling static and a breathless male voice that accelerated toward the
end of a sentence.

"What is it, Dad?"

"*It's a goal!*" He jumped into the air. It was as well that my mother
was out. She tended to be sniffy about football, or "soccer" as she
called it, and why couldn't my father watch "rugger" like Kenneth?

"It's *rugby*, Doreen," he'd said. "And it's for public schoolboys and
Welshmen."

"Well, I don't see why you're so proud of having gone to a grammar. There's no harm in trying to better yourself, you know. Look at
Kenneth."

My father had rolled his eyes at her. "I'd rather not."

"James!"

"Well if he's so bloody perfect, why'd you chuck him?"

"Language! Anyway, I didn't 'chuck' him, to use your parlance."

"Ha!" my father said but didn't elaborate. It was unusual for anybody to answer my mother back, let alone my father. Mostly, he ignored
her, or went to his shed. It was only when she said "soccer" that he'd
turn, Incredible Hulk–like, into another type of husband altogether.

The match had finished and he'd turned off the radio. He looked at me questioningly.

"You don't want to kick a ball around, do you?"

I nodded.

"You do?" He seemed surprised and almost scampered out to the garage to find our old ball.

"Tell you what, you go in goal, okay, and I'll just have a couple of shots."

I stood uncertainly between a pot of geraniums and my father's rolled-up jacket. He ran toward the ball and kicked it toward me. I dived for it and, amazingly, I caught it.

"I caught it!"

My father laughed. "You should be in the England squad! Right, see if you can get this one."

I skidded across the grass, landing on my bottom, acquiring a long green streak across my trousers. My father took another shot and splattered mud up his back. I'd never realized football could be so much fun. Or my father, for that matter.

"Right. Are you ready?" He ran in a curving loop toward the ball, belted it, and it was with a feeling of sinking inevitability that we watched it arc and then smash through the kitchen window, landing with a thud on the draining board, accompanied by the noise of breaking glass.

I looked at my father. The color drained from his face.

"Uh-oh," I said.

We surveyed the damage. One smashed window and three broken cups. We cleaned it up together.

"Tell you what," said my father thoughtfully. "Let's not tell her, eh?"

"What do you mean?"

He chose his words carefully.

"Sometimes it's best that she doesn't know. Saves her from worrying. Go and change then, quick sharp."

I'd never lied to my mother before. And when my father launched into his explanation, I avoided catching his eye.

"Some yobbos playing in the back lane," he said. "Tried to chase them but they'd already gone."

She gave us both narrow-eyed looks and cast a menacing glance at the grass stain on my hand, but never managed to find any actual evidence (it was buried at the bottom of the washing basket).

It had bonded us though. My father and me. Our secret. It was only later that it struck me that we hadn't saved her from anything but our own culpability.

8.4 Love Story (2), Part 4

ALISTAIR WAS READING *when I got into bed. I glanced at the cover. It was a biography of Churchill. Alistair read biographies to relax. He said he liked the casual way they ascribed cause to effect, incident to consequence. He didn't look up as I climbed under the duvet and opened my magazine, but he let out a short laugh. Alistair enjoyed biographies but he didn't believe a word of them.*

It's like with the identical Jims, he says. Imagine Jim Springer flicking through the holiday brochures. His neighbor has told him Florida is great for the kids and he's noticed that the travel agent down the road happens to be offering a special deal for flights to Orlando. He looks at all the hotels in all the brochures and sees one called the San Juan, which reminds him of the great time he had when he went to Mexico. The decor is clean and modern, which he happens to prefer to more fussy traditional hotels, and he books it. He returns there the next year. And the one after that.

Imagine how he feels when he meets Jim Lewis, his identical twin, and learns that he too goes to the San Juan Hotel every year.

We all have free will, but none of us know what it is. We tell stories about ourselves, says Alistair. We construct our past to fit the facts of the present. But none of us have any way of knowing whether we have been influenced by our genes, our childhood experiences, both or neither. What chance on earth does a biographer have?

I opened my magazine and flicked through the pages. I had brought a cup of tea and a slice of toast and honey to bed and ate it as I read. Celebrity stories. I liked to pretend it was work. Recently though I'd become bored with their stories of success, of how they'd always known that they would make it, of how they'd worked so hard and been so talented.

If I had a choice, I'd prefer to read the stories of the ones who didn't make it, the ones who could have made it but ended up stacking the shelves in Safeway instead. The poetics of failure. My kind.

Next to me, Alistair turned his page. I could feel the warmth of his body, the touch of his skin. I put down my magazine and closed my eyes. I found that if I did this and concentrated, I could remember what it was like to have sex. Although not always.

I took another sip of my tea and another bite of toast, taking care to discreetly brush the top of the duvet cover.

"Crumbs!" said Alistair without moving his eyes from the page. These days he resented any incursions into his eight hours' sleep, although when we first met, he used to set his alarm clock for the middle of the night in order to fuck me when I was least expecting it.

In the morning, I often wondered if it had really happened or not. It was only the odd telltale silvery trail of sperm down my thigh that offered material confirmation. But that was before. Before I'd started taking a midnight snack to bed. Before there existed the possibility that it could have been honey. Or maybe marmalade.

"Night." Alistair turned off his bedside light and rolled onto his side.

8.5 abroad *adv* 2 : in different directions

NEWS FLASH! NEWS FLASH! NEWS FLASH! The powers that be (i.e., our mother) had decided that we were going to Majorca! Just like Lucy! It had taken months to make the final choice. Months of deliberating and flicking through brochures until they'd lost their sheen and become dog-eared and creased; months of cross-referencing hotel facilities and swimming pool lengths. Tiffany and I had invented a new form of Top Trumps. We'd sit in the lounge with a brochure each and fire questions at each other.

"Number of bedrooms?"

"Two hundred and ten."

"I've got two hundred and fifty-two. I win. Transfer time?"

"Two and a half hours."

"One and a half hours. Yours."

"Number of bars?"

"Two."

"I've got two too. Draw."

We could do this for hours. The best one to get was the Rio Park in Benidorm, which had 450 bedrooms, three pools and four bars. It was the Top Trumps equivalent of the Ferrari Testarossa.

Our mother had agonized over the final decision. But in the end, we'd all been swung by the descriptions of Majorca. Lucy had told me about the ice creams and the inflatable mattresses on which they lay in the sea for hours, while Aunty Suzanne was always going on about the shape of the mountains and the "singularity" of the sunsets. Uncle Kenneth's brother owned a house there, so they went every year. And now we were going to go too! Two whole weeks at the Hotel Cala D'Or in Palmanova with its Olympic-sized pool, 345 bedrooms, three bars, one restaurant, lifts, en suite bathroom facilities and children's play area.

I was the one who relayed the news to Aunty Suzanne. She was in the garden weeding her herbaceous border.

"Majorca, eh?" said Aunty Suzanne, straightening up. "Well, why doesn't that surprise me?"

I thought about this for a moment or two.

"Because you knew already?"

"Because your mother has always wanted what I've got, that's why." She plunged her trowel back into the soil. "And then she realizes that it wasn't what she wanted after all."

I stood on the path next to the flower bed, searching for some key to enter the conversation.

"Like caftans!" I said, suddenly inspired. My mother had bought an orange, ankle-length one in a fit of enthusiasm, and it had languished guiltily at the back of the wardrobe ever since, like a bad debt.

"Like boyfriends," said Aunty Suzanne. A gobbet of spittle hit the soil. "Like husbands."

She stopped digging and straightened up.

"I'm sorry, Rebecca. What am I thinking? It's very bad karma to get angry like that. Do you forgive me?"

I considered the matter.

"Yes," I said gravely, although I couldn't help feeling she'd missed the point. "It's got a swimming pool!"

Our foreign holiday wasn't the only point of exoticism on the horizon. An Indian family had moved into number 16.

"There goes the neighborhood," said Mrs. Huxley to my mother over the garden fence while they were putting out their washing.

Aunty Suzanne, however, took it upon herself to form a one-woman welcoming committee. She decided to go visiting, taking with her Lucy, me and a tin of Roses' chocolate.

"Come on!" she said. "It's important that we show them that we're going to treat them the same as any of our other neighbors."

Neither Lucy nor I were wholly convinced by the logic of this plan.

"But Roses are to say thank you very much, thank you very, very much," said Lucy, for we were scrupulous viewers of the TV ads. "We should have brought Quality Street chocolates. And besides, when the Fletchers moved in you didn't give them anything."

"Do shut up, Lucy. Or I'll cut your television viewing time." Lucy bit her lip. She already had to time her visits to Beech Drive to coincide with *The Bionic Woman.*

Aunty Suzanne rang the bell.

A woman in a pair of silky pajamas answered it. She had long black hair tied back from her head, and a small gold stud glittered in her nose.

The stud transfixed us. Was she a punk as well as foreign?

"Hello! Suzanne Edwards," said Aunty Suzanne, and she held out her hand. "I just wanted to take the opportunity to welcome you to the neighborhood! A small housewarming present!"

The woman at the door looked a bit startled.

"Well that's very kind. I'm Meera. Meera Ali." We were all taken aback by her voice. She sounded even posher than Aunty Suzanne. "Do come on through." She invited us into the kitchen and put a percolator on the stove.

There was a little boy playing on the floor, but Lucy and I tried our best to ignore him.

"Say hello, Rajiv."

He looked up from the plastic hammer he had been using to pound the floor.

"Hello, Rajiv," he said. Aunty Suzanne chuckled, as if this was a particularly good joke. We continued to ignore him. Little boys were beneath our contempt.

"Is it hot in India?" asked Lucy.

"Lucy!" Aunty Suzanne fixed her with a stare.

Mrs. Ali shushed her. "That's quite all right. We're not Indian, we're Pakistani."

We absorbed this new information, unsure of what it meant.

"And it is hot there, although I left when I was very little."

I stored up the facts to relay back to my mother. There were no particular signs of foreignness in the kitchen, although I wasn't sure what I'd been expecting. The only real touch of exoticism was Mrs. Ali's silk pantaloons, trousers that were gathered at the ankle, worn under a dress. I let the conversation drift over my head and dreamed about wearing silky trousers.

"Would you like some juice, girls?"

We shook our heads.

"Well of course," Aunty Suzanne was saying, "I'm very interested in the East. I think that there's a lot that we in the West could learn."

"Oh well yes I suppose so," said Mrs. Ali, who was busy pulling small, brightly colored cakes from tins and rounding up brown smoked glass plates on which to serve us. She didn't appear to be listening very hard. "Although we went to Scarborough once for our holiday and I don't think we'll bother again."

Although there were still two months to go, packing preparations were already under way. Our mother had started studying the fashion sections of her *Woman* and *Woman's Own*, and had even gone so far as to discuss with us the merits of one-piece bathing suits versus bikinis.

"The thing about one-pieces," she said, "is that you don't have to show your tummy. But then with a bikini you do get a more complete tan." I wasn't sure what I should say. Or indeed whether it was a statement that required a response. Tiffany seemed to have a handle on the situation though.

"Pamela Ewing always wears a bathing suit," she said. "And Sue Ellen wears bikinis."

We all nodded thoughtfully.

Our mother had already bought a new leatherette suitcase that perched catlike on the top of her wardrobe. She'd started to assemble a collection of holiday paraphernalia too: a plug adapter, a document holder, a sun hat and a see-through bottle of factor six Ambre Solaire sun oil. It was the color of deep mahogany, and when my mother was occupied with other matters, I liked to open up the lid and sniff it. It was a rich, fructid scent that I tried to memorize: the smell of abroad.

The weather front had moved on in an easterly direction, settling over the Old Parsonage, where sudden squalls blew up, catching Lucy and me unawares.

"Kenneth?"

"Hmm. What is it, Lucy?"

"Tina Westlake has got a puppy. Can we get one?" She looked at her father. "Please? Please? Please?"

"You don't say 'got' Lucy, it's slang. Tina Westlake *has* a puppy. Can we *have* one?"

Lucy looked at him expectantly. Uncle Kenneth merely looked irritated.

"They haven't even taught you to speak properly at that school, have they?"

We were all in the kitchen. Uncle Kenneth was reading the business pages and Aunty Suzanne was repotting her spider plants. She banged down a pot onto the counter. "Oh, don't start that again."

"Start what again? She's going to St. Edward's next year and that's the end of it."

"She is not! You know my views on private education. It's an elitist anachronism and I won't have it."

"It's her *education* we're talking about, not an excuse for you to jump on your socialist bandwagon."

"Listen, Kenneth, just because you're a repressed public schoolboy doesn't mean that everyone has to be."

"I just don't want my daughter growing up to be a common little shopgirl, that's all!"

"Oh, for Christ's sake! Stop being such a snob! You're beginning to sound like bloody Doreen! You'd have been a match made in heaven, you know."

They glared at each other. Lucy and I had suspended our game of Connect 4. Uncle Kenneth and Aunty Suzanne appeared to have forgotten we were there. Lucy, realizing that they must have misunderstood her question, tried again.

"So, does that mean we *can* get a puppy then?"

Uncle Kenneth walked out of the kitchen, slamming the door behind him.

"I BET YOU BLOODY VOTED FOR HER, DIDN'T YOU?" yelled Aunty Suzanne behind him.

When I related the conversation to my mother, she paid more than usual attention. "Suzanne said me and Kenneth were 'a match made in heaven'? Whatever could she mean? What a funny idea."

I wasn't sure I'd got it right. "Yes. But I don't think she realized I was there."

She stirred her saucepan with a slow, deliberate movement. I tried to tell her about Tina Westlake's puppy, but it was no good; she'd lost interest. I crept away to inhale the pure, sweet air of a bottle of Ambre Solaire instead.

We looked up Majorca in our mother's old school atlas. It showed the world as red countries (which belonged to us) and non-red ones (which didn't). Majorca was a non-red country. We found it eventually, although it didn't look very impressive on paper. My father peered over my shoulder and pointed out other places—Menorca, Ibiza and a whole shower of little rocks hanging off the end of a glove, which my father said was Greece and Her Islands.

"I went there, you know, before you were born."

"You did?" My father had been abroad? I looked at him with new respect.

He lowered his voice. "It was before I married your mother." And he winked confidentially at me. "With a girlfriend."

It was almost too much to take in. I looked at him poring over the page of the atlas.

"What was it like?"

"Fanbloodytastic!"

"Dad! You swore."

But he wasn't listening to me.

"There was this film called *The Moonspinners*. With Hayley Mills. And it was set on Crete, so that's where I went. Took the train to Patras, then the ferry to Piraeus, then another ferry to Heraklion. Took forever, but I wouldn't have changed it for the world."

I looked at my father, unsettled now. He was tracing his finger over the lines on the atlas, murmuring to himself. He looked the same—gray trousers, blue shirt, tie loosened at the neck, eyes with the same slightly hangdog air—but I felt a new sense of awe toward him, this stranger with the exotic past. I had never before considered the possibility that my parents might have other compartments in their lives, that didn't include me.

It was a brilliant stroke of luck that Mrs. Graham, my teacher, should choose to study the Mediterranean in our next geography lesson. Who can name an island in the Mediterranean? she asked. My hand shot up. I didn't often get breaks like that, not like Lucy, who always had odd facts and bits of information up her sleeve, like who won the War and who it was against.

Mrs. Graham scanned the room.

"Majorca!" I said.

"Very good, Rebecca."

"And what country is Majorca in?" This foxed me. I thought Majorca was a country. But no, according to Mrs. Graham, it was in Spain, a piece of information I carefully stored away to relay to my family at dinner.

That evening, we'd eaten and were stretched out in the lounge watching *Nationwide* before I remembered. I was lying across the hearth rug and was about to impress my family with my newfound geographical knowledge when my mother appeared in the doorway wearing her Dannimac.

"Just popping over to Suzanne's to pick up the guidebook," she said. My father looked up from his paper.

"What guidebook?"

"On Majorca. Suzanne said she'd lend it to me."

My father grunted and went back to his book.

"Mum! She's out! And it's in Spain." But she'd already gone. Tiffany and my father didn't even bother to look up.

"Majorca's in Spain! And Aunty Suzanne and Lucy are playing tennis. I told Mum that earlier."

Nobody paid any attention to me so I went back to my drawing, picking a particularly virulent shade of purple to color in the sky. It was then that I felt the first violent stab of pain in my side.

The last thing I remembered hearing was my father calling 999, his panic rising a semitone at a time.

8.6 academic *adj* 3 : scholarly to the point of being unaware of the outside world

ALISTAIR CLAIMS that it's females who choose their mates. It's a Darwinian theory, "sexual selection."

We were at the supermarket. Usually I was the one who went. Or Alistair picked up a few things after work. But we'd decided to cook for a couple of friends, and in the end, we'd gone together.

"Darwin theorized that it was the sexual preferences of females that accounted for the evolution of certain male physical characteristics," said Alistair.

I was examining avocados, checking the ripeness, the coloration of the skin.

"But you crossed the room," I said. "*You* chatted *me* up."

I put the avocados in the basket and stared at him. He never seems to remember that. "The two statements are not contradictory," he said. "It is the male that has to expend the effort to get noticed. This is typical among mammals and some birds."

Sometimes I don't know how Alistair does it. How he manages to make even the simple fact that he flirted with me sound like the script from a nature documentary. But he just carried straight on.

"If, for example, at some point in the past, females preferred more brightly colored males, then brightly colored males would have a breeding advantage, and this, in turn, would lead to even more brightly colored males in the next generation. Hence, the peacock's extravagant tail, the stag's elaborate antlers."

"Most people talk about baked beans or olive oil when they go to the supermarket," I said.

He reached over the shelf and selected two grapefruit. "What?"

"Don't we need olive oil?"

He frowned, and replaced the two grapefruit, for two identical-looking different ones. "An Israeli scientist, Amotz Zahavi, however, proposes that the tails are themselves handicaps. A male, who can afford such a handicap, must therefore be strong and healthy."

A man standing next to us looked up from the vegetable display and stared at Alistair. I stared at him too. Did other people discuss sexual selection in the middle of a supermarket aisle?

"Alistair . . . ?"

He'd walked off though toward the dairy section. I trotted after him, anxious that he'd forget the orange juice.

"There's a new theory now though. A variation on the other theories." He reached for a milk carton.

"No, get semi-skimmed," I said. He put back the carton and selected another one.

"It claims that there's another method that is employed by drabber, weaker males. While the stags lock horns and the peacocks strut, they make their play.

"This, according to the evolutionary biologist John Maynard Smith, is the 'sneaky fucker strategy.'"

An old woman standing next to him looked sharply in our direction.

I stood before Alistair and blocked his way.

"Don't we need olive oil?" I pleaded.

I've read Herbert's Bought Ledger files though, so I'm inclined to go along with the theory. The amended theory. But I didn't choose Alistair. He crossed the room. *He* chose me. But he seems to have theorized his way out of that. Or blanked it. One or the other.

8.7 **relative** *adj* **1** : having pertinence or relevance

AFTER I'D BEEN let out of the hospital, I wasn't slow to appreciate how lucky I'd been. Nobody I knew had nearly died. In fact, nobody I knew had actually died. I was unique! And also famous. All the neighbors had heard the story, and everyone in my class and all the relatives had to be telephoned especially. My appendix had actually burst, and had it taken any longer to reach the hospital, I might have died.

I had three weeks off school, and my mother brought me runny boiled eggs and toast soldiers. She'd missed the whole thing, returning home to find the house empty, her family gone. She'd been satisfyingly distraught when she did finally make it to my sickbed though, so it was tempting to feel that it was worth it.

She brought me cups of tea and sat on the edge of my bed. "Poor Rebecca," she said. And with her hand she stroked the hair from my forehead. A lump came to my throat.

Being ill was like being on holiday. Only better. I basked in the unadulterated attention I received from my mother. Stories were read to me, cooling flannels passed over my brow, and Tiffany was under special instructions to be nice to me. She did this by ignoring me. On the chest of drawers in my room, I displayed my sixteen Get Well Soon cards and a pot of hyacinth that flowered pink and white. Nobody had ever given me flowers before. I couldn't remember feeling happier. Best of all though were the hourly visitations from my mother. She was always hovering by the door, or taking my temperature, or feeling my brow.

"Poor little thing!" she said with concern clouding her eyes. "Poor little Rebecca!" She was really a much better nurse than anybody would have guessed, and I fulfilled the role of patient to the best of my abilities. Even when I started feeling better I found that if I groaned from time to time, it seemed to do the trick.

My mother looked at me sharply. "No need to ham it up, Rebecca." Although even then there was a softness to her voice that she couldn't quite expel.

Nanna was allowed to come and visit too as a special treat. My mother enforced an invitation-only policy toward visits from her parents.

"It's because they're working class," said Tiffany knowledgeably. I looked at her uncertainly. Our mother said the working classes ought to be renamed the shirking classes and that anybody with money to waste on beer and cigarettes could afford a nice, new pair of curtains.

"But they're *family*," I said.

"Mum's bettered herself," said Tiffany. "I've got a book on it." She flipped it over to show me the cover. It was called *Class* and was by Jilly Cooper, who occasionally appeared on early evening chat shows to talk about sex. It was her specialty apparently. Although she said it was better with horses.

"She doesn't like to be reminded that Nanna's common," said Tiffany. "I'd like to be upper middle class. That's what Jilly Cooper says she is. She says her mother wouldn't dream of having guests without putting fresh flowers in the guest bedroom."

"But we don't have a guest bedroom," I pointed out.

"Exactly!"

According to Tiffany the very best people were the upper classes, who ignored all the rules and did outrageous things like eat peas with a knife.

"They don't care what anyone thinks of them and can afford to get on with the working classes because they've been impregnating them for centuries."

I looked at Tiffany, impressed. Would I ever know as much as her?

I lay propped up with the cushions on the sofa when Nanna arrived.

"There you are!" she said and kissed me, her skin soft against my cheek. "How's my little Rebecca?"

I smiled at her. "Hello, Nanna!" I said and beamed.

I knew it was wrong to have favorites, but Nanna was far and away my preferred grandmother. I always had the impression Granny Monroe didn't like me very much. And anyway, Tiffany was her special pet. She received a £5 Boots voucher from her every birthday, whereas I usually got a packet of balloons or a novelty pencil sharpener.

Nanna, on the other hand, was always scrupulously fair in her dealings with Tiffany and Lucy and me. But Tiffany thought she was wet, and Lucy thought she was old, so I was the one who played receptive grandchild to her doting grandmother. I enjoyed it. We had a "Special Relationship." It was a phrase I'd picked up from the news, although we tended to share toffee bonbons rather than nuclear weapons.

"Hello, Alicia," said my father, taking her coat. She wasn't alone. By her side was an old lady wearing a large turquoise hat. She was a relative, apparently. How many more of them were there? I wondered. They kept on appearing, demanding more tea, or rubbing hand cream into their liver spots. This one was called Great-Aunt Betty and she sat stiffly on her armchair, her back straight, her knees pressed together.

My mother had made Victoria sponge cake, coffee and walnut cake, and cucumber sandwiches. I tried to sit up straight and she fussed behind me, propping another cushion under my back. Tiffany sulked on the sofa.

"Poor little Rebecca!" said Nanna. "Who's been in the wars?"

"Which war?" I asked, but my mother had already swooped into view.

"She's getting much better now. Not long before she's back at school!"

I gave a theatrical cough. I was beginning to suspect that my invalid days were numbered. I smiled nervously and let out a small whimper. My mother narrowed her eyes.

"Rebecca . . . ," she started, but I was saved by Nanna.

"And this is your great-aunt Betty!"

"Hello, Great-Aunty Betty!"

Great-Aunty Betty stood up and walked across the room, bending her face toward mine. Her clothes smelled musty, and when she leaned down to kiss me on the cheek, I caught a whiff of her sour breath.

"So? These are the grandchildren, are they?"

She picked a large black vinyl handbag with a big silver clasp off the floor and started to rummage through it.

My mother set down the teapot in the middle of the table. She had laid out her best china, with the cups and saucers and matching sugar bowl and jug. She always made a point of using the best china when Nanna came to visit. Usually, it was kept in a frosted-glass cabinet locked with a key.

My mother fussed with her tea service. She wielded the pot as if she was trying to make some sort of point, pouring the tea into dainty cups with a silver strainer.

The rest of us watched her and sat around in our best clothes making polite conversation. This was what you did when you had visitors.

Nanna looked from me to Tiffany and then said, "Great-Aunty Betty is my sister!"

I thought about this for a moment.

"So you're like me and she's like Tiffany?"

Tiffany turned and glared at me.

"Who's the oldest? You or Great-Aunty Betty?" she asked.

Nanna folded her hands across her lap. "I am."

"Nur-nuh-nur-nur-nuh!" said Tiffany, turning to me. "You're wrong! *I'm* like Nanna. And *you're* like Great-Aunty Betty."

"No," said Nanna, taking a sip of her tea. "I think Rebecca got it right the first time."

Our mother went to put the kettle on again. She liked to keep busy when Nanna came to visit. It gave her a break from saying "Mother!" or "Really!" or "I don't think so!"

Great-Aunty Betty had extracted an ancient pair of horn-rimmed spectacles from her bag and was now wearing them. Behind the glass, her eyes were enlarged and distorted, increasing and diminishing in size as she turned her head. "Let's have a look at them, then. Come here, Tiffany."

Reluctantly, Tiffany stood up from the sofa and walked across the room. Great-Aunty Betty grasped her face and turned it to the light coming in through the patio doors. "Hmm. What's that on your cheek, Tiffany?"

I tried to catch sight of Tiffany's cheek but couldn't see anything. Great-Aunty Betty didn't seem to be looking at Tiffany, though. She was looking at Nanna. "Is it a touch of the tar brush?"

We looked at our grandmother in confusion. Nanna shook her head. "You'll never change, will you, Betty?" And she stood up to leave, even though we hadn't even started on the coffee and walnut cake. "You've had a whole lifetime to change!" She shook her head sadly. "It's all such a waste."

Tiffany and I exchanged a blank look.

"Doesn't she like us?" I asked as we followed her out into the hall.

"Have I got tar on my face?" said Tiffany, rubbing her cheek with her sleeve.

"She's just a miserable old woman, that's all. You ignore her."

They left soon after that.

8.8   **sign** *n* **1** : something that suggests the presence or existence of a fact, condition or quality

IT WAS SEPTEMBER 7 yesterday. I spent all day conscious of the fact that it was September 7 and wondering if Alistair would notice. He never has before, so it's unlikely he would suddenly begin, but I always wonder.

"That smells good," he said when he walked in the door. He threw down his bag, kissed me on the cheek and leaned over to take a spoon of the curry I was making.

I turned my head slightly and looked at him, checking for signs.

"What?" he said.

I hesitated.

"Nothing," I said eventually and went to get a bottle of wine out of the fridge.

He didn't notice. But then, I don't suppose he's ever worked out the dates. September 7, our ghost-child's birthday.

8.9   **pregnant** *adj* **1** : (of woman or female animal) having a developing child or young in the womb

MY CONVALESCENCE was a perfect time. Until, that is, my mother dropped the Bombshell. It was a Tuesday, because we were eating meat loaf for dinner and my mother was holding a spatula of over-cooked sprouts over my plate as she made the announcement. In retrospect, I can't help feeling that she could have picked a more propitious moment. Or at least a different menu.

"So?" she said in the voice she reserved for speaking to other people's children. "How would you like to have a little baby brother or sister?" The spatula was overloaded. The sprouts were precariously balanced. I wasn't sure what kind of question this was (rhetorical? hypothetical? fanciful?) and therefore how to answer it. After a moment's hesitation, I plumped for the truth.

"I'd prefer a puppy."

"Oh, Rebecca!"

I wished people would stop asking me questions they didn't want me to answer. My mother's face was pink. I had assumed this was a result of her proximity to the frying pan, but I now realized it must be due to an upwelling of maternal emotion. She was wearing a strange and unfamiliar expression, and it took me a while to recognize it: she was smiling. My father's face, on the other hand, was less easy to read. He had recently grown a mustache and had taken to hiding behind it. Perhaps he would have preferred a puppy too.

Tiffany was decidedly more gracious in her acceptance of the gift of new life. A tactic, she was right in thinking, that could bear material fruit.

"How marvelous!" she said. It was a phrase she had picked up from Margo in *The Good Life*,* and she was rewarded with a kiss from our

---

**The Good Life*

"This seventies classic British sitcom (released in the U.S. as *Good Neighbors*, and restyled as *Green Acres*) followed the lives of Tom (Richard Briers) and Barbara Good (Felicity Kendal), who had left the rat race and decided to live off the land. In their ordinary suburban home.

"Suspicion of Big Business, the rise in the ecology movement, and back-to-nature principles are shown here infiltrating an ordinary middle-class environment. With vegetables growing, goats, chickens and a pig or two running loose, the pair just about manages to survive, much to the dismay of class-conscious next-door neighbor Margo Ledbetter (Penelope Keith) and her husband Jerry (Paul Eddington).

"Neither couple have children. In the 1970s, as people focused more intensely on their own happiness, and fulfilling their own desires, child rearing came to be viewed as much as a burden as a blessing."

mother and the promise of a new dress "for being such a good little girl." Tiffany did not shrink from such praise. The fact that she had dangled me by the ankles over the hall banisters shortly after my arrival in the Family Monroe had been airbrushed from the official record. Tiffany beamed. But not for long. The ax was about to fall.

"Of course," said my mother, "I've had to cancel our holiday. You can't go around eating foreign food when you're pregnant. It might harm Baby." There was a silence as this news sank in. Surely she was joking. Wasn't she? Tiffany's appetite failed her. Her knife and fork clinked on the plate, a tinkle of doom. Our father went off to the shed to find a bottle of wine from his emergency supply, although I wasn't sure if he was preparing a toast or drowning his sorrows. Our mother smiled beatifically and patted her stomach. We stared at her in amazement. Or was it horror?

"So?" she said. "Which would you prefer? A little brother? Or a little sister?"

"A holiday," muttered Tiffany under her breath. I had a feeling her new dress was about to be withdrawn. But our mother appeared not to have heard.

"Yes. I think I'd prefer a little boy too. I think I've already got too many daughters. I mean I think I have *enough* daughters," she said, correcting herself.

"If it's a boy, you'll be able to play football with him," I said to my father, but he didn't reply. He was sitting in his armchair, hidden behind his mustache. "Football" was our secret code. Our Masonic handshake. My mother looked up and twitched.

"Or rugger," she said, but my father was pretending not to hear.

"So?" she said brightly. "What about Devon then?"

There was an official period of mourning. We all grieved for our aborted holiday. Our holiday that would never have the chance to exist. The memories we would never have the chance to acquire. It was Tiffany whom it hit the hardest. She had told everybody in her class that she was going abroad. The shame would be almost too much to bear. She moped in the sitting room, unable to give up the dream quite yet, and flicked once again through the brochures, looking at the hotels we'd never see, the swimming pools we'd never swim in.

"Mum? Where's the guidebook?"

"What guidebook?"

"The one you went to borrow the day Rebecca got appendicitis." But Planet Doreen wasn't receiving her. She was in the kitchen, rocking back and forth on her chair, smiling to herself.

Tiffany gave up and went to her room. I stole the bottle of Ambre Solaire from my mother's wardrobe and hid it underneath my bed. Neither of us would ever forgive Devon.

8.10 The Gambler's Fallacy

YOU TOSS A COIN. Six times in a row, it comes up heads.

<u>Question</u>

What are the odds of throwing a seventh?

<u>Answer</u>

Exactly the same as the first: one in two.

It's fifty-fifty. The coin will come up either heads or tails. The odds are the odds. The coin has no memory.

Alistair was on television again last night. It was a discussion program about genetic determination. He looked rather handsome, although I think they tend to use too much hair spray. There was a woman on the program whose mother had Huntington's disease. She was good-looking too, in that sort of brisk, efficient, smart-hairstyle, neatly-applied-lipstick, carefully-chosen-brooch-on-the-lapel sort of way. Like a female politician, say, or a news reporter.

I know about Huntington's disease. If you spend any time with geneticists it's one of those things you know about. It's caused by a mutation on chromosome 4, and if you have the mutation, you will, at some stage in middle age, develop dementia. Then come muscle contractions, delusions and hallucinations. After which you lose all control of your motor functions. And then you die. Unless you get run over by a bus first. But as Alistair points out, how many people do you know who actually get run over by buses? Anyway, this woman, Alison I think her name was, her mother had died from the disease. And as her daughter, with half her mother's genes, there's a 50 percent chance she'll get it too. It's fate. As simple as that. There's no prevention and no cure.

She doesn't have a 50 percent chance though. It's like the Gambler's Fallacy: a misconception that arises from applying probabilities to single events. There isn't a 50 percent chance that she has the gene that causes the disease. She either has it. Or she doesn't. There is a 100 percent chance that she will develop Huntington's disease. Or zero percent.

"Which tie do you think I should wear?" Alistair asked me before he left. "The blue one, or the brown?"

"The blue," I said. I kissed him on the cheek and wished him luck, although he doesn't need it. He doesn't even get nervous. He enjoys it, not because he's on television, he's not vain in that way, but because he likes to prove his point. Alistair loves to win an argument.

I watched as the interviewer asked him a question. He threw himself into the answer.

"Huntington's is the extreme example of how your genes can appear to be your fate. But most single genes do not have a single effect; they work in combination." The camera panned to the interviewer and back to him. "And very often, it takes something in the environment to trigger their effect."

The panel nodded thoughtfully. Nobody looked like they were going to interrupt him, so he carried right on.

"However, there is no doubt that personality, or at least what psychologists call personality, is largely genetically determined."

That's one of my favorite of Alistair's phrases, and I have many. "What psychologists call personality" as opposed to what the rest of us call personality. I like that distinction. There's an acronym for it too: OCEAN. The key psychological ingredients of what makes you who you are are these: Openness to experience, Conscientiousness, Extroversion-Introversion, Antagonism-Agreeableness, and Neuroticism. I've never really thought about it like that before, but it makes me wonder what degree of which I've inherited from whom. How conscientious am I?

How neurotic? How open to experience? I always thought personality was about character, the individual quirks and nuances that make you who are. I hadn't realized it could be tabulated.

The discussion programs tend to become heated at this stage. You could tabulate that too. Or describe it as an arc, anyway, a parabola. It goes like this. Alistair says: "But there is no doubt that personality, or at least what psychologists call personality, is largely genetically determined." And then the person sitting next to him starts expostulating. They become outraged, or at least outraged in the television sense, which means their voice increases in volume and they start to talk more quickly and use academic jargon. They tend to end up saying something along the lines of "But what about free will?" They're usually men. But not always.

I like watching though. You don't usually get the chance to examine your partner in this way, five inches high in the corner of the lounge. It's a strangely dislocating experience. I wonder what I'd think of him if I didn't know him, if I wasn't married to him. I am married to him though. We are married to each other. We chose to do that.

Last night, it was a man with a beard. The opposite expert who was sitting to Alistair's left. He was a sociology professor, I think, and expostulated on cue when Alistair said, "genetically determined."

"What about free will?" he said, bellowed really.

But Alistair believes in free will. Your genes don't control you, he says, they created you.

"The imperative of your genes is to go out and propagate, to guarantee their immortality in the next generation. But we are rational, reasoning human beings, with enormous brains capable of complex thought. If your genes controlled you, you would go out and try to have sex with as many women as you could. You would father a thousand children. But we have free will. We commit ourselves to one partner. We have contraception. We are the vehicles of our genes, but we are not impelled to drive them forth into the next generation. And if your genes don't like it, well, that's just tough luck."

The camera panned to the audience and then back to Alistair. The blue tie had been the right choice.

"I am married. And I don't have children. That is my decision. Not my genes'. It is my free will."

The sociology professor was a bit of a walkover, but Alison gave him a run for his money. She called him "the selfish geneticist," which made me laugh. Under the circumstances, she was remarkably cheerful. If it was me, I think I would have given up with the lipstick and the female politician hair and devoted the rest of my life to eating ice cream and lying on the sofa.

There is a test for the Huntington gene but no cure. She could find out if she was going to develop dementia and die a slow, painful, undignified death. Or not. She'd decided against it. What would I do? I wondered. Would I want to know? Or not know?

When the program finished, I turned off the television and made a cup of tea. But I kept on thinking about Alison. Would I want to know? Or not know?

There's a reason, I guess, why this stuck in my mind. You see, I think Alistair may be having an affair.

Although, of course, I've phrased that wrong. Either he is having an affair. Or he's not.

Part Nine

seek *v* : to try to acquire or gain; to strive after; to aim at

9.1 memory *n* **3** : all that a person can remember

I WENT TO SEE Alicia again at the weekend. Herbert said my presence seemed to calm her, so I went and sat in her kitchen and drank cups of tea while she told me about the past. When Herbert went off to his shed, she sat down and patted the table.

"You'll write it down for me, won't you? You will, won't you? You won't let them steal my memories from me?"

"They're not trying to steal your memories. They're trying to make you better."

But I've bought a notepad and I sit there and write up what she says. The chronology's a mess, but it seems to make her happy. She's given me her diaries too, which mostly tally.

"You won't let me forget him, will you?" Her voice was anxious. "You'll tell me, won't you? If I start forgetting him?"

"I'll tell you."

"There's more, you know . . ."

My pen was poised above the page. "Just tell me in order, then it will all be here. Safe."

"You're a good girl."

I smiled at her. "I'm a woman now."

And she smiled back at me. "I know."

"He had the most perfect skin. I've never understood what people had against that skin."

She shows me photos too. My past is contained within muddy-colored photographs trapped inside a vinyl album. But Alicia's is held within small, square, black-and-white prints. It's peopled by strangers in jackets and ties. It's only when she begins to talk to me that I realize if I was dressed in a knee-length skirt and neat blouse, I'd look a bit like her. That people then weren't so different. That it wasn't as long ago as all that.

9.2   sister *n* 2 : woman who is a close friend or companion

ALICIA'S YOUNGER SISTER, Betty, was the first to realize that something was up. Mrs. Cragley ignored the fact that Alicia was acting oddly (staring out of the window when she was supposed to be washing up; sighing at the sight of the flowering cherry tree in the back garden). It was probably as well that as she stood next to her eldest daughter, a tea towel in hand, she was unaware that she was thinking about the smell of a black man's hair. For Mrs. Cragley had a nervous disposition and did not bear shocks well (her wedding night being a case in point). She tried not to notice that Alicia forgot to rinse the cups and put the sugar in the saucepan cupboard.

Betty noticed. She was younger, smaller, skinnier, *less*, than Alicia. She was a teenager at a time teenagers had yet to be invented. Her body, which would fill and plump, was still at the gangly, unformed stage. Her teeth were too big for her mouth, like a puppy that has yet to grow into its paws. She wore her hair in pigtails that from a certain angle in a certain light you could mistake for a pair of horns.

There was a tightness to the air inside the house. The smallest events (a lit match, an over-heavy sigh) acquired weight and significance. Mr. Cragley ate his breakfast in the mornings and his dinner in the evenings without noticing that his wife and both his daughters were circling one another, silken-shorted boxers before the first punch is thrown. He spread yellow margarine onto his toast, taking scrupulous care to ensure that it was evenly distributed, and ate it without realizing that Alicia sat next to him listening for sounds from the street, waiting for a knock at the door. Nor did he notice that Betty too was waiting; waiting for her moment to come. Or that his wife now gave an additional wring to her hands, a new double twist of her wrists; or that there was an extra top note of anxiety and worry to her personality that had created new riffs: a churning stomach and a dark pressing force at the back of her eyes that would momentarily stall her as she cut slices from the loaf.

None of this he noticed. He ate his slice of toast, drank the first of his four daily cups of tea and read his paper. For two weeks, he sat at the table while his wife and two daughters performed their silent masque. He didn't even notice in the third week that Alicia's movements had slowed, her hair had become duller, her face less animated, that his wife had started to fumble the dishes a little less noisily, and Betty had resumed her interest in her comic books. He drank his tea and opened his post.

"Better have a look at that." He handed Alicia the letter. "Witness statement from the police. You need to sign it and return."

Alicia glanced at the piece of paper. "On February 28, 1948, an automobile driven by Councillor Anderson of 7 Alverthorpe Road was seen rounding the corner of said street by one Cecil Albert Johnston, currently residing at 5 Denmark Street."

She read it not realizing that three weeks' worth of dense, stale air was being released through her mouth. Her lungs collapsed, the sacs shriveling, the tubes emptied. Eleanor Cragley, hearing the change in rhythm of her eldest daughter's breath, started. She looked at Alicia's face and dropped the teacup she was holding; its thin porcelain handle smashed on the corner of the unit and broke into three pieces. Betty, looking from her mother to her sister, was aware that something had passed, but she couldn't say what. Cyril Cragley took a bite of his toast and grimaced. The margarine was off.

My grandmother waited for her love affair to start, but now the waiting had changed in texture. It was finite. It could be savored and enjoyed. She treated it like expensive face cream, enjoying the sensation of it against her skin, careful not to squander it.

At work, in Socks, Mrs. Jones found she had to reprimand Alicia on an almost daily basis. She caught her daydreaming at the till, or mixing up the sizes, or shortchanging a customer by sixpence. She'd had to give her a dressing-down there on the shop floor, and as Alicia turned away, Mrs. Jones had caught the after-impression of a certain type of smile. Sex, she told Peggy Simon from Menswear later as they shared a pot of tea in the corner café, you can always see when they've caught it.

Cecil knew none of this. He had a new job at E. Oldroyd & Son's. "Gardener Wanted," the advertisement said and he'd liked the idea of being outside. He hadn't known of the legendary Wakefield rhubarb triangle until he turned up at the farm. He had no idea that between Leeds in the north, Bradford in the west and Wakefield in the south lay a patch of land, rich in clay and nipped with frost, that competed with China, Tibet and Banbury for the glory of rhubarb raising.

Joseph Brunton, the foreman and head gardener, glanced briefly at his references.

"Show me your hands." Cecil hesitated then held them out, palms down. Brunton, a short, stooped man in his sixties whose back had been ruined by almost forty years of bending, and whose milky eyes were set in a permanent squint, touched the tips of his fingers. He turned them over and studied his palms.

"Hmph," he said.

"Now shake my hand." And he held out his arm as if about to close a business deal or greet an acquaintance. Cecil hesitated.

"I said shake it, boy."

Cecil shook it.

"You'll do," said Brunton. "Start Monday, 8 A.M. sharp."

There was no reply.

"You've got the job," he said, since Cecil had shown no signs of understanding. "It's all in the touch. Don't care a fig for qualifications or whathaveyou. They're tender little darlings and they bruise. I won't have any horny-handed oaf working here. You'll do."

It was only then that Cecil discovered the job was inside. In the dark, warm, humid spaces of the rhubarb-forcing sheds. There were no windows, and candles provided the only light. Inside it was dark and still; a world apart; a strange twilight place with row upon row of huge, milky, translucent leaves that rustled as you passed. Beneath them, hidden from view, were long etiolated shafts; not white, but pink; a pink so vivid, so *pure*, that the first time Cecil saw the color, he thought it must be a trick. A sleight of hand. In April, in Yorkshire, in 1948, this pink was preposterous.

Nor was this farming, as Cecil knew it. In Jamaica, a discarded avocado pit thrown into the gutter would sprout shoots and roots and grow into a tree. He came from a land so fertile that the skill lay not in rearing and nurturing, but in pruning and containing. This was something different; a form of gardening that seemed to owe more to the kabbala than to the ripe, untrammeled workings of nature.

"Been growing it here for years," Brunton told him. "Not much after the seeds came to Britain in 1777. Did you know that? Happen not. Most folk don't. Most folk think rhubarb is something common. Like gooseberries. Or raspberries. But that's because they don't know the history, see. Cost three times as much as opium, you know, once upon a time."

Joseph Brunton could talk about rhubarb all day long. He lived rhubarb, had worked with it for the thirty-six years of his working life. He knew how for hundreds of years it had thwarted the attempts of botanists, explorers, traders, gardeners, physicians and pharmacists to discover its inner secrets. How it was used as a cure for constipation, impotence and a broken heart. And he was pleased with the new fellow. Not everyone had the touch.

Cecil found the job suited him. He liked working in the dark. He moved easily between the pools of candlelight, slipping in and out of the dark as if it was water, his face illuminated only by a dull shine. It was the only place in Wakefield where he felt he belonged. In the artificial night of the sheds, he was the same as other men.

He worked steadily, moving along the row, pruning each plant, removing dead leaves, checking them for signs of disease. They grew an inch a day, Brunton said, although never when you looked. You could hear them though, a *creak-creak-creak* like the timbers on a ship.

"So, Cecil, do they have rhubarb where you're from then?"

Cecil bent over the plants, considering his reply. He didn't notice that there was somebody who was listening to this conversation. Someone who saw his face dip in and out of the candlelight, who watched the way he touched the leaves, and noticed how his fingertips caressed the stalks. Someone who had followed him from his boardinghouse at 5 Denmark Street and who stood there now, waiting, knowing that the time had almost come.

All day, Alicia had been waiting for the moment when she'd leave the shop, shrug off her uniform and make her way toward the bus stop. Everything had taken longer. A query about men's sports socks. A complaint about a pair of woollen stockings. Wrapping an awkward-shaped package.

She changed in the ladies', doing her makeup quickly and efficiently, her hands trembling only slightly as she applied the mascara brush to her lashes. She hurried down Westgate, tapping her feet impatiently for the bus, looking at the dark cloud formations looming overhead, wondering if it would rain. Standing at the bus stop, she swiveled on her heel, arched her eyebrows, looked at her fingernails.

The bus heaved and groaned, its gears straining under its weight, the climb up the hills teeth-clenchingly slow. In the mirror of her compact, she checked her face. There was a light shine of perspiration across her forehead and the skin above her lip. Her eyes were darker than usual. There was an excitement, a glitter, that made her own reflection seem strangely unfamiliar.

The bus stopped. She was the only person to get off, and she watched its retreating back, the sound of its engine slowly fading away. The wind was stronger out of town. Gusts whipped her skirt as she walked; cold penetrated her coat. The sky overhead was dark, but in the west, the hills were still lit. Where they crested the horizon, there was a thin gap in the clouds through which shone shafts of red and orange and gold light as if, somewhere in the distance, the hills were burning.

She knew the way; she'd been before. Just to watch him. She slipped easily past the watchmen into the yard. There were men carrying boxes and pallets and sacks of manure, but they didn't see her. She sidestepped them, treading carefully in her heels over the clods of mud and earth. When she reached the door of the shed, she took a deep breath and walked inside.

The door closed behind her, leaving her submerged in darkness. The air was warm and still. Slowly, her eyes adjusted and she saw first the candles and then the floor, an undulating sea of gently rustling leaves, and then noticed the fresh clean smell like a sack of new potatoes.

"So, Cecil, do they have rhubarb where you're from then?"

The voice came from the corner. Alicia squinted. Slowly, she made out a bending form. Next to it was a patch of darkness that was darker than the rest of the shed; more intense. And then it spoke.

"Dere ain't no rhu-barb, Mis-ter Bruhn-ton."

There was a rhythm, a cadence to his speech. She breathed more heavily. Conscious that he was in the same space, breathing the same air, somewhere out there in the darkness. She felt her shoulders lifting and her rib cage expanding to enable her to take down more oxygen. Her back arched. Her pelvis tilted upward. Mrs. Jones, who had been watching Alicia through narrowed eyes all day long, had seen that movement too. Like a cat in heat, she told Peggy Simon from Menswear.

Cecil was wiping his hands against his overalls and thinking about the journey home when he saw the pale gleam by the door.

He stopped. There were a few strands of what looked like hair, a shape that could have been a face, the faintest waft of semolina. He squinted his eyes and stared. Joseph Brunton had gone off to the office, and apart from him, the shed was empty. He closed his mouth and took a long deep breath of air through his nose.

"Al-eesha?" he said eventually. Although it was more of a statement than a question. He knew it was her.

She could see only the whites of his eyes, the swell of his lips, a faint burnish on his forehead. He walked forward, dipping in and out of the candlelight, illuminated, then not illuminated. She saw the paleness of his palms, his teeth, but the rest of him was blurred, fuzzy; his body was semi-merged with the darkness of the shed, part of it.

Alicia took a step forward. Outside, far away, a dog barked. A car climbed the hill, its engine straining. She reached out and touched his hand. It juddered, the skin shocked.

She closed her hand around his, and felt its rough smoothness, its dry warmth. For a fraction of a second, she saw his face illuminated as he moved through a pool of candlelight. His eyes were wide open, his lips parted. In the yard outside, men were calling out good night to one another.

They were so close now, she could feel his breath. It was sweet and rich and fell in hot waves on her cheeks. She held his hand tighter and felt the darkness press around them. They were enveloped by it. A candle hissed.

Alicia, who had practiced this moment, and rehearsed how her lips would part, and her face upturn, forgot it all.

"Kiss me," she demanded.

And Cecil, lost in a sea of gently creaking rhubarb, leaned down and kissed her. Alicia, feeling the soft, wet muscle of his tongue, shivered as he entered her mouth.

She reached out, and with her right hand, she touched his right hand. It was warm and smooth. She stroked it lightly, her lips feeling his lips, his tongue, his breath. It was the underside of his lips that made her breathing increase, become lower, deeper. The fleshiness of them, the plump softness of them. With her tongue, she explored the ridge of his teeth and felt a tiny chip on the front incisor. Her tongue caught and worried it as if it was her own.

The air was cold on her cheeks, her nose; her ears had started to turn pink, but underneath her coat, her lambswool cardigan, she was perspiring. She reached out and put her hand inside his jacket, and encircled his waist, feeling the muscles of his back beneath the cotton of his shirt. With his hand, he reached up and stroked her hair. A gust of air extinguished the candle next to them, sending them deeper into darkness. Alicia's right hand traced a line from his back to his stomach, and in the slit of his shirt, between two buttons, she slowly, carefully, worked her fingers inside, feeling the soft flesh of his underbelly, the wiry hairs of his abdomen. He swallowed hard.

"Al-eesha?"

But Alicia could hear nothing but the roar of the rhubarb stalks growing. Her lips rubbed his. Her hand, insistent now, unstoppable, was working its way lower. The skin was warmer, hairier, the waistband of his trousers pressed against him, but she created a gap, burrowing into his flesh. Her fingers probed. They were searching for something.

Cecil quivered, the whites of his eyes increased and expanded. Alicia moved closer. The beating of the blood against the skin of her thighs grew more persistent.

The leaves creaked but the sound of her pulse echoing inside her inner ear quickened, grew louder, and overpowered them.

"Al-eesha!" said Cecil, but it was too late. She knew it was there.

Part Ten

hypothesis *n* : proposition made as basis for reasoning

10.1 Occam's Razor

THE PROPOSITION, in science, that simple explanations are more probable than complex ones unless given reason to suspect otherwise.

<u>Question</u>

Alistair has gone off sex. Is this because . . .

    a. He has gone off me?
    b. He is having sex with somebody else?
    c. Of another reason entirely unconnected to either of the above, e.g., tiredness, overwork?

10.2   **sign** *n* **3** : an indicator, such as a dropping or footprint, of the trail of an animal

WE'D BEEN ARGUING about it for weeks. I thought that Cliff Barnes had done it. And Tiffany insisted it was Marilee Stone. We'd argued it back and forth just as we argued over who was the prettiest: Victoria Principal or Charlene Tilton (Victoria had the big bosom and the heart-shaped face, but Charlene had the waist-length blond hair that we all coveted. Even if she was a midget.) Roderick Huxley, next door, had a T-shirt that claimed "I shot JR" and my mother said that frankly she wouldn't have put it past him.

But it was definitely Cliff. It was always Cliff. He always thought he'd got the better of JR, but JR always pulled the carpet from under his feet. It was as predictable as anything in our lives: Sugar Puffs for breakfast, meat loaf on Tuesdays, our mother losing her temper when you mentioned Aunty Suzanne. We'd all watched the episode where he was shot. Even our father had watched it. *Even* Aunty Suzanne had watched it. And she never watched television, and kept on asking Lucy questions like "Who's Bobby?" and "Why does that woman have such big hair?" She reckoned it was Sue Ellen. "Emotionally battered wife," she sniffed. "Don't blame her either."

It was a period of strange and unnatural calm in Beech Drive. I couldn't quite understand why being pregnant should make my mother so happy (it certainly wasn't thrilling me to my very core), but there was no doubt that it did.

My mother, pregnant, was somehow more than my mother with bump. She was serene, almost stately, like the *QEII* sailing into Southampton. We knew all about the *QEII* on account of the fact that the Huxleys had photos of it from their honeymoon; a fact my mother had never let my father forget. He took her to the Peak District, only back then it was called Derbyshire.

She had changed. She began to eat with the nonchalance of a grazing heifer. She placed thick, heavy English puddings before us, and smiled between spoonfuls. We began to look forward to mealtimes. The angst that was as traditional an accompaniment as salt and pepper and Heinz tomato ketchup had gone. As had her morning weigh-in. Now when we lay in bed waiting to be summoned, we couldn't hear the creak of the dial swinging to and fro searching for the 8 stone, 2 lb. mark. Instead, she appeared dressed and made-up and ready to launch us into the day.

"TiffanyRebeccaJamesit'stimetowakeuuuuuuuuuuup." The "uuuuuuuuup" bounced off the landing walls and the bathroom mirror and my eardrums as if they were mountaintops and she was reenacting the yodelling scene from *The Sound of Music*.

The Special K sat in the back of the cupboard, ignored. The new cupboard. It was called a "carousel" and swung out of the corner. We didn't go on holiday at all that year. We made the ultimate sacrifice. With the money saved from the holiday-in-Majorca-that-never-was, my mother was finally able to afford her heart's desire: a brand-new fitted kitchen.

She gathered catalogues and magazines, took notes of other people's cabinets and fridges, and spent weeks umming and ah-ing over the merits and demerits of an electric fan oven over a combination gas-electric twin cooker. The choice of sink delayed her for a week. The floor tiles a fortnight. In the end though she went for American cherrywood with a granite-effect Formica work surface, and when the money had been handed over, and the final decision had been made (a double sink drainer in cream enamel versus a single in stainless steel), it all happened surprisingly fast.

Tiffany and I ate our cornflakes surrounded by the old white units, but when we came home from school, they'd gone. Our mother was in a state of high excitement.

"Tra-la!" she said as if she was a hostess on *The Sale of the Century*.* I was very impressed. She opened cupboards and made sweeping gestures along the counter in exactly the right way. All she needed was a swimsuit and a glittery pair of heels.

"What do you think?"

"It's amazing!" said Tiffany.

"Look! It's an integral fridge-freezer! I can't tell you how long I've wanted one of those. It's frost-free too! No more squatting on my knees with a hair dryer."

Tiffany stroked it lingeringly.

"Cooker hood with concealed lighting and extractor fan with three different speed settings!" our mother said, giving us a mini-

---

* *The Sale of the Century*

"Running for twelve years, *The Sale of the Century* remains the highest-rating game show in British television history—when the BBC went on strike in 1978, 21 million turned over to watch the ITV show. A fast-moving general knowledge quiz with the allure of big prizes, it was hosted by Nicholas Parsons, who was assisted by a number of 'hostesses,' all of whom were dressed in revealing outfits and forbidden from speaking.

"Like its American-inspired predecessor, *The Price Is Right*, *The Sale of the Century* used these women to sexualize the rather banal selection of consumer durables on offer. Prizes were (male) sexual rewards exchanged for 'knowledge', available only to 'winners'; female sexuality was a commodity to be traded by men. Parsons repeatedly informed the audience that these were 'glamorous' women lucky enough to have a 'glamorous' job."

demonstration of its main features. "And look!" She opened the kitchen door to the back porch, where we kept our shoes and coats. The old kitchen sink had been installed next to the door. "It's a Utility Room."

I was confused. "Where?"

"Here."

"The back porch?"

"No, Rebecca. Like I've just told you, it's now the *Utility Room*."

She was so happy she cooked a three-course meal that began with melon and ended with Delia Smith's crème caramel. In between was something that could have been pork or could have been lamb. She hadn't quite got the hang of the new fan oven yet.

"That was delicious!" said our father.

"I'll do the washing up!" said Tiffany.

"I'll help!" I said.

"Well, well," said our father. "Never thought I'd see the day."

We cleared the table quickly, keen to try our hand at the exciting new dishwashing technology. We swung down the door and started to place the plates on the rack, but she was already bearing down upon us.

"No! No! No! They've got to be rinsed first."

We both looked up, confused.

"You've got to rinse them before you put them in, otherwise you'll ruin the machine."

"But it's a *dish*-washer, Mum. It washes dishes."

Our mother shot us a look. "In the sink first, please."

Reluctantly, we took the plates out and put them on the draining board.

"NOT THAT SINK! THE ONE IN THE UTILITY ROOM!"

"Why can't we use the new sink?"

"Because it'll get ruined. That's why!" She looked at us and sadly shook her head. Her hair-sprayed curls quivered slightly. "You've got no idea, have you? No idea at all."

There was no getting around it: she was getting fat. Not just her stomach, with its tightly stretched skin and distended belly button, but other bits of her too. Her cheeks had filled out, hamsterlike (was she storing cakes in there, we wondered, for lean months ahead?); her bottom had gained shape and substance; her arms wobbled.

These were the days of chocolate pinwheels and Victoria sponges filled with proper cream. Lucy and I temporarily abandoned *The Joy of Sex* at her house for *The Joy of Home Baking* at mine. Sugary smells wafted through the house at all times of the day and night. We were even allowed to scrape the mixing bowl, the kind of treat that was unheard of in pre-pregnant times.

"Was it like this when I was born?" I asked Tiffany in her role as family archivist. But Tiffany seemed to have blanked that particular episode of her life (holding me by the ankles over the landing appeared to have played havoc with her space-time continuum). She was pleased that Lucy had taken to playing at our house, however. It gave her an opportunity to hone her interrogation skills. Tiffany was possibly the only child in Middleton who watched films about Nazi POW camps in order to pick up interviewing tips. In fact she had many ways of extracting information (a training that would come into its own when she acquired a job in future years as an interviewer for a celebrity magazine). With me she tended to favor the Chinese burn, but with Lucy she took the softly-softly approach. "So, Barry Manilow, you've had an interesting life, perhaps you could tell me about it?" was only five steps down the line from "So, Lucy? Your mummy and daddy seem a very happy couple, how did they meet?"

"Suzanne was a nurse, and Kenneth was a doctor."

"Really?"

"Yes. Although they knew each other already of course. Because they went to school down the road from one another. And he used to ride the bus past her and wolf-whistle."

"And then they fell in love?"

"Yes. And they went off to India in a campervan."

"How romantic!"

"Yes, although Suzanne says that if she knew then what she knows now, she'd have realized she was the victim of a stereotypical female fantasy of the dominant male."

Tiffany and I looked at Lucy. We were both impressed by "stereotypical" (although I, for one, had no idea what it meant).

"And what brand of washing powder does your mum use?"

"Tide. I think."

"A-ha! I knew it!" Tiffany had a firm belief that by your brand names are you judged. Our mother used Bold, which she'd long suspected was wrong.

"Hmph," Lucy said and walked out of the room. After a moment's hesitation we took out our dolls. I had Princess Barbie (you could tell she was a princess because she had long hair all the way down her back), while Lucy had Secretary Barbie and Horse-Riding Instructor Barbie. Aunty Suzanne kept trying to encourage Lucy into Sindy dolls (Sindy wore sensible flat shoes and had an almost nonexistent bust) or Meccano, but we wouldn't have it.

"It's ludicrous!" claimed Aunty Suzanne. "No woman on earth looks like that! It's American consumerism gone mad!" We ignored her. Our Barbies had a fine selection of strappy high heels, tiny waists and enormous Dolly Partonesque bosoms that didn't wobble like Aunty Suzanne's or require a Playtex twenty-four-hour girdle like my mother's, but jutted proudly out.

First, we played Barbie is a secretary and goes to the office and types lots of letters, although Horse-Riding Instructor Barbie had to stand in for the boss, which wasn't wholly convincing: she was wearing jodhpurs but she still didn't look much like a man. Then we played Princess Barbie marries Prince Charles (Horse-Riding Instructor Barbie was better suited to this role). And then we became bored of this and decided to play Barbies go to a nudist camp. The Barbie dolls walked around with no clothes on and played a lot of netball, for which we imaginatively substituted a Ping-Pong ball.

It was Lucy who struck on the idea of the Barbies undertaking an experimental bout of Cuissade and Coitus à la Florentine. Princess Barbie, obviously, landed the girl role on account of her hair. Horse-Riding Instructor Barbie, once again, had to play the man, although her riding crop finally proved a useful accessory.

"No!" said Lucy. "He's supposed to take her from behind! It's to heighten her pleasure!"

My mother's head appeared at the door. "Girls?"

We looked up guiltily.

"Are you playing dolls? How nice. Christine has come to play."

"Oh."

"She's right here. Go on through, Christine. They're playing dolls."

Christine Huxley from next door walked into my bedroom, and I experienced the same feeling I had when Tiffany undertook one of her periodic spot checks of my possessions (to ensure that I didn't have more than her). Christine was small and what my mother called "petite," and we called weedy. We didn't like Christine. She was a bad loser. Her voice became instantly whiny when she didn't get her own way, and her eyes narrowed when she was being mean. Just like her mother's. We were reluctantly bound together for all eternity due to the fact that we lived next door to one another and were the same age. We eyed each other suspiciously.

"What are you playing?" said Christine.

"Dolls."

"Shall I fetch my Tiny Tears?"

Lucy and I looked at each other and rolled our eyes. Christine was very proud of her Tiny Tears and called it Maxine. When you fed it water from a bottle, it wet its pants. Christine seemed to think that this was a great plus. Without discussing it, Lucy and I concluded that Christine was not to be party to our game of strip Barbie and threw the dolls into the corner. To make matters worse, Tiffany reappeared. She would always deign to join us if we were playing any game she knew she had a statistically higher chance of winning. We took out Operation, a favorite of all of ours on account of the fact that it was battery operated and made a buzzing noise if you failed to extract the patient's funny bone or bread basket with one clean stroke of the surgical tweezers. It raised certain biological questions however. We all wondered what bodily function the "bread basket" performed.

Tiffany, who liked to pull rank, particularly if there was no possibility of being proved wrong, said it was the stomach.

"It's where bread goes, dumbo."

"No it's not," said Christine. "It's the bit that they cut babies out of."

"They don't cut babies out," said Lucy. "They come out of your bum. It's like doing a number two." This was news to me. I wondered if I'd find my new baby brother or sister floating at the bottom of the toilet bowl, like one of Grandpa Monroe's famously unsinkable turds. I made a mental note to check before flushing.

"No, they don't."

"Yes, they do."

"No, they don't. They have to go hospital and have them cut out by a doctor," said Christine, her fingers grasping the electric tweezers and making for the Adam's apple. "Although my mummy says your mummy won't need a doctor to cut the baby out, because she already had a doctor put the baby in."

Bzzzz! She'd failed to hook the Adam's apple. The trouble with Christine was that she wasn't only mean but stupid. The previous week she had copied all her sums off me in class, and when she was caught (I had perhaps jerked my exercise book away a touch over-flamboyantly), she'd burst into tears. For weeks she had insisted that the earth was flat. "Well why don't ships sail off the edge then?" she'd wailed. Sometimes being with Christine was like hanging around with Dark Age man waiting for the Renaissance to arrive.

Lucy and I raised our eyebrows at each other and mouthed "Thickie." Maybe if we played hangman instead, she'd go away. Christine's ability to spell was only marginally better than her ability to lose a game without throwing a tantrum. Hangman was a particularly potent combination. ("You don't spell cow with a k!" "*You do, you kow!*")

Tiffany looked at Christine in silence and then left the room. Christine, however, was determined to stay. We couldn't tell her to go home; we'd get told off. Our only hope was that she would get bored and flounce off on her own accord (not a wholly unlikely scenario). In the end we went downstairs, where she tried ingratiating herself with my mother in a way that trumped even Tiffany's best efforts.

"Oh, Mrs. Monroe, you look lovely! Have you thought of any names yet for Baby?"

My mother had spent hours poring over *The Bumper Book of Baby Names* and had been thinking of little else, flicking between the "Traditional" and the "Modern" sections with occasional forays into the "Creative" chapter. At that moment she was moving toward Charles for a boy, on the grounds that it was good enough for the Queen, although she also liked Damien, Bradley and Warren.

"A few," she said, for although she was susceptible to a compliment, she hadn't moved into Beech Drive yesterday. She'd had enough dealings with Mrs. Huxley over the years to be wary of Christine.

"Would you like a little boy or a little girl, Mrs. Monroe?"

"Well, I have to say that I would like a boy. Every mother wants at least one boy. It's just one of those things. And they're easier than girls, so they say."

"Mrs. Monroe?"

"Yes?"

Our mother was undertaking her weekly cleansing of the inside of the kitchen cupboards, and had laid her jars of spices and herbs and baking powder and glacé cherries on the work surface. Christine seemed uncertain about something.

"Mrs. Monroe?"

"Yes, Christine? What is it?"

"Who put the baby there?"

There was the tiniest pause.

"Goodness, Christine. Nobody put the baby there. He's growing inside me."

"Or she."

"Yes. Or she." It was a deft interception, even by my mother's standards. For a minute I thought she was going to launch into the Daddy-places-a-little-seed thing all over again, when we all knew that he actually had to wee into you.

10.3 The Necker Cube

IT WAS A FEW YEARS after we married when Alistair told me how certainty is created. How can you be so sure? I said. Although I don't think he got the joke. He didn't laugh anyway; he just carried straight on explaining. We were on holiday in Edinburgh at the time, sitting in a café, and I was absentmindedly playing with the sugar lumps in the bowl when he doodled something on a napkin.

"It's called the Necker Cube."

I looked at it.

"What do you see?"

"A cube."

"Okay, now stare at it."

I stared.

"What do you see now?"

"Another cube."

"Exactly!"

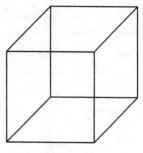

Figure 11.
The Necker Cube

I waited for the explanation. It would come, when he was ready. It always came.

"It's because it's a fundamental tendency of the human mind to create certainty. The Necker Cube has ambiguous depth. There is nothing to show which face is the front and which is the back."

I nodded and wondered where we should go for dinner.

"However, when you look at it, you don't see ambiguity. You see it one way, or the other. When you stare at it, after a couple of seconds, the image will switch. That is, you see the other cube instead, but again unambiguously."

He was getting into his stride, wearing the slightly worried look he has when he's thinking, and had started scribbling over napkins. There were paper napkins strewn across the table. I ordered another coffee and stared out of the window, wondering if we still had time to get to the castle before it shut. I daydreamed while Alistair scrawled.

"Different people resolve this ambiguity in different ways. And individuals resolve it differently at different times. What you think of something, *someone*, at one time, is not constant."

He had stopped doodling and was staring at me. He was fiddling with his wedding ring, twisting it round and round his finger, worrying it. He got up suddenly from his chair and motioned for the bill.

"Time to go," he said. And I stood up too, unsure of what had passed.

If I'm honest, it was only later that I resolved the scene in this particular way. At the time, I remember looking at him and wondering if he'd put the serviettes in his pocket. Or if he had an erection.

10.4   **pregnant** *adj* : having a hidden meaning, significant, suggestive

MY MOTHER had become so fat she could no longer walk. She waddled. But it wasn't just that her body looked like it had been inflated by a bicycle pump; her brain had gone missing again. Although it was different from the last time. She seemed, well, *happy.* She was obsessed with her bump. She spent all day stroking it and talking to it, or else she'd just lie on the sofa watching television. There were no taboos. I spilled crumbs at breakfast time and it wasn't even mentioned. Tiffany scuffed her new school shoes and it was dismissed as "an accident." What had happened to *"There's no such thing as an accident, just a child who doesn't watch what they're doing!"*? Bye-bye *"I want doesn't mean I get!"* In today's Beech Drive, if I wanted (a biscuit, another helping, a trip to the park), I generally did get. Au revoir *"You'll feel the back of my hand if you're not careful."* For there was no need to employ the threat of physical violence in this halcyon age. The family stock of proverbs was depleting, old friends who'd just vanished overnight. If Tiffany didn't watch it, they'd all have disappeared by the time she finally swung her *Family Affairs* column and she would have nothing left to put in it (a false alarm).

Although there was one fly in the ointment. Our mother was planning to send us back to the den of the child-eating wardrobe. Granny Monroe had volunteered to take us in for the duration of her hospital stay. I caught a mystical whiff of Lily of the Valley talcum powder and felt instantly depressed. I wasn't optimistic about my chances in a rematch with the furniture. In the end, we were saved by providence. Or at least Aunty Suzanne, who telephoned our mother and insisted that we should go and stay with them.

"Well I don't know," she said. "I'd *hate* to put you to any bother . . ."

In the end though the enormous psychic force of Tiffany's displeasure forced her to back down. My father dropped us off at the bottom of the driveway and looked wistful as we clambered down from the car and grabbed our suitcases. "See you next week!" we cried and bounded off toward the house. Tiffany was overjoyed: the guest room boasted a vase of freshly cut dahlias.

Staying with another family but not being of that family was certainly an eye-opener. All sorts of things were different. Aspects of our domestic routine that we'd thought of as universal, as immovable as Everest, that we'd never suspected might be different elsewhere, turned out to be local peculiarities. At the Old Parsonage, for example, there were two bathrooms, a seemingly bottomless hot water tank and no accusatory looks when the water ran out (because it didn't). You didn't have orange juice with your dinner (which was called supper) but water (which tasted terrible, there was nothing in it). Cups did not have to be washed, dried and put away in a cupboard immediately after use; they hung around on the side for ages before finally being loaded into the dish-washing machine. Rice was brown and tasted like cardboard. If you dropped a piece of bread on the floor, Aunty Suzanne picked it up and put it back on the table. "You'll eat more than a speck of dirt before you die," she said. And when I spilled orange juice over the cream-colored carpet, she fetched a cloth and said "No use crying over spilled milk." She appeared to have inherited an entirely different set of family sayings than my mother, who said that a tidy home showed a tidy mind and that cleanliness was next to godliness.

("But we don't go to church!"

"I've had quite enough of you for one day, madam.")

There was more: bedtime was later, and pretty loosely enforced. Our clothes smelled of Tide washing powder. Aunty Suzanne had a habit of walking out of the bathroom without any clothes on. There was a mid-morning snack and a hot drink before bed. There were seconds of anything you wanted, including pudding, although they were shop-bought, and not as good as our mother's. We went to visit Nanna twice. (My mother would only go if there was news of a special nature to pass on, such as the time we got a new car or Tiffany won the regional heat of the Brain of Britain Junior Competition.) There were so many small but astonishing differences between the households. When Uncle Kenneth came downstairs with a button missing off his shirt, Aunty Suzanne said: "Well you know where the sewing box is." And on the evening that he was late home from work, she scraped his lentil casserole into the bin.

"I don't suppose your father forgets to call, does he, when he's going to be late home from work?"

"Suzanne?"

We were all in the kitchen and Aunty Suzanne was busying herself at the sink, an expression of sour disapproval on her lips.

"Suzanne?"

"Yes, Tiffany."

"Lucy said that you used to be a nurse." Aunty Suzanne sighed and stopped plunging potato peelings down the waste-disposal unit.

"I did. If I've got any advice for you, it's to never give up your career for the sake of a man. It won't make you happy."

Tiffany considered this.

"Suzanne?"

"Yes, Tiffany?"

"Why don't you wear lipstick?"

I was playing Connect 4 with Lucy but looked up with interest to hear the reply. Our mother would never dream of leaving the house without an application of lipstick. Putting on her face in the morning was as much a part of her routine as breathing.

Suzanne seemed pleased with the question and turned to look at us.

"You see, Tiffany, as women we're trapped in a male-dominated society, and some women feel that they have no choice but to try to conform to men's idea of femininity by, say, wearing lipstick. It's not their fault, of course, they're just lacking awareness."

"But don't you think it makes people look pretty?"

"That's really not the point."

"Oh."

We stood waiting for her to explain.

"The point is why are they trying to make themselves look pretty for the sake of men? That's the point. And it is because women have been conditioned to compete with one another in order to win the approval of men."

A thought seemed to occur to Tiffany, although she looked doubtful. "Suzanne? Are you a Women's Libber?"

Aunty Suzanne paused, looked Tiffany meaningfully in the eye and said, "Yes, Tiffany, I am. Although feminism is the modern word for it."

Neither of us knew what to say. Our mother said that Women's Lib was just an excuse not to keep up with your dusting and that any woman who couldn't be bothered to shave her legs shouldn't be surprised when her husband ran off with his secretary.

"Golly."

They sometimes appeared on *The Benny Hill Show*: a bunch of ugly women who burned their bras in the street and looked on disapprovingly as Benny chased a large-breasted woman with long hair around a tree.

"But you're nice!"

Suzanne looked as if she was going to laugh but then changed her mind. "Why can't feminists be nice?"

"Because they're supposed to be ugly."

"Oh dear." Suzanne sighed. "So ugly people can't be nice, then?"

"No . . . ," said Tiffany, although Anthea Randall, officially the Ugliest Girl in the School, was also a bully.

"Or feminists can't be pretty?"

Tiffany looked helplessly confused.

"Being a feminist means that I believe that women are equal to men, that's all. Do you believe that boys are cleverer than girls?"

Tiffany shook her head.

"No. Well then you're a feminist too."

I looked at my sister. She appeared shocked. I couldn't say I was surprised. She'd get a hell of a row if our mother ever found out.

Finally, after months of waiting and wondering, and speculating, and people on television making jokes about it, we were going to find out who shot JR. Lucy and I ran around the house singing the *Dallas* theme song and practicing our Texan accents.

"Why, Miss Ellie, you shuh look mighty fine!"

"Why thank you, Bobby, you're one hell of a bwoy, you know!"

The Edwardses didn't watch television (which Aunty Suzanne called "the box") in the lounge (which Aunty Suzanne called the "drawing room"). They had a "television room," a little room upstairs with an old battered sofa and an odd assortment of furniture and ornaments that had failed to find a home elsewhere in the house. It was my favorite room, the only one that wasn't crammed with valuable-looking antiques and dangerously pale carpet. You could relax in the television room. We carefully prepared for the 8 P.M. kickoff, assembling bowls of crisps and glasses of Coke and the special edition of the *Radio Times*. Tiffany joined us, and at the last minute we persuaded Aunty Suzanne to come too. Uncle Kenneth was still at work.

"It's Cliff," I said.

"Marilee," said Tiffany.

"Sue Ellen," said Aunty Suzanne.

"Vaughn Leland," said Lucy.

"Duh-da-dah, duh-da-duh-da-duh, duh-da-dah, duh-da-dah!" We sang along with the theme tune, breathless with anticipation.

Bring bring! Bring bring! It was the phone. Aunty Suzanne got up to answer it, and the sound of her voice ringing through the hall was distracting us at the crucial moment.

"How marvelous!" we could hear her saying. "Of course I will. Would you like a word with Tiffany or Rebecca?" Our ears pricked up and I prayed I wouldn't be made to go to the phone. They were showing flashbacks to the scene where JR was in his office, and somebody had just come up in the lift and walked through the door.

Bang!

JR keeled over right by his desk. We could see the gunman (gunwoman? gunperson?) lower the weapon.

"Righty ho! Take care!" Aunty Suzanne had replaced the receiver.

JR looked up, gasped, and then said, "Kristen!"

"You've got a new little baby brother!" said Aunty Suzanne, flinging open the door.

We all looked at each other in disbelief. It was Kristen Shepard. Kristen Shepard shot JR! It was a terrible anticlimax. We'd waited months to find out who it was, and then this. There'd been no real lead-up. No significant pointers. There should have been clues. There are always clues.

"It's a boy. Seven pounds, three ounces. What do you think to that?"

Tiffany and I nodded. We weren't sure what we thought of that. It was an awful lot of information to take in at one go. Kristen Shepard shot JR. And we had a boy in the family.

10.5 experience *vt* 2 : meet with, feel, undergo (pleasure, pain, fate, etc.)

ALISTAIR HAS CHANGED his area of research recently.

"Why aren't identical twins identical?" he asked me, but I knew better than to try to answer. His questions have a nasty habit of tripping you up backward.

"I don't know," I said. "Why aren't identical twins identical?"

"I don't know either," said Alistair. "That's the point. No one does."

And his eyes had the excited glitter that they used to have right at the moment before he'd push me down onto the bed and tear off my clothes. For a moment, I thought that was what he was going to do.

"They're clones," he said. "They *should* be identical. It's why they're *not* that's the interesting thing."

And I felt a pang of lust-nostalgia. A ghost-tangle. A black hole where it used to be.

He didn't tear off my clothes. He showed me a computer printout instead. I did my best not to look disappointed. He'd used chaos theory to model the development of a pair of twins.

It showed a pair of wiggling lines that began from a single point and then steadily diverged. He'd made one tiny change to one of the developing embryos, and then ran them both through a set of algorithms, a computerized version of life circumstances. By the time they were adult, half of their characteristics were different.

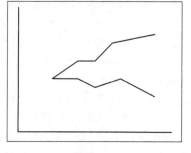

Figure 12.

"Isn't that chance then?" I asked. He hesitated. "Chance is just a word expressing ignorance," he said. "All you are saying is 'determined by some as yet unknown, or unspecified, means.'" Sometimes I think he's kidding himself.

I used to fantasize about being an identical twin, although thinking about it now, I can't understand why. They turned up a lot in fiction, I suppose. The identical twins who could be told apart only by a freckle or an eyebrow. Maybe it was because they could deceive adults, play tricks on them. Or perhaps it was just the idea of having a sibling who was similar to you. Possibly it was because I liked the idea of wearing matching outfits.

When I went to see Alistair yesterday at his department, one of his graduate students showed me the latest tables. Alistair's surrounded by graduate students. They're all young and keen and they all want to work with him. This one was young and keen and female. I'm jealous, I suppose, but then sexual jealousy is a defining characteristic of what it is to be human, Alistair says, so I don't give myself too hard a time about it. She had big tits too. I was looking at the table but kept thinking how fertile she looked. Female songbirds are attracted to power and status; male songbirds look for youth and fertility. Most other animals too.

"It's very exciting," she said. She had long brown hair, plump, white skin and an ever-so-slight lisp that made her sound even younger than she actually was. "I think we really may be on to thomething." There was an edge of admiration that she didn't quite manage to expel from her voice. I sighed. Every year, I get older. And every year the students stay exactly the same age.

This is his new project, figuring out what makes identical twins non-identical. Until now, scientists have tended to shrug their shoulders and put it down to "noise." Noise is science's coverall term. It's the insignificant but unquantifiable background detail. It just is. In this instance, it's everything you've ever seen or heard or read or smelled. A snatch of music. The touch of a feather against the skin. The taste of papaya. It's the sum of everything that has ever happened to you, in the womb, out of the womb. Life. Or, as scientists put it, noise.

10.6   **mother** *vt* **2** : to watch over, nourish and protect maternally

OUR FATHER CAME to pick us up in the car, and when we arrived at the hospital, Granny Monroe was already there, with freshly set hair and a bunch of carnations.

She looked me up and down.

"You look like you've been dragged through a hedge backward. That T-shirt is almost gray."

I looked down and shrugged. Nothing gave Granny Monroe greater pleasure than to catalogue the deficiencies in another woman's house-keeping.

She fingered my sleeve. "Not even ironed!"

We walked through to the ward. My mother was propped up in a high, steel bed, wearing a new nightgown with blue flowers on it, and although she'd applied lipstick and powder, she looked exhausted.

I leaned down and kissed her, but Tiffany hesitated.

"You shouldn't wear lipstick. You're conforming to outmoded male ideas of female beauty."

My mother looked at her sharply and said, "Don't you let her fill your head with nonsense, Tiffany. I don't want any daughter of mine growing up to have hairy armpits."

We stood around awkwardly until the nurse appeared holding a baby. Not any old baby. My new baby brother. He was amazing, tiny and wrinkled like a little baby alien. He had big blue eyes and black hair, and although he was swaddled in a blanket, we caught a sight of his *thing* when the nurse picked him up to see if he needed changing. It reminded me of the worms our father used when he went fishing. I felt a pang of pity for him. Imagine having everybody looking at your parts. His head was powdery too, as if he'd been sprinkled with fairy dust.

"Cradle cap," said my mother dismissively. She seemed distracted and wasn't really looking at him. His fingers were tiny. Like the fingers of my old doll, except that they moved.

"So, what's he going to be called then?" said Granny Monroe.

My mother looked up from the bed and made her pronounce-ment. "Damien Bradley Monroe!"

My father looked surprised. Although not as surprised as Granny Monroe.

"*Damien?* What's wrong with Richard or David or Peter?"

"I wanted something a bit more *modern*, Cynthia."

"He'll turn into a gayboy if you're not careful." But she was smil-ing and cooing. Everybody was pleased.

"Girls are all well and good, but there's nothing like a son," she said.

Nanna and Grandpa Arnold arrived next and Nanna fell upon

him, exclaiming, and bursting with smiles. They'd bought presents for everyone.

"Oh! Isn't he beautiful?" She leaned down and stared into his eyes. "Isn't he handsome? Who's handsome? What a lovely little boy! Oh, Doreen, he's absolutely perfect."

It was always funny to see our mother being fussed over by Nanna. It made her seem as if she was still a child like us. But she batted away Nanna's hands impatiently.

"It's a bit late to start mothering me now," she said, causing Nanna to breathe suddenly inward, as if she'd just seen a spider or forgotten something off a shopping list.

I looked from my mother to Nanna, uncertain what had passed. Nanna stepped back an inch or two from the bed and stood to one side. I wormed my way next to her and took her hand, in my role as Special Relationshipee. Tiffany gave me a scathing look and patted my mother's head.

"Tiffany, I'm not a dog," she said. She turned then to Grandpa Arnold. "Dad?"

Grandpa Arnold shuffled forward.

"Don't you want to say hello to your grandson?"

"Hello," he said.

"Look!" said my mother. "He's got your nose!"

"No," said Herbert looking down briefly. "I don't think so."

Lucy was jealous that I had a brand-new brother. "You'll be able to dress him up," she said. "And take him for walks. And when he's older, you'll be able to boss him about."

"You can borrow him if you like," I said, for we shared all our toys.

We were sitting at the breakfast table and having grapefruit followed by whole-wheat toast. It was another seminal difference between the households. At home we helped ourselves to cereal and ate it at the breakfast bar listening to Radio 2. At the Old Parsonage, we had to sit at the table and were expected to talk to one another.

Kenneth was reading the newspaper. We'd hardly seen him all week. He was always at work or playing tennis or attending one of his enthusiasts' rallies (he owned a vintage Morgan). I'd had a problem looking him in the eyes ever since we found the book in his sock drawer. Tiffany, on the other hand, was always trying to draw him into conversation. Although not with much success.

"Well," he said, not moving, "I suppose I'd better go and save some lives!"

Tiffany and I looked at him, impressed. Our dad never said that before he went to work.

Suzanne banged the dishwasher shut. "And I'll just stay at home and clear up after you while you play God, shall I?" This wasn't strictly true, as we all know that she had a cleaning lady, Steven German's mother, who came in and "did" for her, although our mother said that no one with any sort of pride would allow another woman to rummage through her knicker drawer.

"Suzanne?" Lucy tried to get her mother's attention. "Suzanne?"

Aunty Suzanne was standing over the stove watching her coffee. Nobody made coffee like Aunty Suzanne. She spooned it into a little copper pot that she boiled on the stove, and drank it from a tiny cup. When she'd finished, a layer of what looked like mud sat at the bottom.

"Yes, Lucy."

"Why don't you have a baby? I want a baby brother too."

"It's not as simple as that, Lucy."

Simple as what? We waited for elaboration but there was none forthcoming.

Uncle Kenneth grunted from behind his copy of *The Times*. He looked at his wife and said, "No. They don't appear by bloody magic, do they?"

"Kenneth!" said Aunty Suzanne sharply. I couldn't say I blamed her. My mother wouldn't have let my dad get away with "bloody" at the breakfast table either.

10.7   sister *n* 3 : a woman who advocates, fosters or takes part in the feminist movement

I TURN UP in Tiffany's columns sometimes. I'm The Sister. I come off better than The Husband, but not as well as The Best Friend. Mostly

I'm invoked for compare and contrast purposes. For example: "The Sister thinks that fashion is for wimps. She says you shouldn't judge a book by its cover" (*Family Affairs* 42). Or "The Sister wears her heart on her sleeve. I tend to prefer Armani" (*Family Affairs* 16).

There's only one constant: I'm always misquoted. I have never said, "You shouldn't judge a book by its cover." There are enough people quoting proverbs in my family without me joining in.

It's Charles (aka The Husband) I feel sorry for though. He tried to ban her from mentioning him, but Tiffany's never been known not to get her own way, so he's still there, week after week, tottering ineffectually in the background of her domestic trials.

We went to dinner at her house last week. She invites us over about once a month and cooks something impressive while Charles juggles bottles of vintage claret. Alistair was looking forward to it, I could tell. He was singing in the shower, and appeared with a red towel wrapped around his midriff. There were little globules of water meshed in his chest hair. They glistened in the light. His physical beauty still has the capacity to surprise me. He rubbed his hair dry so that it stood up in tufts. I reached out to touch him, clean and newborn beneath my fingers.

"Come on," he said. "We'll be late. And you'll get the blame." He was right about that. Tiffany is still Tiffany, although she's a great fan of Alistair's. She's always stealing his ideas and shoehorning them into one of her columns. She's never understood what he sees in me. But then, I wonder about that too sometimes.

"Mwuh! So glad you could make it. Do go on through. Charles will fix you a drink. I heard you on the radio this morning, Alistair. You sounded frightfully fluent."

You have to admire Tiffany. Or at least I do. I have to admire Tiffany. She's got everything she's always wanted, and how many people can you say that about?

"Ah, there you are, Rebecca," Charles said and kissed me on the cheek. I get on well with Charles. Tiffany married him mainly, I think, because he's an old Harrovian who makes lots of money in the City. I don't know if she noticed his gentleness, his small, unobserved kindnesses. We both tend to regard Tiffany with similar emotions (awe, incredulity). He drinks too much, but then if I lived with Tiffany, I would too.

Damien turned up late with his boyfriend, Michael, giggling and already drunk. He's a designer and is the most angst-free person I know.

"How's my sis?" he asked and kissed me on the cheek. Tiffany doesn't approve of homosexuality, but she loves to talk about interior decor, and Damien will indulge her for hours at a time. He's too good-humored to mind when she says things like "I don't care what people get up to in private, but I just don't want their sexual preferences rammed down my throat." He tends just to look at Michael and roll his eyes.

"Go and look at my new bathroom cabinet," she told him. "I want to know what you think." She calls Michael "Damien's little friend," even though he's six foot three and barrel-chested.

I watched her tossing the salad with vinaigrette and expounding to the room, although mostly Alistair. The rest of us weren't listening.

"It's like all this nonsense about institutionalized racism," she was saying. "What rot! Anybody can do anything with a bit of hard work. It's just our moan, moan, moan poor-little-me culture. It's like all these talentless nobodies who just want to be famous."

Sometimes I take Tiffany on, but not often. She just steamrolls right over the top of you.

"It's like these women who go on about sexual discrimination. Ha! They don't complain when they show a bit of leg at the interview and get the job, do they? Doors open to women who wear heels. Believe me, I know!"

Once upon a time, I would have argued with her, but instead I sighed and looked at Alistair for help. He was too busy pouring him-self another glass of wine. And anyway, he tends to agree with most of what she says.

"Well, it is very interesting, the genetic research into gender issues," he said, taking a swig of wine. "There are very real, very innate differ-ences. But then I think we've probably always known that; it's just been a matter of political correctness that we're not allowed to say it."

"Exactly my point!" said Tiffany.

I looked at her and opened my mouth but then closed it again. I wondered if Alistair would say anything, but he simply poured himself another glass of wine. I used to think that Tiffany was a dinosaur, that the world had changed, that Britain wasn't like that anymore. Now I'm not so sure.

I looked across the table. Tiffany was patting her mouth with her napkin. She was talking Alistair through her Nigella Lawson mushroom risotto. Charles leaned across the table and refilled my glass.

"My mother used to make risotto with soy sauce and bits of carrot," he said. "Bloody marvelous it was too."

Tiffany looked at him briefly, annoyed. "You can use white wine in it," she said. "But personally I prefer vermouth."

I took a sip of my wine and tried to follow Tiffany's conversation. She's my sister so I guess we're related. But, even now, I can't work out exactly how.

Tiffany and Alistair spent the evening talking about the media while Damien and Michael touched each other's knees beneath the table. Charles got drunk. I ate three portions of risotto and felt the waistband of my trousers digging into my waist.

"Super to see you both," said Tiffany on the doorstep as Charles swayed imperceptibly behind her. "You must come again soon! Keep up the good work, Alistair." And she kissed him hastily on the cheek.

He wandered out into the street to look for our taxi. Charles went back inside. I was left alone on the doorstep with Tiffany.

She kissed me on the cheek and looked at me. I saw her hesitate.

"You'd be much happier, you know, if you lost a bit of weight."

10.8   fallout *n* : airborne radioactive debris from nuclear explosion

THE HOUSE FELT funny when we went home. Our family had expanded by 20 percent, and although Damien was only tiny, he took up more space than anybody else. There was his cot and his baby carriage, and his bottle warmer and the various mysterious unguents that had appeared in the bathroom. The air inside the house seemed to have been shifted around, as if it had been displaced to make way for him. There was a strange new smell too: a fresh pungent aroma that drifted from room to room.

But it was more than that. It was our mother. She looked like she did when she was a hump under the duvet. It filled us all with a sense of dread. None of us wanted to go through that again. Her movements were listless, and although she got up from bed to feed Damien (formula not breast), she kept on crying. We'd all seen the jar containing her little pink pills in the bathroom cabinet, but I didn't know if it was they that made her eyes go cloudy, or something else. Sometimes, a dribble of saliva would escape from the corner of her mouth without her even realizing it.

"Children, babies," she muttered. "And I have to do everything!" Although Tiffany and I had become quite good at looking after ourselves, since Damien now occupied most of our mother's attention. Still, at least the sayings had returned.

"Claire Dougal in my class got a new bicycle when her mother had a baby so she wouldn't feel left out."

"Did she now? Well you can have a clip around the ear if you want one of those." I concentrated hard on trying not to annoy her, but there were so many unforeseen pitfalls and it was easier to fall into them than ever before. "Can't you do that any quicker?" she asked as I tried to tie up my shoelaces before school. But I couldn't. My hands were small. I was a child! It was that which seemed to annoy her more than anything else.

My father walked around wearing a pinched expression, although he wouldn't allow us to bad-mouth our mother behind her back.

"She's ill, Rebecca!" he said, turning on me. "You could try and make a bit more of an effort, you know."

"How's she ill?"

When other people's mothers got ill, they went to bed with the flu and a hot water bottle.

"She's very . . . tired. Grown-ups sometimes get a bit tired, and they're not quite themselves for a time."

I was feeling quite tired myself. I exiled myself to my room and took out my sketch pad and tried to remember what it was like when my mother was pregnant and the house was filled with expectation and the smell of cakes rising, but when I looked down, I'd drawn another of my mushroom clouds. A great atomic plume of smoke that looked a bit like a tree but that could wipe out the entire world in seconds. Just like that. One minute you were there, the next you weren't. Although it was worse if the bomb didn't get you immediately; then you died a slow, torturous, agonizing death from the radiation. We'd studied it at school.

Everybody thought that I would hate Damien and dangle him by his legs over the landing, but I didn't. I felt sorry for him. He looked so fat and happy. Wait till you grow up, I told him.

10.9   inherit *vt* 1 : receive as a bequest or legacy

I WAS DRUNK, perhaps, which was why I asked the question.

"Is it hereditary?"

We were in the taxi on the way home, and Alistair was flicking through his diary, making small, neat notes.

"What?"

"Adultery."

He looked up startled. "*What?*"

"Is adultery hereditary?"

I saw him hesitate, his pen poised over "September," not moving. "That's a new one on me."

But I'd thrown him a challenge, and I knew that Alistair-the-Intellectual would rise to it. Alistair-the-Husband might have asked a different follow-up question. But then, Alistair had never been that sort of husband.

He worried the end of the pen against his teeth. I could see that he was thinking about it.

"Not *per se.*"

"But?"

"Well, there are lots of reasons why people might commit adultery, and of course monogamy is itself a cultural construct . . ."

"Yes." I waited patiently. Alistair was enjoying himself. He loved being set an intellectual conundrum. I watched as he teased out the idea in his mind.

"But there's an argument that it *could* be genetic. For example, the D4DR gene, which controls the body's responsiveness to dopamine, has been shown to correlate with thrill-seeking in individuals. People with the long version of the gene are six times more likely to engage in dangerous sports. They're more likely to take risks in their financial dealings. They sleep with more women."

"Or men."

"Yes," he said. "Or men."

I directed the driver down our street.

"Does your mother know about your father's affairs?" I said.

Alistair turned toward me and opened his mouth, but paused before speaking.

"What makes you think he has affairs?"

"Oh, come *on*."

He looked at me for a moment before replying.

"I could ask you a very similar question," he said.

The driver pulled up outside our flat and left the engine running. Neither of us moved.

"Touché," I said eventually and opened the door.

10.10 relative *adj* 3 : considered in comparison with something else

IN SPITE OF Tiffany's pleas to be allowed to go to boarding school, she'd gone up to the comprehensive like everyone else. Everyone else, that is, apart from Charlotte Wilson, who had been sent to St. Edward's School for Girls and wore a purple gingham dress and a straw boater. Sometimes we saw her looking out of her bedroom window at us riding our bikes in the street. We didn't ask her out to play anymore though and she didn't ask us. Our mother said it was because she thought she was a cut above the rest of us now. We thought it was because she was a lesbian (an exciting new word that we'd been introduced to via a *Nationwide* item on Denmark). I caught Tiffany looking wistfully at Charlotte's purple gingham uniform, and for months she harangued our mother to buy her a lacrosse stick. She seemed to think that without one, she might be marked down in later life, and Tiffany never liked to come anything other than top in anything.

She had homework these days too and would shout at the rest of us to turn the television down or stop talking so loudly. She wasn't going to allow her family to ruin her prospects just because we were over-assiduous *Crossroads* viewers.

"You have to work hard, pass all your exams and go to university," she said. My mother raised her eyebrows at my father.

"I don't know where she gets her brains from. It must be my side of the family, I suppose. Herbert's very sharp in his own way."

My father looked up from behind his newspaper as if he was going to say something, but then changed his mind. Neither of our parents had been to university.

"Uncle Kenneth went to the University of Sussex. You could go there," I pointed out helpfully.

"Shut up, Rebecca. Everyone knows the redbricks aren't worth bothering with." Tiffany had decided to go to Oxbridge. It was where all the best people went, apparently, although even she had been thwarted in her attempts to find it in our father's AA road atlas.

She turned back to her books, then looked up and snapped. "And turn the television off!"

I sighed. Tiffany's new status as family genius meant my viewing schedule had been radically restructured. I was watching *It's a Knock-out* and the teams had just appeared to wild cheers from the audience. "I'm watching it!"

"Rebecca!" My mother was in the kitchen trying to follow a complicated recipe for Chicken Chasseur, and the tone of her voice suggested it wasn't going well.

Damien, who was teething, started to grizzle.

"Now look what you've done!" she said, fixing me with a stare and throwing a tea towel melodramatically over her shoulder.

I went to check the mail, and among the brown manila envelopes and electricity bills was a blue airmail letter with an American stamp.

"It's from the Americans!" I cried and ran into the kitchen. We got one every year. A roneoed piece of paper in faint blue ink with our names written in Biro at the top and scrawly signatures at the bottom. Usually there was some personal message added as a PS, something along the lines of "Hope you guys are doing well! Best seasonal greetings!" although it did vary. One year it said, "See you at the B-B-Q!" We'd wondered about that for ages, but in the end, we decided that it was probably an oversight, seeing as how our cousins lived in America and we lived in Middleton. It seemed unlikely that we'd see them at a barbecue. Particularly in December.

This year's letter contained a different PS again. "Will be over later this year. Would love to see you all. Will write soon, Aunty Susan, Uncle Bob, Celine and Joe XXXXX." They'd all signed it individually, Celine dotting her i with a heart. They wrote every year, even though they weren't real cousins, or a real uncle and aunt. Not even a great-aunt like Aunty Betty or a great-great-uncle, like Uncle Reginald. It was more complicated than that.

"Aunty Susan is my father's sister's daughter," said my mother. "So she's my mother's cousin too, but that just complicates things." She stirred a sweetener into her coffee. "Her mother is Elizabeth, who is my father's, your grandfather's, sister. She married a GI at the end of the war. Let me see, that makes her my niece. No, that's not right. She's my cousin. So her children are your cousins once removed."

"Removed from where?"

"From Britain stupid," said Tiffany.

Our mother hesitated.

"No, removed from you."

None of it made sense. We stared at the photo of four brightly dressed strangers standing in the garden of a large white house with pillars and a porch. They looked as if they were advertising something, although I wasn't sure what. Toothpaste? Shampoo? Good health? They were smiling and screwing up their eyes against the sunlight. Our mother was right. They did look removed from us.

They were coming on holiday to Britain, at an unspecified date at some point that year, and were planning to pass through Middleton. I tried to imagine them in Beech Drive but couldn't. It wasn't sunny enough. The houses weren't big enough. Our Aquafresh toothpaste wasn't strong enough.

"Well," said our mother, "they'll have to take us as they find us. I'm not going to keep my best linen out just in case a bunch of Yanks happen to show up."

She tended to be sniffy about Americans, even if they weren't related in some way. She claimed they had "no culture."

"What about *Dallas*?" I said.

"Exactly!" she said. Although she had recently started experimenting with shoulder pads and little jackets with nipped-in waists. She'd regained her pre-Damien figure too. The trick was to eat Ryvita and steak, although not together. I lifted my T-shirt and stared at my stomach in the mirror.

"Am I fat?" I asked her. She surveyed me with a critical eye.

"Well, you could probably do with dropping a couple of pounds."

"Suzanne says fat is a feminist issue."

"Ha!" she said, drawing in her stomach. "It's willpower is all it is. There's no gain without pain."

The Americans were circling. There had been sightings of them up in Yorkshire, and a telephone call suggested they might descend at any moment.

"Typical Yanks!" said my mother. "No consideration for anyone other than themselves."

She was scrubbing the inside of the kitchen cupboards.

"If we were born in America, would we be American?"

She shook more Ajax onto her cloth and reapplied herself to an invisible stain. "Yes."

"Even though we're English?"

"Yes. If you're born in America, you're American. If you're born in England, you're English."

"So if you had been in America when you had me, I'd be American?"

She hesitated.

"Yes."

"So I'd still be me but I'd be American?"

"Yes, Rebecca," she said in semi-exasperation.

"Weird." I tried to get my head around this. "Because I'd be different, wouldn't I, if I was American?"

My mother snapped. "For goodness' sake, Rebecca, haven't you got anything better to do than to hang around here and annoy me?"

But what was better than contemplating the mysteries of life? If I had been brought up in my aunt and uncle's house, would I be an Edwards? If . . . A question occurred to me, however, and I went back downstairs.

"What about if you were in Pakistan when you had me, would I be Pakistani?"

"That's completely different," she said, grappling with her dish cloth. Although she didn't say how.

10.11 Love Story (2), Part 5

The conversation at Tiffany's must have buoyed up Alistair. Or maybe it was the bottle of claret and three large glasses of Laphroaig. He woke in the night and pulled me toward him. I could smell whiskey on his breath. He grabbed one breast in each hand and started rotating them. It wasn't precisely what you'd call erotic, but after that amount of alcohol, I figured it was about the most I could hope for. He didn't look at me, satisfying himself with a quick glance to check that there was no clothing impeding his way. He kept his pajamas on. It was the kind of sex only married people have: methodical, no-frills. His climax was short and perfunctory.

"There," he said. As if he'd proved something.

When I woke up, there was a rash across my torso. A friction rub produced by sweat-dampened polycotton. As I moved onto my side, my legs stuck together. Was it marmalade? I wondered. Honey? But no, there was Alistair, back from his run, saying, "You'll have to get the morning-after pill, I'm afraid. Forgot to get your cap, eh?" He wagged his finger good-humoredly. "Don't forget now, will you?"

10.12 plan *v* 1 : to formulate a scheme or program for the accomplishment, enactment or attainment

DUNCAN ROGERS FROM two doors down had taken to wearing a badge that said, "Stuff The Wedding! What About Jobs?" But it was not a sentiment that was echoed at number 24. The buildup to the Big Day had been going on for weeks, with special reports on *Nationwide*, free commemorative mugs distributed at school and endless speculation about The Dress. The last time anything this exciting had happened was the Silver Jubilee, when we had a street party and I'd worn a plastic bowler hat with the Union Jack on it.

"Anyway," said our mother. "He should be wearing a badge that says 'What About A Wash?' or 'What About A Haircut?' If I was his mother, I wouldn't let him out of the house looking the way he does." There was a sense of female solidarity about our sudden interest in the news. Our father harrumphed behind his paper whenever there was a Lady Diana item, but our mother would always call Tiffany and me and we'd race into the lounge to see the latest pictures of her. Usually she was making a dash for her car or looking up from under her fringe. I practiced doing it in the mirror. The trick was to lower your chin and raise your eyelids up toward the ceiling. But my hair was mousey and refused to flop over my face. My forehead was too high.

Was the wedding so exciting because she was young and pretty and in love? Because she was marrying the heir to the throne? Or because the television said it was? The question troubled me, although mostly I just liked looking at her clothes.

"Ooh look. She's had her eyebrows plucked. Not before time. She was beginning to look like Mr. Brezhnev." We watched as she dashed out of the Emmanuels' studio looking up coyly to smile at the cameras. "I wonder if she'll go for something with a bit of a modern twist. Maybe asymmetrical, you know."

"No, Mum," said Tiffany. "It has to be traditional. The Queen told her. I saw it on the lunchtime news."

Our father rustled his paper. "Waste of money if you ask me."

"Yes, well nobody did ask you, did they?"

"It's ridiculous. This isn't news."

"Well we don't think so, do we, girls?"

It wasn't only our father who seemed curiously indifferent to The Wedding. The gender divide was repeated in homes up and down Beech Drive.

"But, Dad! It's an Historic Occasion!"

"Ha! Load of media hype. It's just to distract attention from the economy." He refused to be drawn into our mother's increasingly elaborate plans to mark the occasion (fueled by some dim ancestral memory of the Coronation), but she wasn't going to be put off by a mere man. She had a finger buffet to plan.

10.13 family *n* 3 : a group of persons sharing common ancestry

I FELL BACK TO SLEEP after Alistair left for work, and it was only after the clock-radio turned itself off that I remembered it was the first Tuesday of the month. I had a rushed shower and a few scalding sips of coffee before I hurried off to his department. I saw his back retreating down a corridor, but he didn't come and say hello. A researcher, the young one with the lisp whom I'd met the last time, took me through to the lab.

She didn't introduce herself, but then she was only young. I tried to put her at ease.

"What's your name?"

"Cathy," she said matter-of-factly. She didn't bother to look when she replied.

I sat waiting for her while she studied the paperwork, and glanced around the room. There wasn't much to look at, only the standard-issue university plastic stacking chairs and a yellowing poster about fire regulations.

"I thought you worked with Alistair," I said eventually.

She looked up at me briefly. "I do."

I thought about this for a moment.

"But it's not his project."

The eyes flickered up again. "No."

I waited for elaboration.

"He *ith* the head of the department," she said eventually. He is, it's true, although somehow this hadn't really occurred to me before. "Anyway, I'm just helping out for a month."

I sat and waited some more and then she finally got down to doing the tests. When she'd finished, I filled in the usual forms. I'd almost finished when I noticed that she'd brought my file in with her too; another sign, I assumed, of her inexperience. I stared at it while thinking of the answer to the last question. I twiddled the pen in my fingers. There was something in my line of vision that was bothering me. I couldn't work out what it was at first, and then I saw it. Underneath a sheaf of papers was a pink document folder. It was marked "Doreen Monroe."

I stared at it for a full minute and then said, "What's that?"

She looked up. "What?"

"That folder."

"Oh, it'th your mother's medical noteth, I think."

I stared at her then. "*You* have my mother's medical notes?"

I looked at her in astonishment, and she must have realized, then, that she'd slipped up. She picked up the pile of papers and tidied them, banging them against the side of the table to make them square.

I thought for a moment.

"So, have you found what you're looking for?" I fished.

"Thorry?"

"The study . . . Is it proving successful?"

She hesitated, suspecting a trap.

"It's still the preliminary stages."

I paused, leaving a silence and waiting for her to fill it.

"But we're making a certain amount of progress. As I'm sure you're aware, mental illness isn't carried by any one gene. It's not as thimple as that . . ."

I sat absolutely still and let the words hover in the air. "Mental illness." I should have known. Or, perhaps, I did know. Perhaps that's why I'd never asked. "You'll be perfect for it," Alistair had said. The perfect guinea pig. The perfect fruit fly.

"But you think that it could be . . . genetic?"

"Well, it's a pothibility that we're looking at . . . the consanguineous relationship . . . your mother's . . . We're looking into the mitochondrial DNA to see . . ."

I let the sentence hang, but she didn't finish it. I looked down at the final form she'd given me, signed my name and gathered up my jacket. I gave her a TV smile. "There you go!" And walked out the door.

When Alistair arrived home, he found me crying on the sofa.

"What's the matter?" he said, taking off his coat and loosening his tie.

"Alistair . . . ?" But my tongue clotted in my mouth. I couldn't form the question. Or perhaps, I just didn't want to hear his reply.

He looked down at me.

"It's only the hormones," he said. "It happened last time you took the morning-after pill. It would really be much easier if you remembered your cap, you know."

Part Eleven

lose v : to be deprived of (something one has had)

11.1   memory *n* **4** : act of remembering; person or thing remembered

HERBERT CALLED ME. I felt a stab of panic as soon as I heard his voice. Alicia.

"Maybe you could come up?" he said.

I breathed a sigh of relief. She wasn't dead then. It's what you always think, when you have an elderly relative. Every phone call could be the one.

"She's not so bright. But she'd like to see you, you know."

Panic, relief, then guilt. Are all families like that? Or just mine? I caught the train the next morning. Alicia was smaller than before. She seemed to have shrunk. She hadn't forgotten me though. Not yet.

"Rebecca!" I hugged her close. "How's school?"

"It's university these days," I said. "I'm doing my Ph.D., remember?"

Her eyes clouded. "Herbert, did you get the buns?"

"Aye. I got the buns."

"Always have buns on a Wednesday," said Alicia. "Buns on Wednesdays. With a nice bit of jam."

It was Tuesday. Neither of us felt like correcting her.

"Suzanne said she'd pop round later," I said.

Alicia turned to Herbert. "Did you get the buns?"

"Aye, I got the buns."

"Always have buns on a Wednesday."

"Did you hear me? I said Suzanne said she'd pop round later."

"Suzanne?"

"Suzanne. Your daughter."

"My babies," she said. "I loved them. All three of them."

"Two," I corrected her, but I don't think she heard me.

.   .   .

Everything's confused with her. She dips back through time telling me details that happened forty, fifty years ago as if it was yesterday. She's given me more of Herbert's files. The ones marked "Outgoings." I can't help but think what her life might have been like. How it could have been different. How her time's running out. I've so many questions that I want to ask, but every time I try, my throat swells up and I can't form the words.

Later I did the washing up, while Alicia watched me.

"Have you got a Brillo pad?" I asked.

"Ooh no. You can't get those for love or money. Terrible the shortages are. An ounce of sugar, only. And hardly any butter at all."

"Cup of tea?" I said.

"Lovely! Proper Yorkshire tea. It'll put hairs on your chest, you know."

"I don't want hairs on my chest," I said.

She smiled at me, suddenly lucid. "Am I going mad?"

"No, you're not going mad."

"I don't know who I am anymore."

We sat at the table and drank our tea. Hot, sweet Yorkshire tea. Join the club, I thought.

11.2   collector *n* : one who collects (specimens, books, stamps, etc.)

I ALREADY KNOW most of my grandmother's secrets. I know about Cecil Johnston. I know that on an uncharacteristically warm evening back in September 1948, shortly before he married my grandmother and became my grandfather, Herbert was in the shed in his parents' backyard feeding his ferrets.

I've put together the pieces. It wasn't so hard. I'm good at collecting facts. But then, I expect that's the Herbert in me.

.   .   .

Herbert was in the shed in his backyard feeding his ferrets. He had been breeding ferrets for years. He liked the feel of their slippery little bodies. The way they wound themselves around your wrist and sat in your lap, docile and obedient.

Mustela putorius furo. From the Latin: *mus*—mouse; *putor*—to stink; *furo*—a thief. From the same family as the stoat, the weasel, the polecat and the otter. People misunderstood ferrets. They thought of them as wild, untamed, unbiddable, but Herbert knew that ferrets were a domestic breed, that they existed only in captivity, and had done so for the past three thousand years: longer than the cat. But cats were not verbs. A ferret, on the other hand, you could conjugate (**ferret** *v* : to rummage, to search out [secrets, etc.], to bring to light).

Herbert knew all about ferrets. He knew the difference between the smell of a male ferret (a hob) and that of a female (a Jill). He knew about the coloration of their coats. He knew about their fondness for dark, hidden places. He knew that if a Jill comes on heat and isn't mated, she would die a slow, painful death from aplastic anemia.

A flock of birds. A gaggle of geese. A business of ferrets. There were currently two ferrets in Herbert's business. A brother and a sister: Norma and Norman. Norma was a red-eyed albino, Norman a tawny-colored sable with a dark facial mask. Initially they had shared the same cage, but they chased each other, bit each other, scratched and complained. Herbert separated them. He would have them neutered, but not yet. He liked the smell of uncut ferret, the stink—a high, musky smell that made other people wince and stretch their eyes. But then other people misunderstood ferrets. They didn't recognize their capacity to love. Not in the dopey, gullible, misguided ways of a dog. They were more intelligent than that. More curious. Herbert liked to pick them up and groom them, to scratch them behind their ears and stroke their soft, delicate underbellies.

"Herbert?" His mother walked into the shed. "It's dinnertime."

Peggy Arnold wore a flowered apron and, in the presence of her only son, an expression of infinite disappointment. He wasn't the kind of son she'd dreamed about when she walked down the aisle of the West Parade Methodist Chapel in an organza dress. She carried a posy of delphiniums and a meager bag of expectations for the future. Still, a son like Herbert had not been among them.

"Are you coming in?"

She watched her son for a couple of minutes, watched the ferrets run up and down his trouser leg and escape to corners of the shed, and then walked out again. He just wasn't that kind of son.

Herbert used a mallet to grind up the mouse. He caught them in a trap set in the lane that ran down the back of the house. The mouse was still warm, and as he brought the mallet to bear on the light brown fur, it twitched. But he'd got used to that. He divided it onto two plates, set them down on the floor and watched the ferrets eat, fighting for the last scraps. Norman won, but then he was almost twice the size of Norma. Herbert returned them to their cages, fastened the clasps and went inside for his dinner.

Even his mother considers Herbert odd, but being odd has its uses. There he is now standing in front of Cecil waiting at the Westgate bus stop. Cecil doesn't see Herbert. He stares into the middle distance, humming to himself, waiting for Alicia to come tip-tapping down the road in her new black court heels. Cecil tipped his hat and tapped his feet. A tapping that was almost a jig, that resonated with the sound of Alicia's black court heels on the paving slabs to create a rhythm that Herbert suspected was best described as syncopated.

"Al-eesha," he said and took off his hat. She turned quickly at the sound of her name and her face changed, transformed. She smiled—a full, broad smile that Herbert had not detailed before.

"I've missed you." And her face, the face that should have been looking into Herbert's eyes, that should have been shining toward him, turned the other way.

As they walked away together down the street, Herbert's ears were filled with the sound of their feet tip-tapping. He very nearly missed the sight of his cousin Alicia, *his* Alicia, reaching out her hand and touching the inside of Cecil's wrist. It was over in an instant, but recorded forever, a double entry in both Bought Ledger and Outgoings.

The overlaps were becoming increasingly frequent. Herbert tracked them both, tracked their haphazard progress to parks and cinemas, tracked the changing expressions on their faces. Alicia's repertoire had expanded. There was a new smile to document; a new look that persisted on her face, in her eyes, even when Cecil was not there. Herbert recorded it all in black and white, wrote it up in columns, contained it within tables, enumerated it in lists.

Herbert understood the power of the list. It was a method of containment that he had happened upon by accident in the unhappy long Sunday hours in his room. There were other methods too. He discovered, for example, the particular male alchemy of transforming emotion into objects: he became a collector. Herbert collected stamps, train numbers, military blunders, facts, lists, whatever. He hunted down Penny Reds and rare-issue Helvetians. He pasted them neatly into albums and corresponded with dealers in London. He spent long hours at Westgate Station tracking the elusive Black Five loco. He acquired obscure facts about the Battle of Okinawa and hoarded them. But mostly he collected Alicia. He wanted to know everything. Possession was all. To possess was to control.

It was a week after Norma came into season that Herbert followed Alicia and Cecil up Lindale Hill. He knew the date for a fact because it was written in his book. Herbert did not make those kinds of mistakes. They were having an Indian summer, and the heat of the day was not the crisp, hollow heat of autumn; it was close, oppressive. His jacket was too hot; the tweed itched his skin. Scrabbling through the undergrowth, he cut his ankle on a bramble, and blood seeped down his leg, drying into dark brown flakes, matting his hairs together. Large circles of sweat gathered in the armpits of his shirt. He saw his cousin hold up her face to the black man's. He saw their lips touch. Back at home, the smell from the hutches in the shed in the backyard hit him in waves. Norma panted. Her eyes were glassy, her belly flopped. In the next cage, Norman scratched and worried the chicken wire. Herbert knew what he had to do and undid the clasps.

It didn't take Norman long. He cornered Norma in the space under the worktop and stuck it to her. Herbert crouched down to watch. Norman pinioned her down and went at it hammer and tongs.

When it was over, Norma didn't move. She flopped on the floor, her tongue hanging out. Herbert picked her up. She looked at him with her ferret eyes, eyeball to eyeball. And then she sank her teeth deep into his thumb, drawing a warm, wet stream of blood. Herbert yelped and leaped to his feet. Norma clung onto his thumb, until he beat her body against the gate. Once, twice, it took three increasingly violent bashes before she let go, and shot out through the chink in the door. The skin on Herbert's hand never quite grew back. He would retain a long silvery scar that was forever Norma.

11.3   black hole *n* 3 : a great void; an abyss

THERE'S A GENE for Alzheimer's, I've discovered. Or at least there are several genes that are under investigation. But then Alistair says it's a popular misconception that there are genes "for" diseases. It's the absence of the gene usually that does for you.

I've been reading about it again. There's this case all the Alzheimer's books refer to, although it's not about forgetting, but remembering. Shereshevsky, he's called. He was a newspaper reporter in Moscow in the 1920s and was discovered to have perfect recall. There was nothing he could not remember. After seeing a table of random numbers for a few minutes, he could remember it. He could still remember it twenty years later, having seen thousands of similar tables of similarly random numbers.

    Scientists study mutations to understand nonmutations. They study the extreme to make sense of the ordinary. The Russian psychologist A. R. Luria studied Shereshevsky's amazing ability to remember in order to understand our amazing ability to forget. I'd never thought it was amazing until I read about Shereshevsky. He could forget nothing. It was his cross. He tried writing down his memories and burning them, but still in his mind's eye, he could see charred pieces of paper and the words underneath. He remembered everything. But he understood nothing.

    He could remember this:

8	6	3	0
4	8	3	1
2	6	1	0
1	7	6	3
9	0	0	2
1	6	3	5
3	2	0	5
6	8	4	3
9	0	3	2
8	4	6	3
0	0	2	1
8	7	8	4
2	4	0	5
0	1	4	3
0	4	9	2
1	9	0	8
1	4	2	6
9	1	4	8
0	5	5	3
8	7	0	9
3	6	1	2
7	3	7	9
0	1	2	8
4	5	2	9
0	0	5	4
1	7	1	9
0	6	8	3

Figure 13.

But could make no sense of this:

1	2	3	4
2	3	4	5
3	4	5	6
4	5	6	7

Figure 14.

His mind was a mass of detail, but there were no patterns. Shereshevsky saw trees, but not woods.

I watched Alistair at the breakfast table this morning. Pouring himself a coffee, opening his newspaper, bringing the cup to his lips. Trees but not woods.

11.4   innocent *adj* **1** : uncorrupted by evil, malice or wrongdoing; sinless

HERBERT KNEW about Cecil. Alicia's mother knew (although she denied she knew). Betty sensed it but couldn't understand it. And Sylvia, Alicia's best friend, guessed it.

Sylvia worked in Lingerie and was therefore well acquainted with the workings of love. She was frequently called upon to find a hankie for a lady in distress. They had a habit of breaking down when they looked at themselves in their new underwear in the mirror of the changing room. In Hosiery there was none of the feeling of female camaraderie that came with discarded outer garments and wobbling bosoms. Alicia saw less, knew less.

It was a Monday morning. Sylvia looked at Alicia, scrutinized her face, cast her eyes up and down her body, noted the movement of her hands.

"You've changed," she said finally.

Sylvia was not big and blowzy, as her name and job title might have suggested, but rake-thin with a long stride. She spent her days finding suitable armature for heaving maternal bosoms, vehicles that would lift and separate outsized cleavages, although where her chest should have been, there was nothing, two empty pouches. "Flat as a pancake I am. Runs in our family."

She paced through Lingerie, her tape measure ever ready to puncture myths and uncover the truth beneath the layers of petticoats, liberty bodices, thermal underwear and reinforced pants in which her customers chose to arm themselves against the world, and in some cases, their husbands.

"A 34B, madam? Well, of course, I'm sure you *were*. Might I suggest Madam try a 34A?"

It was no coincidence then that it was Sylvia who saw straight through Alicia's secret. That she was the one who observed the changes that Cecil's gifts of mango and starfruit and bitter-tasting lemons had wrought upon her face. The subtle change in the set of her eyebrows, the clouding that occurred in that portion of her eyes between her pupil and her iris, the wrinkle on the left-hand side of her mouth that pointed to the development of a late-onset dimple.

"Where did you find him?"

"Find who?"

Alicia looked at her friend wide-eyed. She tended toward awe in her relationship with Sylvia. Alicia, who had no older sisters, whose mother was known within the family as Nervous Nelly, who did not read much, and who had never enjoyed many friendships of the intimate, confidence-sharing variety, relied upon Sylvia for instruction in the ways of womanhood.

"Alicia Cragley, don't come the innocent with me! You've got a man!"

Alicia blushed. It was a habit she had been born with. Her emotions passed directly (from where? her head? her heart?) through her skin and onto the cheeks of her face and the palms of her hands, without bothering formally to notify her mouth or her tongue. Her armpits prickled. Her toes expanded. It was true. She did have a man.

She was waiting for him at the top of Lindale Hill. Herbert was there too, also waiting. He was in his observation position, crouched low, behind a horse-chestnut tree, his body frozen, his eyes fixed.

Cecil arrived late holding a picnic blanket, a woollen Utility weave large enough for them both to sit on, and a brown paper bag. Wherever he went, ripples of people flowed around him, staring and looking, and stepping out of the way. He tried to ignore the ebbing and flowing Yorkshiremen, but it wasn't easy. With Alicia, the quality of the staring changed. Curiosity gave way to something else, something edged with hostility and laced with an ugliness that neither of them wanted to look in the eye. They preferred to meet out of town, on the hill, where the gritty Yorkshire soil was not sprinkled with gnomes and edged with begonias. They were freer up there.

Herbert, who had recently started working as a clerk for West Riding Council, was wearing a new set of clothes his mother had helped him pick out. They were somehow, indefinably, wrong. His jumper sagged. His jacket hung. His trousers flapped. Alicia cocked her head to one side and listened to the noise.

"Is that a bird?"

"What?"

"That noise?"

"Crickets," said Cecil, who had a habit of forgetting that the Yorkshire's fauna and flora was not the same as at home.

He held up his paper bag, and after a theatrical pause, he extracted a fruit from it with an elaborate flourish.

"Ta da!" he said. It was small and brown and looked as if it was several months old. "Guava!" he said in triumph.

"Ah," said Alicia. "What is it this time? Mold or mildew?" Teasing Cecil was the highlight of her week. She watched him pare back the skin, her eyes focused on his hands. The fruit was drippingly overripe.

He peeled it slowly, methodically. Alicia waited. She anticipated the taste of it, the texture of it, the brush of Cecil's skin against her as he placed it in her hands.

The flapping of the bird in the tree increased in intensity. The sun overhead burned her back, scorching her through the blue cable-knit cardigan and thin cotton dress.

"Eat!" he commanded finally and held a piece of fruit up to her lips. Alicia ate. And felt the sweetness slipping down her throat like a sudden rush of pleasure. She watched as Cecil took a slice and swallowed it, a drop of golden juice trickling down his chin. She reached across and licked it, taking a taste of him, the salt on his skin mingling with the juice, sour sweet.

What neither of them noticed, as they ate slices of guava and sat looking at the view, was the shadow that had fallen over the gray-weave Utility rug. Somebody was standing between them and the sun. Somebody with horns. It was Betty.

Neither Alicia nor Cecil saw her, but Herbert did. He wrote a whole page of notes in "Outgoings" as he watched his cousin watch her sister. He watched Betty watching Alicia. He watched her staring at Cecil, at his hands and face and hair and wrists. He watched as she gazed at him. And he analyzed her stance and face and eyes and the shades of envy and resentment and bitter sibling love therein that he knew and understood all too well.

That night, Herbert enjoyed the best night's sleep he'd had in months. In his dreams, the behavior of the dwarfs had been held temporarily in abeyance. Snow White leaned slowly down toward him, revealing her breasts trembling in their low-cut smocked blouse. She reached forward to kiss him gently on his lips. There was an unfamiliar taste on her tongue. It was guava. Not that Herbert realized this. It would be thirty years and a revolution in international air-freight management before he'd taste a guava again and realize this.

11.5 The Hedge Sparrow (1)

I'VE TAKEN TO walking in the park in the mornings. With the old ladies and the junkies and the underemployed. We sit on the benches and watch the commuters walking briskly to work and admire their purposefulness. There's a bond between us. We sit and watch the great stream of humanity passing us by before drifting back off to our half-lives.

It's not that I'm unemployed. I have my research. I even have a grant. And Peter, my supervisor, is encouraging. He seems to think that my work has merit. But I can't help thinking that's academia for you. If he didn't believe my thesis was worthwhile, he'd be out of a job.

It was Alistair's idea that I go back to my Ph.D. Two years ago my boss at the consulting firm where I was working called me into his office. It was the end-of-year review, and I thought I was going to be given a pat on the back and sent on my way. He motioned me into a chair on the other side of the desk.

I sat down awkwardly, but that was the fault of the chair. We both knew I was good at my job. He smiled at me.

"So, Rebecca. You know that I don't have a problem with your work, of course." He shifted in his chair, his gut hanging forward.

"Oh," I said. "That's good."

"But in any plane, there's only one pilot."

I hesitated.

"Yes . . . ," I said eventually.

"Do you understand what I'm saying?"

I shook my head.

"Only one person can fly the plane."

"Right."

"The rest are crew."

I stared at him. It reminded me vaguely of a conversation from a long time ago.

"Like an air hostess?" I asked. He laughed magnanimously.

"I think you'll find they're called 'flight attendants' these days, but yes, you get the picture. I lead, and it's your job to follow that lead. To keep things running smoothly."

I opened my mouth, but I wasn't sure what response was required. I closed it again.

I felt my face go hot. My tongue stuck in my mouth.

"And I'm afraid that I make the decisions. You're doing a good job. That's the important thing. I'm sorry that we couldn't give you a pay raise this year. But we'll see what we can do next year."

He folded his arms to show the interview was over. I walked back out into the office, uncertain what had just passed.

Later I found out that my six male colleagues had received an 8 percent pay raise. I was the only female member of staff. And I got nothing.

I simmered for a week. And then I confronted him.

"I can pay my staff what I want," he said and shrugged his shoulders. "It's as simple as that."

I sat and waited.

"You can," I said eventually. "I just want to know what I'm doing wrong."

"It's not to do with doing anything *wrong*. Don't be so reductive."

"Reductive?"

And then he lost his temper. "There's an argument that middle-aged men with children should be paid more. I'm not saying I agree with it, I'm just saying there's an argument, that's all." He leaned toward me, his face red, angry. "If you're going to be a *troublemaker*, life could become very uncomfortable for you."

I walked back to my chair. For a week, I did nothing. I went over and over it in my mind but I didn't understand. Why *tell* me that he was paying me less? Why tell me that he was paying me less because I was a woman? I rang Lucy and asked her.

"It's power," she said. "It's not enough that he screws you, he wants you to know you're being screwed. It's absolutely textbook bullyboy behavior. It's also illegal. Sue him."

I didn't sue him. I walked. I wrote to my old supervisor and Alistair offered to support me. He seemed vaguely pleased.

"My salary's big enough for both of us these days anyway," he said. As if that was the point.

I sat on the bench and watched the world sweep by. The women in their uncomfortable heels. The men with dandruffed collars. I thought I'd enjoy going back to academia. But I'm struggling. Alistair leaps out of bed every morning and rushes off to his department. He whistles and hums. I can tell he's happy. He believes there are answers. He even knows what the questions are. The great god Science is his metanarrative. I thought that went out in the nineteenth century, but I'm wrong. As ever.

Me? What do I believe? I'm not sure anymore. I watch *Coronation Street* and see trees but not woods.

I take bread sometimes and feed the birds. The squirrels too. They're urbanized squirrels; they've evolved to their environment. They come right up and take food out of your hand, strutting across the grass, stealing crusts from the blackbirds and the small brown sparrows.

Alistair told me about the hedge sparrow once. The dunnock. How it had been studied by generations of ornithologists, bird-watchers, zoologists. It mates for life.

"And then they discovered DNA testing," said Alistair. "And found that ten to fifteen percent of all dunnock offspring are not biologically related to the father. The tabloids had a field day with it."

I shredded another piece of stale bread and threw it onto the grass. A bird (a common or garden sparrow? a cockney sparrow? a hedge sparrow?) hopped forward. It looked at me sideways, its eye gleaming brownly. I tried to imagine it sneaking around its partner's back, booking hotel rooms, buying lingerie. I'd always assumed the animal kingdom was above that kind of thing.

"It's because you see what you want to see," Alistair had told me. He had a point to make, of course. There was always a point that had to be made. "You screen out data that doesn't match your expectations. Human observation in any experiment is never enough. It is why you must always cross-check your results. The brown hedge sparrow. The red herring."

I pulled another piece of bread out of my bag.

"They're quite tame, aren't they?"

I looked up. The voice was coming from a man standing a few yards from my bench. I held my hand up to my eyes to look at him, squinting against the sun.

He was young, in his twenties, wearing a uniform, and was looking at me.

"They've probably been drinking Special Brew." I motioned to the pile of empty cans next to the bin.

"Can't say I blame them."

He had a dog on a lead. It was an Alsatian and sat, complacently, preserving its energy.

"Hello, dog." I reached down and patted its head.

"He's called Duke," the man said and leaned down to adjust the dog's collar. As he straightened himself, I caught him, just for a moment, looking at my legs.

"Hello, Duke." I petted his ears. "Are you a . . . policeman?"

"Dog patrol. With the council. We go round the parks. You know, check on the junkies, the alkies. Makes a nice change to talk to someone normal, I can tell you that. All I have is weirdos all day."

I tucked a strand of hair behind my ear. "Well at least you've got Duke . . ."

"Too right. I'd get a dog, if I were you, for protection. Young lady like you. I bet you get some offers."

I couldn't be sure, but I think he leered. Was he chatting me up? I perked. He wasn't bad-looking. He was male, anyway, and young. Youngish.

"So, is he trained?"

"Oh yeah. I've trained him. I get him to go for the blacks. They're the ones who cause all the trouble."

I stood up quickly, as if I'd been caught looking at child pornography or peeing on someone's grave.

"Bye," I said and walked briskly out of the park. I spent the rest of the day nursing my fury.

How dare he? I felt weak with anger. It was only later, when I'd calmed down a bit, that I stopped and wondered if my anger was caused by the fact that he was a racist. Or that a man had fancied me, and he had turned out to be a creep.

That evening, as I was cooking dinner, I told Alistair what he'd said.

"So?"

"So? Don't you find it depressing?"

"Hmm," he said. I was cooking and he was checking through his post. I hesitated. His face was a study of inattention. He skimmed the contents of a letter and took a sip of his wine. "Uh-huh."

I stirred the sauce and watched Alistair as he turned over the piece of paper and started to read the other side.

"He tried to make a pass at me."

Finally, he looked up from his letters and turned toward me. "Did he?"

He hesitated. I waited expectantly. He stood up and walked toward the stove. "So? What's for dinner then?"

Part Twelve

experiment *n* **1**: a test under controlled conditions that is made to demonstrate a known truth, or to examine the validity of a hypothesis

12.1 The Hedge Sparrow (2)

THERE'S A RUSSIAN PROVERB that Alistair likes to quote: the only exact science is hindsight.

It's called "retro-fitting." Evolutionists do it all the time. It's where you know the end result and work backward from there. You amend your hypothesis to account for a new piece of evidence. Like with the dunnock, for example, the hedge sparrow. You know the female dunnock is unfaithful, so you work out how and why and then form a coherent thesis to account for it. The only problem is that it may be true. But then again, it may not.

I've started going through his pockets. Looking at his credit card bills. I'm not sure what I'm looking for. I'm just looking.

12.2 noblesse oblige *n* : benevolent, honorable behavior considered to be the responsibility of persons of high birth or rank

THE AMERICANS never arrived. There was a letter instead, typewritten this time, filled with a list of job promotions ("Bob is now a Vice President of his company!"), favorable school reports ("Celine has won a scholarship for being the Most Promising Student at Meadow High!") and athletic endeavors ("Joe is captain of his football team for the third year running!"). At the end of the letter was the usual handwritten PS.

"We're real sorry that we never got to meet you all. However, we remember you nightly in our prayers and hope that God will bless your family in this year as he has blessed ours."

My mother threw down the letter. "Ha! God botherers! I knew it! There had to be something wrong with them." There was a PPS too.

"PPS. What do you think of the new computer? Neat, huh?"

"A computer?" said our father. "Well, well."

My mother started gathering up the dishes but she couldn't quite cover her disappointment.

"Well," she said. "Not good enough for them, were we?" I checked the envelope and found some photos of their British holiday. Snaps taken outside Buckingham Palace and the Tower of London. I looked at them longingly. I'd never been to London.

I kicked my legs back and forth beneath the breakfast bar, studying the photographs and the faces of my American cousins. You could tell they weren't English, although at first I couldn't put my finger on why. Perhaps it was their shoes. They wore brilliant white tennis shoes that didn't look like they'd ever been grass stained or stepped accidentally in dog poo.

I read through the letter again and its roll call of achievements. I suspected that my mother was wrong. I could never have been an American. Even if I'd been born there.

She was banging plates into the dishwasher. "Actually, I'm pleased that they're not coming. I simply don't have the time."

It was true: preparations for the Big Day were snowballing. I was thoroughly enjoying being swept along by the national mood of excitement and looking forward to Doing My Bit. Tiffany, on the other hand, was experiencing mixed emotions toward The Wedding. She enjoyed watching the pictures of Diana as much as the rest of us, but she still found it hard to believe that it would never be her.

"Never mind, Tiff," said my father, ruffling her hair. "He probably picks up the BBC with those ears anyhow." She scowled, and not just because he'd called her Tiff. She didn't like it when my father made rude remarks about the Royals. She had her sights set on a new target. Not Randy Andy (too much of a playboy), but Prince Edward. I found a notepad covered with pages and pages of swooping signatures. "Tiffany Windsor," they said. "Tiffany Windsor, Tiffany Windsor, TIFFANY WINDSOR!"

She was in the lounge practicing her deportment, walking back and forth with a cookbook on her head. I looked at her doubtfully.

"Isn't he a bit old for you?"

She frowned. "Charles is twelve years older than Diana," she said. "And everyone knows that they're a match made in heaven."

The cookbook slipped off her head and fell to the ground. Her voice assumed a cruel edge.

"When I do marry Edward, *you're* not going to be invited to the wedding."

She was wearing a high-collared frilled shirt and a string of fake pearls she'd bought in the sales that made my father choke on his coffee.

"Blimey!" he said when he saw them.

Tiffany frowned. "Really, Daddy, one shouldn't swear."

"Oh, shouldn't one?"

"Not in front of children or servants, no."

He raised an eyebrow. Tiffany sighed then walked out the room, slamming the door behind her.

Worse was to come, however. She borrowed a copy of Nancy Mitford's *Noblesse Oblige* from the library and started to berate my mother for saying "serviette," and on the evening when we had smoked haddock with poached egg for our tea, she refused to use her fish knife on the grounds that they were "pretentious."

"But, they're Sheffield Steel those, top quality," said my mother. "I got them as a wedding present!"

Tiffany looked at her pityingly. "The upper classes don't use fish knives. They're déclassé."

"I'll de-class you if you're not careful!"

"I like them!" I said. It wasn't often I had this kind of opportunity. Tiffany scowled at me and headed for the door.

Just as Lady Diana and Prince Charles had struggled to keep the numbers down to the twenty-five hundred who would fit inside St. Paul's, so my mother agonized over her invitations. She wrote list after list, adding names then crossing them out. There were no heads of state or foreign dignitaries among our immediate neighbors and family, although I pointed out that Aunty Suzanne and Uncle Kenneth had been abroad an awful lot. My mother chewed the end of her pencil.

"Do be quiet, Rebecca." A thought occurred to her. "The Alis!"

She added their name to her list with a triumphal flourish. It was the start of the campaign for the Big Day, and since Tiffany had taken to locking herself in her room with her new personality, my mother had no choice but to promote me to second-in-command. It was hard to say who was more surprised at this development.

"I'm relying on you." She wagged her finger at me. "Don't mess it up now, Rebecca." I nodded then shook my head, relishing the prospect of my new adult responsibilities.

"Right," she said. "You can start by helping me change Damien's nappy." I was about to object (Damien seemed to be going through a stage of excreting liquid manure) when I caught sight of her face and changed my mind. It would be a pity to be demoted so quickly.

Together we hefted him into the bathroom. "He's such an easy baby," said my mother as I handed her a cotton wool ball and he gurgled away on the changing mat. "Unlike *some* I could mention."

Afterward we went back downstairs and Operation Royal Wedding commenced in earnest. There were invitations to be designed and written and delivered. A menu to be planned, outfits to be considered. It was in more minor areas, however, that my expertise was employed. Running up and down the stairs, for example, or licking envelopes shut.

"Rebecca, could you go and check how many serving dishes I've got?" My mother was sitting at the kitchen table, her lists splayed out in front of her. I leaped to my feet and opened the cupboard door.

"One . . . two . . . three . . . four . . . Do I count this one? Five!"

"Five? Hmmm. Okay, thank you."

My ears burned with rare pride. I couldn't help but feel I was an important, perhaps vital, member of the task force. I returned to my position at the table and awaited my next instruction. My father rustled his newspaper impatiently.

"Really, Doreen. They're a bunch of upper-class twits who live off our taxes. I really don't see how this is something to celebrate."

My mother looked up briefly. "You always did have your Bolshie tendencies, didn't you, James? You'd probably prefer it if Lenin was getting married, wouldn't you?"

My father looked as if he was about to say something, but then changed his mind. "Doreen? You're not getting too worked up about this, are you?"

She glared at him. "What precisely do you mean 'worked up'?"

He opened his mouth as if he was about to say something, but then seemed to think better of it and went back to the football results.

My mother stared at him for a moment or two longer and then turned her attention to me. "All right, Rebecca, could you go and check the number of tumblers? At least *someone* is being helpful around here."

I ran into the lounge. Was I the only member of the household apart from my mother who appeared to fully comprehend the gravity of the occasion?

Tiffany was steadfast in her refusal to be involved.

"It'll be fun!" I said. She looked at me with pity.

"Don't we know *any* baronets?"

My mother was revising her menu and didn't look up. "Pardon?"

Tiffany wagged her finger at her. "You shouldn't say 'pardon.' You're supposed to say 'what.'"

My mother looked up from her paperwork. "If you're trying to be funny, young lady, you can go to your room."

Tiffany slunk out of the lounge while I bounced on the balls of my feet, Martina Navratilova at the baseline, waiting for the next shot.

"Rebecca, could you fetch volume three of my *Supercook* cookbook and bring it in here?"

I leaped up and scampered back to the kitchen.

"Thank you," said my mother when I handed it to her. "We make quite a good little team, don't we?"

And we smiled at each other; imperfect reflections of the same pair of lips.

12.3 The Universal People (1)

ALISTAIR WAS HAVING DINNER with his editor, and for reasons I didn't understand, or that he hadn't made clear, I was expected to attend.

I spent a long time getting ready, although I wasn't sure why. I dallied in the bathroom, had a long hot soak, experimented with hair products, used blusher on my cheeks. I wanted to give myself color, animation.

There are all sorts of things pinned up in our bathroom. Postcards, pictures, cuttings from magazines. Alistair put up a new one the other day. He's ripped it out of something, because the edges are all ragged and the paper is already starting to yellow. It's called "Donald E. Brown's List of Human Universals," and according to the explanatory note, it was compiled in 1989. An anthropologist, Donald E. Brown presumably, created it by examining a selection of ethnological and historical records. From those, he compiled a list of traits common to all people across space and time. Only those traits that are shared by all are included.

The Universal People

The list includes:
Snakes, wariness around
Economic inequalities
Economic inequalities, consciousness of
Envy
Envy, symbolic means of coping with
Memory
Black (color term)
Conflict
Mealtimes
Marriage
Jokes
Metaphor
Right-handedness as population norm
Rape
Statuses, ascribed and achieved

Sexual jealousy
Self as subject and object
Fear of death
Figurative speech
Judging others
Preference for own children and close kin
Private inner life
Onomatopoeia
Proverbs, sayings

I'm not sure why the bathroom should be the place to ponder the nature of humanity, but in our flat that's just the way it is.

I unscrewed my new lipstick, carefully applied it, then wiped it off. Too pink. Not me. I tried an old browny-colored one instead. It seemed to work a bit better. I stared at my hair in the mirror and squeezed out some gel onto my hand and rubbed it over my scalp. This was a mistake; it felt sticky, unwieldy. I decided to wash my hair again and hung my head over the edge of the bath and showered it with water.

I wrapped it in a towel and sat on the edge of the bath to wait for it to dry off a bit. I read the list. I've become slightly obsessed with the list. It's like a stock take of the human condition. What is universal, what is particular. There are 352 of them in total. Envy is there. That's a universal. Family. Marriage. Memory. They're all universals. Sexual jealousy, that's a universal too. I've considered making a photocopy of it and sending it to Tiffany. I'm sure she could find a use for it. Sibling rivalry is not there. Nor ambition. These, apparently, are more localized concepts.

I plucked my eyebrows. I looked in the mirror and tried to decide if this was an improvement or not. It was hard to tell. I still looked like me, just with thinner eyebrows.

"Proverbs, sayings" pleases me the most. Although they vary, of course, from culture to culture. I heard a good Japanese one the other day: if the father is a frog, the son will be a frog. Tiffany, surely, would be able to find a use for that.

The Darwinian interpretation of proverbs is that they are clichés that have proved their fitness over time. The survival of the tritest, perhaps. Or, as we in the Monroe household would have said: if it ain't broke, don't fix it.

·   ·   ·

The restaurant was, predictably, uncomfortable and overpriced. Alistair was in his element. He and the editor swapped pieces of gossip. His wife seemed to be there to prove that this was an informal social occasion. I assumed I was fulfilling the same role and ate my way steadily through the breadsticks.

"So?" said the editor's wife. "How many months gone are you?"

Alistair stopped his conversation mid-flow. I blushed.

"She's not pregnant," he said. "She's just big-boned."

When we got home, Alistair put on the kettle. He seemed to be on the point of saying something to me, then changed his mind.

"What?" I said. "What is it?"

He hesitated then shrugged the palms of his hands at me. "You could try and make a bit more of an effort, you know."

12.4 observe *v* 4 : to say casually; remark

LATER, when my mother and father had gone to look at bedding plants at the garden center, I went through to the lounge and switched on the television.

"Turn that down!" Tiffany was sitting at the dining table, her brow furrowed in concentration. "I'm doing my biology homework!"

I sighed and reluctantly turned the volume down.

"Rebecca?"

I turned to her suspiciously. "What?"

"What color eyes did Grandpa Monroe have?"

"Blue, I think."

"He can't have."

I frowned and looked at her. Tiffany had a habit of only asking questions to which she already knew the answer.

"Why not?" I said.

"Nanna and Grandpa Arnold have blue eyes. Mum and Dad both have blue eyes. Grandpa Monroe had blue eyes, and Granny Monroe has blue eyes. It's not right. Blue's recessive."

"So?"

"I've got brown eyes!"

Tiffany was always trying to catch me out. I suspected it was a trick question. "So?"

"Nobody's got brown eyes in our family!"

I couldn't be bothered to follow her. *Happy Days* had just started and I was keen to watch.

"Why don't you get the photo album?" I said.

"You get it."

"You're the one who wants to know."

"If you don't get it, I'll tell Mum it was you who spilled tomato sauce on the hall carpet."

Tiffany was staring at me through narrowed eyes. I went and fetched the photo album. We flicked back through the pages, but the only photos of Grandpa Monroe were in black-and-white.

"Look!" I said. "They're the same color, see, as Granny Monroe's. And hers are blue, so his *are* blue."

Tiffany studied the album intently. "Blue's recessive. I've got to have got a brown-eyed gene from somewhere."

It was as I'd suspected all along: a trick question. I turned off the television with a sigh and made to leave the room. As usual, Tiffany had won.

12.5 The Deductive Fallacy (2)

Question.

I am . . .

a. *Big-boned?*
b. *Fat?*
c. *Pregnant?*

THEY'RE NOT mutually exclusive of course, but when I peed on a stick this morning, there were two blue lines.

Part Thirteen

fruition n : enjoyment, attainment of thing desired, realization of hopes, etc.

13.1   memory *n* 10 : the capacity of a material, such as plastic or metal, to return to a previous shape after deformation

I WENT TO SEE Alicia again yesterday. It was a good day, Herbert told me when he met me at the station, and she was surprisingly lucid when I arrived. We dug out the old albums and looked at the photos of my mother and Suzanne as children. Herbert pottered around in the background, so quietly that most of the time I forgot he was there.

"That was the day your mother learned to ride a bicycle," she said, pointing at a photo of a small, plump toddler standing on the doorstep, a huge smile across her face. "She was so proud of that. We got training wheels and she had this little red bicycle that she rode up and down the street."

We stared at it together. I found it hard reconciling this clean, unmarked, all-smiling version of my mother with the one in my head. I hesitated then looked at my grandmother.

"Did . . . When . . . Was she always prone to . . . ?"

Alicia turned and looked at me. "It came on later. She was always a very happy little girl. Well, until my . . ."

"Until?"

"Very happy," said Alicia quickly. "Very determined to make something of her life. And look, there's Suzanne."

She pointed at a different photo. Suzanne was standing by my mother's side, looking intently into the camera.

"It's funny, isn't it, the way they were so different," I said.

"They were. From the day they were born. Chalk and cheese. Your character is something you're born with, you know. You'll find that out when you have children."

I turned sharply toward her but she didn't look up.

"Maybe I won't have children."

She reached across and patted my hand and smiled at me. Her head shook from side to side. I flicked over the page in the album and felt my ears start to burn.

"We don't have much of a track record in our family," I said.

She didn't say anything. We sat in silence for a minute or two and stared at the photos and then she squeezed my hand.

"Lightning doesn't strike twice," she said. Although of course it does. All the time.

Later we sat and watched television together. It was the news and then a documentary about something or other. I wasn't really paying attention and Alicia nodded off.

She woke with a start. "He wouldn't let me go, but I went anyway."

"What?"

"Filey."

I looked at her, trying to catch her train of thought. "Filey?"

"What was the old bat called? The one in Filey? I always forget that." She stared at the ceiling for a moment or two. "He was the first man I ever went to bed with."

I felt disorientated in time, in space. Did she really just say that? *"Cecil?"*

"Al-eesha Crag-lay, he said when he saw me. He couldn't believe it. I couldn't believe it either, but there you go."

She smiled and stared at me.

"So ignorant," she said. "I was so ignorant."

There was a cough. I turned around. Herbert was there standing by the door.

"Anyone want a cup of tea?" he said.

13.2 Filey (1)

IT *WAS* IN FILEY. It's all there. In Alicia's diary. I just hadn't got to it. Cecil had a day off from the rhubarb sheds and went to Filey, on the long, straight Yorkshire coast.

"Can I come?" Alicia had asked. "Please?" But he'd just shaken his head. He caught the train and wandered along the front watching the waves. It was plain that summer was over. The sea already had a wintry gray tinge to it, and there was a nip to the air. The seasons had turned.

Filey was where he'd done his basic training. Marooned up at Humanby Moor. On his days off, he would promenade with Glen, his friend from home, along the sea front. They ate fish and chips out of newspaper, watching the waves, and drank pints of bitter in the pubs, protected from disapproving stares by the double flash on their airman's berets. In the Palace Dance Hall, they'd done the two-step and the tango with the bolder of the land girls and the off-duty munitions workers.

It had been different when the country was at war. They'd been accepted, welcomed even. In peace, the country had changed. There was a new edge of hostility that punctured the air around him.

"Sunnyside" was a handsome Victorian guesthouse with gables and a smartly mown lawn. A few late-blooming flowers lined the sides of the path.

"Hel-lo?"

The voice rose up from the flower bed. Cecil could make out the firm flowered haunches of a middle-aged backside. The rest of what he assumed was the landlady was hidden behind a bush.

"Can I *help* you?" The woman straightened up, her eyes narrow with suspicion.

Cecil removed his hat and smiled at her. "Yes, ma'am. I've booked a room."

"*You?* You have booked a room?" She parroted his words, not understanding.

"Cec-il Johns-ston," he said and extended his hand. She didn't take it but watched him as if he was a greenfly on one of her prize-winning roses.

"You're Cecil Johnston?"

"Uh-huh."

"And you've booked a room?"

He nodded his head.

But Mrs. Wetherby was not going to be taken in like that. "Well I'm afraid that, well, I didn't realize. I take cash payment in advance, you know."

She'd blown it. She'd become flustered, and now there wasn't any choice. She'd have to let him stay. She'd told her husband that telephone would be the death of them, but oh no, he said it was progress.

"Dining room," she said, pointing at a dark room at the back of the house. "Breakfast is at eight. Sharp if you don't mind."

The hall was filled with dark, wooden furniture, the carpet a blood red, frayed at the edges. "You're in here," she said, leading him to a small, cold room on the first floor. She called it the "Green Room" for no immediately obvious reason. "No visitors. No noise. No food in the room. No hot water after 7 P.M. I'll take the cash now if you don't mind. And I don't want any trouble."

He wandered along the front and, as the sky darkened, walked toward the Old Copper Kettle. Its electric light spilled out on the street, a puddle of orange. He opened the door, the bell tinkling as he went inside. A waitress, bored and sullen, was reading a magazine at the counter. She studiously ignored him for fifteen minutes and, when she finally brought his tea, made a point of letting it slop into the saucer. He drank it, lukewarm, three-quarters full, without complaint.

By the time he returned to Sunnyside, the house was completely still. The heavy Victorian furniture, the thick velvet curtains and the moth-eaten old carpet swallowed all noise and condensed it to occasional creaks and groans. In his room, he opened the worn, flowered curtains an inch or so and climbed into his narrow, hard, single bed. The sheets were cold. He shivered then said a prayer (of which Felicia would have been proud) and thought of Alicia (of which she would have been less proud). Almost immediately, he fell into a deep and heavy sleep.

. . .

He was woken by the sensation of something tickling his nose. Or maybe it was the smell he noticed first. A rich, milky smell like rice pudding or oatmeal porridge. Something was brushing against his skin. He lifted up his hand to bat it away, but it fell back again, filling his nose with a scent of heavy English puddings. It was then that he saw what looked like strands of hair. Strands of pale cream hair. He lay quite still. And then he sat bolt upright. "Al-eesha?" he said. Although it was more of a statement than a question. He knew she was there.

13.3 Filey (2)

THE HOUSE WAS SILENT; the only noise was the far-off sound of the sea, the waves plowing back and forth on the beach. Delicately, Alicia lifted herself inch by inch, then lowered herself into the tiny space on the mattress next to Cecil. Leaning over him, she let her hair fall and brush against his face. Her breasts fell forward and pressed against the cotton of her nightgown. It was cold in the room. Her arm goose-pimpled, the hairs rising slowly erect. Cecil lay with the sheet carelessly thrown off, his long thin frame loose-limbed in sleep. She'd never seen him sleeping before. His eyes shut, his long black lashes upon his cheek, his breathing heavy and regular.

He shifted in his sleep. She leaned over his face again and blew gently on his eyelids. He stirred, opening his eyes, but not seeing her. He lay motionless, taking deep breaths through his nose. And then he sat bolt upright in his bed.

"Al-eesha?" he said.

She didn't answer him, but blew gently against his cheek.

"Al-eesha. 'Ave you lost po-ssession of your sen-ses?"

But Alicia merely smiled at him.

They lay next to each other, their faces turned to each other, and breathed each other's breath. There was a gap in the curtains, and the moon had risen, almost full, but not quite, beautiful in its imperfection.

Their arms brushed against each other and the hairs flared in a static embrace. Cecil reached out a finger and touched Alicia's face.

"Al-eesha." It sounded like wind blowing under the eaves. He stroked her cheek.

"You should'na be here." The "shh" of "should'na" hung in the air. His words were soft, barely audible.

"Al-eesha," he said. "You should go." It was like the sound of the shingle moving on the shore, pushed by the waves, in and out. "You should go, Al-eesha." And he kissed the corner of her lips. Or perhaps he just breathed. A cloud passed over the moon, leaving them in darkness.

Slowly, Alicia reached out her hand and touched his face. She leaned forward and kissed the tip of his nose, his eyelids, his chin.

Outside, a car hooted its horn. A cat screeched. She felt his breath on her face, hot like the sun. With his finger, he stroked her hair. Then her face. Then his fingers, slowly, softly, inched downward. She felt him touching her lips, her chin, her neck.

The first few drops of rain rattled against the window.

"Cecil?" she said, but he didn't answer. She took deep breaths of him, memorizing him, imprinting him upon her nostrils, taking him down to the bottom of her lungs. The smell of cocoa-nut on a February evening mixed with coal smoke and malt. Of papaya overlaid with disinfectant. Of bloodred oranges and the juice of guava. And a very faint hint of sprouts.

"Al-eesha Craag-lay," he said, rolling the syllables around in his mouth and shaking his head. "Al-eesha Craag-lay."

And after that, they listened to the sound of the rain, more insistent now, beating against the window, and watched the final shimmer of moonlight sink beneath the window frame, knowing that there was nothing else to say.

13.4　Filey (3)

NEITHER OF THEM heard the telephone. Downstairs it rang and rang, until eventually Mrs. Wetherby appeared in a pink flannelette dressing gown and a head full of curlers. It was seven o'clock in the morning.

She picked it up reluctantly.

"Hel-lo?" Her voice was heavy with distrust. She had disliked the device from her very first acquaintance with it, and the previous day's events had only served to convince her of its natural perfidy.

She held the earpiece half an inch off her head, and listened. Her head cocked in a display of suspicion.

"*No!*" she said finally. The line went dead and she returned the receiver to its cradle with a small metallic tinkle that echoed through the house. She walked through the hallway with heavy deliberate steps and mounted the stairs, a grim satisfaction stationed on her face. And there in Room 3, she found the colored man molesting the young lady.

13.5　repercussion *n* : echo; recoil after impact; indirect effect or reaction of event or act

NOBODY ASKED Alicia what she was doing in Filey. She'd said she was going to Scarborough. To visit Sylvia's aunt. The question hung in the air of the house, air that wasn't moving. It was trapped, suspended. The curtains were drawn, the windows locked shut. Nobody asked. Apart from Betty, and no one listened to her.

Alicia was woozy and confused; her skin was sallow; the shadows around her eyes a bluey gray. The police doctor had injected her, she remembered that. She remembered the blood running from Cecil's head. And then nothing. Where was Cecil? Where was he? Dr. Allen prescribed a course of sedatives, sleeping pills and psychiatric evaluation. Mrs. Cragley ground up the pills into teaspoons of jam, which she put into Alicia's tea. Alicia's head moved in and out of fuzziness.

She wrote Cecil long, rambling letters in an unsteady hand. She covered pages and pages with spidery writing and sent them first class to Filey. Mrs. Cragley brought up trays of food that wouldn't be eaten, and washed her face and combed her hair and said, "There, there." She sat by her bed and said, "There, there, Alicia. You're all right now."

"Where's Cecil? Where is he?"

"Sshh. Your father will hear."

"I want Cecil."

"You're all right now."

"We were lovers, you know."

But Mrs. Cragley refused to be shocked. It was common in convalescents to want to test the boundaries. Alicia had had a tremendous shock. Things were bound to be confused.

"I love him."

Or at least blurred.

"Sshh. There, there. It's all right now."

"When will he come?"

But he didn't come. And he didn't write. Dr. Allen said that she must be kept calm and quiet. Her nervous system had suffered with the strain. No loud amusements or anything too exciting. Bed rest, he said.

Mrs. Cragley sat by her and wiped her forehead. Through the wall, Betty could hear her mother padding across Alicia's room delivering a hot cup of tea or a cold flannel. Betty didn't understand. When she'd made the telephone call, she really thought that even Alicia wouldn't be able to weasel her way out of this one.

When her mother was downstairs, she put her head around the door to Alicia's room.

"He's been put away." She waited for a reaction. "I heard them talking. The policeman said they were going to throw away the key."

Alicia stared at her. Betty waited for a moment in order to give her final statement its fullest impact.

"You're *never* going to see him again."

Alicia spat out the sedatives. She placed the sleeping pills on the roof of her mouth with her tongue and pretended to swallow, and when her mother left the room, she took them from her mouth and stored them in her bedside drawer.

Dr. Bryanston, a new doctor, came. "Delusional," he told Mr. and Mrs. Cragley, a common occurrence in cases of severe shock. Transference, too. Believed her attacker to be her lover. He prescribed her more tablets and went away again. Every day the pile of tablets grew. Alicia wondered how many would be enough.

And then she realized she was pregnant.

Part Fourteen

count down *vt* : repeat numerals backward to zero, esp. in procedure
for launching rocket, etc.

14.1 The Science of Happiness (3)

IT WAS THE FIRST Tuesday of the month yesterday. I wasn't going to go. I sat in the kitchen and drank coffee and looked at the clock, but eventually I got up and put on my coat. I was feeling queasy and hot. The Tube was overcrowded. In the end, I got off and walked. I had to fight my way through the station. Everyone seemed to be going in the opposite direction to me.

At the end of the usual tests, I was given a questionnaire to fill in. I ticked box after box until I reached the final page. My pen hovered over the paper. The final question said:

Are you:

    a. Very happy?
    b. Quite happy?
    c. Neither happy nor unhappy?
    d. Not very happy?
    e. Not at all happy?

I hesitated. I looked out of the window and chewed the end of my pen. Alistair was somewhere out there, I guessed, in the department, being important. I sat in the room, while the researcher, a man, looked on dispassionately.

Sometimes, I find science too bloodless a sport. He sat examining his nails, waiting for me to fill in the form. I crossed my legs and tapped my pen against the piece of paper. Was I (a) very happy? or (e) not at all happy?

.   .   .

Finally, I ticked a box, put on my jacket and walked out of the door. The researcher picked up my questionnaire with a bored expression.

(E). I ticked (E). Not at all happy.

14.2　**pregnant** *adj* 3 : teeming with ideas; imaginative, inventive

ALICIA FELT BETTER almost immediately. She got up from her bed and washed and put on a clean dress. Mrs. Cragley breathed a sigh of relief. Finally her daughter was beginning to mend.

She had that wonderful early pregnancy glow that some women experience, when their faces turn pink and their hormones sing. Being pregnant was a revelation. She could feel Cecil's child growing inside her. Every day her body changed. Her breasts became large and sore. Her belly swelled. She flushed the sleeping pills down the toilet, and looked out of the window for the first time in weeks. It was her baby. Cecil's baby. She couldn't believe that her body was capable of such a miracle. Her stomach became bloated, and she fed it starchy foods. The baby was crying out for potato and rice and tapioca.

It pleased Mrs. Cragley to see her girl's appetite return. She must be getting better, a good sign. With extra milk rations she begged from the neighbors, she made thick creamy rice pudding cooked in the oven, and watched with satisfaction as Alicia ate bowlful after bowlful. There were very few things that a spot of home baking couldn't cure.

"Mum? Dad?"

It was a Thursday night and they were all in the kitchen. Mrs. Cragley was cooking. It was a hot pot and she was only at the braising stage. A worry line creased her forehead; she hadn't even started on the potatoes. Mr. Cragley was doing the crossword. Betty sat at the table with her schoolbooks. Alicia made one last look around the room. She took it all in—the linoed floor, the cooking range, the calendar of *England's Glorious Roses*, the teapot sitting on the table wearing its tea cozy, the tea towel from Scarborough illustrating "Nautical Knots" that hung on the wall. A recipe book from the Ministry of Food called *Make Your Meat Go Further* lay open on the counter; the radiant heater on the wall was throwing down heat and light; the oilcloth on the table had the slight nick in it where Betty had rested a too hot saucepan. On the corner of the dresser sat the meat grinder in its cardboard box next to the dish containing spare buttons and a prewar postcard, faded now, of Skegness. Everything was in its place, where it had always been.

Alicia took a snapshot of the scene to file away in the back of her head with all her other Momentous Moments. This one would be entitled "The End of Childhood."

"I'm expecting," she said. There didn't seem to be any point in beating about the bush with it. Mrs. Cragley dropped her braising dish. Mr. Cragley breathed suddenly, painfully inward. Betty's mouth formed a wide, self-satisfied smile.

"I'm having a baby," Alicia said, in case they thought she meant visitors.

14.3 D-Day Minus Two

I STOOD with my arms outstretched while my mother unhooked all the curtains and threw them down to me. Together we loaded them into the washing machine, then out onto the line to dry, then back into the house to be ironed.

She had composed a strict schedule of chores to be completed before the Big Day, "D-Day," my mother called it.

"What does the D stand for?" I asked. My mother hesitated.

"It's just an expression," she said decisively. "It doesn't *mean* anything."

"I thought . . ." but I trailed off after that. I thought all expressions meant something.

We ticked the completed tasks off our list as we went. Skirting boards, cleaned? Check. Rubber plant, dusted and polished? Check. We scoured the shops for the correct size of cocktail sausage, paper doilies in gold and silver and a jar of glacé cherries that would decorate the trifle.

"It's a family recipe," she said.

There seemed to be some dim ancestral blueprint for party giving that my mother felt bound to follow.

"There's always got to be a trifle. It's your grandfather's favorite, you know."

I stood next to the ironing board with a spray bottle in my hand. Vaporous clouds of steam rose from the iron, misting my mother's glasses and settling as condensation on her nose. I skipped off to find some paper towel and handed it to her.

"Thank you, Rebecca."

I smiled at her and sprayed more water, anxious to get it just so. Together we worked out where the table for the buffet would stand, and I was assigned to fetch Aunty Suzanne's extra set of cutlery and folding director's chair. Damien had recently reached the crawling stage and had a habit of maneuvering himself into my mother's flight path, until she bought a playpen and caged him in a corner of the lounge like a gerbil. My father, marooned in his armchair, surrounded by an ebbing and flowing tide of cookbooks and china, met each new development with the same unbelieving shake of the head.

Forty-eight hours before D-Day, my mother put on her jacket, picked up her handbag and said, "Come on, then."

I looked around, but there was only me in the kitchen.

"Me?"

She smiled and nodded her head.

"Where to?"

"The hairdresser's."

"The hairdresser's?" I waited uncertainly for an explanation. My mother cut my hair in the bathroom with a pair of red-handled scissors and a look of acute concentration on her face.

"Well, you're too old for me to still be cutting it really, and besides you deserve a bit of a treat."

I couldn't believe it and ran and put on my shoes before she could change her mind and remember that it was Tiffany who deserved a treat, or somebody else. Anybody else. A cousin, perhaps. Or a neighbor. I jogged out to the driveway.

"Mum?"

"What?"

I hesitated.

"Can I sit in the front?"

She looked at me, her hand resting on the door handle.

"Oh, well, I don't see why not."

There was always a reason why not, but this seemed to have slipped her mind too. She opened the driver's door and I opened the passenger's door, and we both got in. My hands trembled on the seat belt.

The salon was called Curl Up and Dye and was presided over by a woman called Peggy, whose hair was like no hair I'd ever seen before. It was bright red and floated four inches off the top of her head.

After my hair had been washed, I sat in front of a mirror that reflected against the other mirrors. It showed the room as tiny rectangles, repeated and re-formed in other reflections. There were women everywhere, only women. Women with their hair wrapped in curlers and cotton wool and plastic bags. Women staring into mirrors. Women submitting to machines and contraptions, their heads encased in plastic hoods, or under attack from metal tongs. One woman had her head in a turban and was biting her lower lip anxiously. She reminded me of someone. I gazed at her uncertainly. And then I realized it was my mother. I hadn't recognized her. Her hairdresser, a woman called Cheryl, with dirty blond hair, unwrapped the towel from my mother's head and made loud tutting noises.

"Doreen! What did I tell you? I said you make sure you don't leave it three months the next time!"

I waited for my mother to launch a retaliatory reply, but none came. She made a spluttering noise that if I hadn't known better, I would have said was a giggle.

"I know," she said. "I know!"

"Honestly! And you've got such lovely hair, after all!"

I expected my mother to tell Cheryl to put a sock in it, or to get a move on because she didn't have all day, but instead she folded her hands and looked straight into the mirror in front of her. I sat in the corner of the room, waiting for Peggy to come and cut my hair, and realized that there was a part of my mother to which I had no access, where I didn't exist, where she was a woman sitting in a salon having her hair cut, not a mother in the kitchen cooking my dinner, or a wife in our car reading a map. I shivered slightly. It was as if I didn't know her at all.

14.4 The Science of Happiness (4)

I TRIED THE QUESTION on Lucy later. We were having lunch together at an old-style Italian restaurant where they flourished pepper grinders and Parmesan and called you "signora."

"Are you (a) very happy?" I asked her. "Or (e) not at all happy?"

"What?"

"It's a questionnaire I had to fill in."

She leaned over and selected a bread roll from the basket in front of us. "My therapist says I have issues. You know. Parents. Blame. That kind of thing. But I don't tend to let it bother me."

"I didn't know you saw a therapist."

"Doesn't everybody?"

"Alistair says it's a load of mumbo-jumbo."

Lucy put a breadstick in her mouth and rolled her eyes. "Alistair says a lot of things but I don't suppose even he believes half of it. He's professionally obliged to have certain opinions."

I shrugged my shoulders and studied the menu.

"So? How is our resident television star?"

"Oh, you know. Busy. Important. The usual."

"I don't know why you don't leave him. That would wake him up a bit."

"I'm married to him," I said.

"So?"

I hesitated and thought about it for a moment. I put down the menu and looked at my hands.

"I love him," I said simply.

.   .   .

When the pasta arrived, Lucy launched into a detailed dissection of her sex life. She'd just started seeing someone new and she was never one to spare the details.

"He's got huge balls. Do you think that's a *good* thing?"

I laughed and opened my hands in a noncommittal gesture.

"No, I'm not sure either. They get in the way, I can't help thinking."

"Lucy . . . ?"

"Hmm?" She took a mouthful of salad.

"Nothing," I said, quickly changing my mind.

We ordered espressos, and Lucy sat slowly stirring in three teaspoons of sugar.

"I need the strength," she said.

"Why?"

"To face the faceless men."

"What?"

She looked up. "I didn't get the promotion."

"Oh, I'm sorry," I said, surprised. Lucy is so capable, so confident, I couldn't imagine her failing at anything.

"Oh, well, " she said.

"Who got it?"

"This bloke they brought in from outside who I've spent the last three months training up."

"But why?"

She shrugged her shoulders. "What *really* annoys me is this idea that they try and make you think *you're* being paranoid. That if you think he's got the job because he's one of them—male, public school–educated, clubable—that *you're* the one who's got a perse-cution complex, when all the time they systematically discriminate against *anyone* who is not exactly the same as they are. You know how many nonwhite people my firm employs?"

I shook my head.

"Oh, quite a few. The cleaners are Bangladeshis. There's a couple of black secretaries. And it's rumored that there's an administrative assis-tant in accounts who's Asian. And that's it."

She was stirring her coffee so fiercely it slopped over the sides and into the saucer.

"You know how many female board members there are? None. I used to think that Suzanne was barking up the wrong tree, you know. That if you were good and worked hard, anyone could get on. But it's all bollocks."

We sat in silence for a while.

"So, what are you going to do?" I said. "Go elsewhere?"

"The hell I am. I'm a lawyer. I'll litigate. I can't believe you didn't let me sue your boss."

"Life's too short."

"Not for sexist pigs, it's not. It's far, *far* too long."

I've always wished I could be more like Lucy. Bolder, braver. More determined. Seeing her always cheered me up.

She flagged down a waiter and ordered two brandies.

"What are we toasting?" I asked.

"The level playing field," she said.

14.5   propose *vt* 1 : put forward for consideration, propound; set up as an aim

HERBERT WAS readying himself. Ahead of him was the Big Push. The Final Assault. He had been to the barber's and had a cut and a wet shave. He had applied antiseptic cream to his spots. In front of the bathroom mirror, he had practiced his walk. It was a John Wayne swagger with a touch of the Gary Cooper. A rolling of the hips; an attitude as much as a means of locomotion. It exuded precisely the mixture of manliness and authority that he required. He dabbed a touch of Brylcreem across his fringe. He was wearing his one good suit, a freshly laundered shirt, and a black and gray Viyella tie. He looked as good as he ever would. He stood upright, feet square upon the ground, and staring at the mirror, he saluted himself. The runt's time had come.

It was early evening, and there was an edge of light left in the sky as he walked down the street. He had reviewed the Alicia files. It was important to have all the information at one's fingertips. In his mind, he ran through the pages and columns, the facts that went back years. The facts that he had collected and written down and gathered into himself. The obscurer the fact, the more pleasure he felt. The first item Alicia sold in her capacity as a junior sales assistant? A pair of size 16 support stockings, made of a spiral loom to alleviate the pain and discomfort of varicose veins. The make of her three-piece electroplated brush set? Superbe. The place where she'd first kissed the black man? The rhubarb shed.

He'd reached Westgate, and crossed the Calder, passing the Chantry chapel, where traditionally travelers stopped to say a prayer. He paused, not knowing to which saint he should make his appeal. St. Casimir of Poland? The patron saint of bachelors. St. Peregrine Laziosi? The patron saint of skin disorders. How many times had he walked along here? A hundred? A thousand? But tonight, it was different.

By the time he reached the end of their road, his palms had stopped sweating and he felt nothing but an almost religious sense of calm. This was his destiny.

Alicia didn't even hesitate. She just said, "Yes. Okay then." Without bothering to look into his eyes. "Yes," she said. "I'll marry you." Herbert stood with his hands clenched into fists in his pockets, his face even more lopsided than usual from the strain of concentrating, and felt what? What was it he felt?

"Oh," he said.

It wasn't like he'd thought it was going to be. Not at all. He'd expected the sort of triumph he felt when Wakefield Trinity beat Sheffield in the Cup. Or when Yorkshire County cricket team wiped the floor with Lancashire. He thought it would be like that. The sudden overwhelming joy that made you want to jump up and down and hug someone, anyone. But it wasn't like that. He felt curiously deflated.

"I'll be off then," he said. "Shall I?"

"All right then," said Alicia. Herbert picked up. Those eyes, that hair. That skin. His. He leaned forward to kiss her. She turned very slightly so his lips hit her cheek. And it was only then that Alicia looked at him. Her eyes reminded him of something, someone, although he couldn't put his finger on what.

"I'll be seeing you soon then."

"I expect so," Alicia said and went back upstairs.

14.6　The Science of Happiness (5)

THE WAITER appeared with the bill and a final flourish. Lucy leaned down to retrieve her wallet from her bag. I hesitated, watching her riffle through her credit cards, then, finally, spoke.

"I'm pregnant."

She looked up, wide-eyed. *"No!"*

I nodded.

A huge smile spread across her face. "Rebecca!" She looked amazed, overwhelmed. "I can't believe it! Congratulations! You must be thrilled."

I hesitated.

"Yes," I said. "Of course."

"What did Alistair say?"

"He hasn't."

She looked at me puzzled. "What do you mean?"

"I haven't told him yet."

Lucy stalled. "Why not?"

"You know his views."

"Yes, but . . ."

"I'm not sure. Anyway."

"Oh!" she said, as if suddenly seeing the light. "You haven't done a test."

We signed the checks, stood up, gathering our coats and bags around us, and made for the door. Outside on the pavement, I turned to her.

"I'm thinking of having an abortion."

She turned and looked at me. Her mouth fell open, undecided.

"Because of Alistair?" she said eventually.

"A bit. Partly."

"Well, *why?*"

I didn't answer for a while.

"They think it's genetic, you know, my mother's illness. I could pass it on."

She looked at me and put her arm around my shoulder.

And then I started to cry.

"Rebecca?" Lucy rummaged in her handbag and found a paper tissue and handed it to me. "You don't have to, you know. If you believed Alistair's line on the world, you'd never manage to get out of bed in the morning."

"Sometimes I don't."

"There's drugs for everything these days."

"I know." I struggled to find the words but couldn't.

"It wasn't *your* fault."

I didn't say anything. She hesitated.

"You know what Suzanne would say, don't you?"

I blew my nose noisily. "What? A Woman Has the Right to Choose?"

"No. Biology Is Not Destiny."

I managed a smile in spite of myself. "Yeah," I said. "Right."

Lucy opened her mouth to protest but closed it again. Neither of us were able to believe that anymore.

14.7 D-Day Minus Two (cont'd.)

WE WALTZED OUT of the salon as light as air and drove carefully home with the windows shut. I flipped my head from side to side, but my hair didn't move. It had been cemented into place by Peggy with "a little bit of spray," a chemical shower that I could still taste on my lips.

My mother paid with a check. I peered over her shoulder as she wrote it out. Twenty-nine pounds!

"Don't tell your father!"

I searched for a suitably conspiratorial reply.

"A nod's as good as a wink."

She snapped her handbag shut. "There's no need to be pert, Rebecca."

When we arrived home, my father was standing in the kitchen, an orange juice carton clamped to his lips, frozen in the spotlight of our unexpected entrance.

"Tra-la!" said my mother, launching herself into a 360-degree twirl. She seemed to have decided to pretend that she hadn't seen the orange juice carton.

My father stared at her as if she was a particularly difficult crossword clue. "You've had it cut?"

"Don't be obtuse, James. Of course I've had it cut. Well? What do you think?"

"Very nice. Very nice."

"Haven't you noticed?" She pouted at him, and turned down the corners of her mouth.

"Noticed . . . ?"

"I've had it highlighted."

My father looked visibly relieved. "Ah. That's what it is. It looks very nice, my dear." And he leaned over and kissed her on the cheek. "You look lovely."

She simpered and lowered her head and looked up through her eyelashes. I couldn't help but be impressed. I wondered if she'd been practicing it in front of the mirror too.

"You look like Diana!" I said.

She gave a high tinkly laugh. "Do I?"

My father did a double take, his spoon of Maxwell House hovering over his cup. "Oh dear God, no."

My mother pulled on her Marigold washing-up gloves with an abrasive rubber squeal. "The hall carpet is going to have to be cleaned, James. If you leave now, you should be able to get to the hire shop in time."

"Doreen!" Steam started to rise from the spout of the kettle. "This has gone too far, it really has. The reception is at Buckingham Palace as far as I'm aware, not our living room."

"It's a sitting room!"

I looked from my mother to my father. My mother was staring straight ahead of her, her lips pinched tightly together, my father at her back. I hopped from foot to foot and wondered if I should try and intervene.

"Dad! It's an historic occasion!"

"It's got to stop, Doreen. You're . . . getting too worked up over this."

My mother turned on the hot tap and started filling the washing-up bowl. When she spoke, there was a new, hard edge to her voice. Her words were precise, sharpened at the corners.

"I don't ask for much, James. I don't think I've been an overdemanding wife. All I am asking is that you *try* to support me. Do you think that is too much to ask for?"

The kettle was in full boil now. Steam rose and filled the kitchen. The plastic lid rattled against the stainless steel.

"We are *having* a party. I have invited *our* friends and *our* family and *our* neighbors. And I have worked my fingers to the bone preparing for it. It's always *me*. I had to fight to get you to marry me in the first place, although God knows why I bothered, and now I have to fight to get you to do anything at all to help me. Why is it always *such* a struggle?"

Her face had gone red. Her hair juddered under its hair-spray pelmet. It was one of the longest speeches I'd ever heard her make.

"Do you think that just this *once*, you might *try* and understand what it's like to be me?"

My father stood transfixed, the teaspoon of Maxwell House still in his hands. He turned, switched off the kettle and muttered something under his breath.

My mother recoiled, viperlike, and then spat. "*What?*"

I saw his shoulders slump and we all knew then that it was over. He fired a couple of dejected salvos above her head, but nobody was in any doubt that he'd lost.

"Nothing. I'll go. I'll go to the hire shop."

And he slouched out of the back door, while we put on our aprons and prepared to start on the pastry cases. My mother took a packet of flour and began sifting it into the bowl.

"Once a wimp, always a wimp," she said, lifting the sieve high into the air. Plumes of white powder filled the air. "He's got no backbone at all, your father. Right then, butter from the fridge please, Rebecca, look smart."

14.8   **trial** *n* **2** : a state of pain or anguish

THE TRIAL was held at York Crown Court. I know because I've seen the court transcript. It's there in my grandmother's box of documents. I don't know how she got it, but I've seen its yellowing pages and can testify for its veracity.

Mrs. Wetherby appeared as a witness for the prosecution. She had put on her best brown worsted wool suit and had worn a hat. She knew there was something rum about him, she told the jury, from the moment he appeared at her door. There was something suspicious about the way he walked and looked around him. She'd been worried all night, although her husband told her she should shut up and go to sleep. She wouldn't have let him stay, obviously, had he said he was colored, but that's the thing about the telephone, there's no way of telling. Anyhow, she hadn't slept well and then at seven o'clock in the morning, the telephone rang.

It was a woman's voice. A girl's even.

"There is an impropriety occurring in your house," she said. Those were the exact words. An impropriety. And then the line went dead.

She'd known immediately and had climbed the stairs with a sense of dread. Her heart was pounding. Knocking right up against her ribs, it was.

Anyway, she'd pushed open the door to Room 3, the Green Room they call it, the small one at the back, and there she saw with her own eyes the offense being committed. The colored gentleman—and at that point, Mrs. Wetherby pointed at Cecil in the dock—had pinioned the poor young girl to the bed with his arm. They were very still, which had made her think initially they were asleep, but of course, she knew now what was going on! And to think, it had all happened while she and her husband were sleeping under the same roof.

Mrs. Wetherby drew her handkerchief out of her bag.

The *poor* child, she said, and at this she let out a theatrical sigh. The *poor* child had been screaming and gibbering when the police arrived.

There were no witnesses for the defense.

Cecil's war record was read out in court, and then both sets of counsel were asked to sum up.

The prosecuting lawyer made a good deal of the word "wicked." "A depraved act of a wicked man," he said. "A man whom this country has welcomed with open arms, and who has turned around and spat in the face of the mother country." Alicia was variously "defenseless," "poor," "innocent," "the victim of an unspeakable crime" and "in all likelihood will be scarred by this incident for years to come."

It was no surprise to Cecil that when the jury shuffled back, none of them would look him in the eye. Guilty. The judge sounded thoroughly disappointed when he told the court that the maximum tariff the crime carried was a year.

14.9   couple *vt* 1 : to link together; connect

I WAS WRAPPING the scarf I'd bought for Barbara, Alistair's mother. I'm not sure when it was that I assumed responsibility for remembering his parents' birthdays, and choosing their Christmas presents. It was just something that happened. One of those hundreds of moments that you don't even notice, until you wake up one day and discover that you've bled into each other; that you are no longer distinctly you; that you've merged, coupled.

"What do you think of it?"

I held up the scarf. He studied it for a moment.

"She'll love it."

He said it with the absolute conviction that he was right. Alistair has this confidence that the world will bend to his will. And it usually does. Was that it? I wondered. That he believed it would, and therefore it did? He was standing by the kitchen window, his face half-lit by the sun outside, the curve of his lips highlighted, his eyes shadowy.

"Okay. Ready." I attached the final piece of tape.

There was something about the light on his face, his stance as he leaned against the table, his eyes, semi-focused, that made me lean toward him. I couldn't help myself. I've always loved him like that, when he was thinking; when he was half in, half out of the world. I could smell toothpaste on his breath and the faint whiff of fresh sweat from underneath his shirt. I was struck by his solidity. By his thereness. Without thinking, I slipped my hand down the front of his trousers. His penis lay flaccid in my hand.

"We've got to go," he said. And he reached for the car keys, shaking me off like a dog after a bath.

14.10   marry *v* 1 : join (persons one to another in marriage)

THE SERVICE was short and to the point.

"I do," said Alicia. "I do," said Herbert. They signed the register, kissed each other quickly on the cheek, and then Herbert finally got to look into the eyes of his bride. It was then that he realized where it was he'd seen that expression before. The expression Alicia had worn on the day that he'd proposed. The one he recognized but couldn't put his finger on. He looked at her and Norma the ferret's eyes stared right back at him.

14.11 **couple** *n* **2** *phys.* : a pair of forces of equal magnitude acting in parallel but opposite directions

BARBARA APPEARED at the door in her best at-home smart casual wear. Tailored black trousers, a cotton silk top, discreet but expensive jewelry. Her hair was freshly colored and blow-dried. I always half-expected to see her in her tennis gear, glowing from the exercise but still perky and fresh. Barbara was in her late fifties yet retained a certain debbish youthfulness.

"Rebecca! Don't you look well. Come on in."

Martin, Alistair's father, stood behind her, with a hand resting on her shoulder in a way that struck me as posed.

"Hello, Rebecca."

He leaned down and gave me a kiss. He looked like an actor, I always thought. Somebody you'd seen playing the handsome, older surgeon or the high-flying barrister in a soap opera you couldn't quite remember. I always found it hard to believe he really was a professor and not just playing one.

We walked through the hallway to the dining room. I made a point of looking at the paintings on the wall. There was a pair of pictures above the hall table that I liked to study, a legacy of a watercoloring holiday in Tuscany. They showed the same hilltop town, the same foreground of wheat fields and sunflowers, the same distant views. But one was by him, and one was by her. It was only when you studied them closely that you realized they weren't the same at all. One had a fence, where the other had nothing but rolling fields. One had three cypress trees puncturing the sky, the other four.

"Which one's right?" I asked Barbara.

"Sorry?"

"The pictures. Which one's right?"

She gave a brittle laugh. "Oh, Martin, I expect. He usually is. You know the Betterton men."

She hurried off to the kitchen to check on the food, and the rest of us sat down in the dining room, a sanitized, airless, over-vacuumed room that looked out over the garden. The house was Barbara's kingdom, a territory she defended with new paint schemes and conservatories and bathroom suites.

I felt a sudden, overwhelming weariness. How many meals had I eaten here over the years? There was always the same studied politeness to the proceedings. Nobody was ever rude to one another. No one drank too much. I suspected it had always been like this. The carpets exuded the kind of hushed quiet that had never been disturbed by raised voices or overexuberant ball games.

"So how's the book coming on, Dad?"

Martin's subject was mechanical engineering. He wrote a book a year. A habit, he'd often remarked to Alistair, was good discipline.

"Oh, not so bad, not so bad. Got a new research assistant and she's cracking on with it, so that's been a big help."

I'd met a number of Martin's "research assistants" over the years. Who would have imagined that mechanical engineering could yield such a ready supply of blond, large-chested young women? He had once told me in a confidential manner that he thought female employees were more "malleable."

Barbara brought in the roast chicken and put it on the sideboard. In a carefully rehearsed maneuver, as Martin stood up to carve, she stepped back then hurried out again, to bring in vegetables arranged on flawless silver platters. A matching silver gravy boat followed, and large unwieldy serving spoons.

I watched while she apportioned the meat to four plates, surreptitiously reserving the choicest, most succulent pieces for Alistair. Her only son.

We passed vegetables around the table ("Carrots, Rebecca? Make you see in the dark, you know."), and then I watched Martin pass a forkful of chicken through his lips and chew it thoroughly and methodically before swallowing.

Barbara brandished a jug at me. "Gravy, Rebecca? Or are you dieting?"

I gave her a forced smile. "Yes please, Barbara!" I said, my voice bright and cheery.

Over the years, I've almost come to admire the determination with which she has tried to remake me in her image. Barbara has a trim, size 6, tennis-firmed waist and schoolgirlish calves. She'd never understood why her son hadn't married a woman more like her, less like me.

I watched her fastidiously place the tiniest amount of food on her own plate. Poor Barbara. She'd spent almost fifty years watching her figure, only for her husband to lust after fleshy twenty-five-year-olds.

Martin turned to me. "So, how's your thesis going?"

"Okay thanks!"

"What's it again? Popular music?"

"Popular *culture*."

"Oh yes. TV and whathaveyou, eh?" The end of the sentence drifted off into nothingness. I could see him struggling to find something else to ask.

"And what then? When you've finished it?" he said eventually.

I smiled at him but didn't offer any reply. I shrugged my shoulders instead.

"You could always teach," said Barbara, looking up from her plate. "I've always thought it's quite a good little job for women. You get all the school holidays, which is useful if you have children."

"Mum . . ." Alistair stared at his mother from across the table.

"Oh, Alistair, don't be tiresome. We all know what *you* think. But what about everybody else? Everybody I *know* has grandchildren; it's almost become embarrassing."

She gave a tinkly little laugh, to show that this was just another piece of familial small talk.

Alistair put down his fork and prepared to launch his reply, but Martin beat him to it.

"Barbara!" He turned to his wife, reproving.

"It's evolutionary whatsits, isn't it?"

Alistair responded automatically. "The desire to have children is hardwired into our bodies by evolution. But we're not slaves to our genes. We don't go round clubbing our rivals. We don't *have* to have children."

I wondered how many times I'd heard him recite that. I could have said it with him, word for word, although possibly I wouldn't have been quite as convincing.

Martin put down his knife and fork and looked at me sympathetically.

"I wouldn't take it personally, Rebecca." And he leaned across the space between us and patted my knee. "*I* think you're a little cracker."

There was a silence while I sat and felt the pressure of Martin's hand on my knee. I opened my mouth to say something. And then I saw Alistair's face. The chicken stuck in my throat. My cheeks burned. He looked away, but it was too late. I'd seen his eyes.

And it was then that I realized. All this time I'd thought Alistair didn't want to have children. When it was just that he didn't want to have children with me.

14.12 D-Day Minus One

MY MOTHER was preparing sausage rolls in the kitchen and I'd been exiled. "Too many cooks," she said. "Go and get your sister and you can start blowing up the balloons. And you can change Damien's nappy then, if you don't mind."

I walked up the stairs. It was like Christmas Eve. The house was spotless and stacked with goodies we weren't allowed to touch. My father had been banned from the living room and had hovered on the patio until my mother finally packed him off to the pub.

"Well . . . If you're sure," he said and made a grab for his wallet before she could change her mind.

It was a warm evening. The air felt charged. Everything inside the house was expectant. My outfit for the Big Day was laid out, freshly ironed, on my bed. I couldn't believe that after all the waiting, the time had almost come.

I walked into Tiffany's room. She was lying on her bed, studying a piece of paper.

"Tiffany?"

"Knock before you come in!"

"Tiffany?"

"I'm busy."

"Mum says we've got to blow up the balloons."

Tiffany chewed the end of her pen, and then drew something on the piece of paper. I looked over her shoulder. It was a family tree.

"Let's have a look!"

I snatched it out of her hands. There were the names of all our family, with "BB" or "Bb" written under our names. There was me and Tiffany and Damien. There was our mother and father, but from Tiffany's name was a stem leading up to "Kenneth Edwards & Doreen Monroe."

"You've made a mistake."

Tiffany looked at me and said tartly, "I don't *think* so."

"You have! Dad should be there, not Kenneth!"

"No, Rebecca. I think you'll find that I'm quite correct."

I studied the piece of paper.

Tiffany hesitated and said nothing. Then her need to be right reasserted itself.

"I've got brown eyes. Nobody in our family has brown eyes."

"Well nobody's got my forehead either."

"That's different."

"How?"

"It just is. Blue's recessive. And brown's dominant. Mum and Dad both have blue eyes. So do all our grandparents. It's impossible. We studied it at school."

I couldn't see what she was getting at. "So?"

"So. Therefore it follows that my father is not my real father. It follows, furthermore, that Kenneth is my real father."

I looked up at Tiffany. Her eyes were shining.

"Kenneth?" I said. "*Uncle* Kenneth?"

Tiffany was wearing her triumphant air, the same one she used when she came top in maths or managed to procure the biggest helping of pudding.

"I don't understand."

"That's because you're still a baby. Kenneth and Mum. Mum and Kenneth."

I still didn't get it.

"They've been having an 'affair.'" She placed the word "affair" in quotation marks. It wasn't the kind of word we'd had much practice at saying in Beech Drive.

"What's an 'affair'?" I asked.

She looked at me dismissively.

"And *I* am their love child!"

I stared at her.

"You have to gather your clues. There was the guidebook, and the photograph . . . Nanna told us that Kenneth used to be sweet on Mum, you must remember that! You were there. And of course, I've always known that I was different."

It was like watching *Scooby Doo*, with Tiffany playing the girl with glasses who always figures everything out in a way that you'd never have thought possible but suddenly makes sense.

"What about me?" I said. I was always being left out. Couldn't I be a love child, not just an ordinary child?

Tiffany surveyed me with a critical eye.

"No," she said firmly. "You're too common to be Kenneth's."

14.13　　black hole *n* 4 : a dungeon or prison cell

I was in bed when Alistair came home.

"Headache," I said. He went off and brought me a cup of tea and sat by the edge of my bed.

"Time of the month?" he asked. I tried to drink my tea but couldn't. There was something stuck in my throat.

Later, I rang the clinic to make the appointment. The nurse started telling me the drill but I interrupted her.

"I've had one before," I said and replaced the receiver with a click.

I went back to bed and picked up my book and tried to read but I couldn't see. My vision was blurred. I put my hand to my face. And it was only then that I realized I was crying. Big salty drops fell onto the page, wrinkling the paper.

Alistair walked into the bedroom to look for something. I tried to cover my face with the duvet but too late.

"You'd feel much better, you know," he said, "if you got up and did something."

14.14   **result** *vi & n* **1** : have outcome or end in specified manner, *esp* in failure, success, etc.

A Party
To Celebrate the Wedding of
Prince Charles and Lady Diana Spencer
July 29, 1981, 24 Beech Drive,
Middleton

Invited Guests
Alicia Arnold
Herbert Arnold
Cynthia Monroe
Kevin Huxley
Gloria Huxley
Kenneth Edwards
Suzanne Edwards
Lucy Edwards
Meera Ali
Rajiv Ali

Menu du Jour
Cheese straws
Chicken croûtes
Mushroom vol-au-vents
Ham bites
Sausage rolls
Scotch eggs
*
Bacon and cheese quiche
Coronation chicken

Ham "on the bone"
Mixed salad
*

Sherry trifle
Strawberry pavlova
Delia's squidgy chocolate log
Fruit salad
*

Coffee and "petits fours"
*

In the event, we never got as far as the trifle, the strawberry pavlova or the chocolate log. They sat in the fridge for days, until Tiffany eventually threw them out. And by then, our mother was dead.

14.15 The Universal People (2)

I WENT TO SEE if Alistair wanted lunch. He looked up, surprised, when he saw me, then kissed me quickly on the cheek.

"Why aren't you at the library?"

"Thought I'd have lunch with my husband."

He frowned and looked at his watch. "I'd love to but I've got a department meeting at two, and . . ."

"Don't worry. Just a thought. There's something I want to talk to you about."

Alistair looked at me, suspicious. "Is it . . . anything important?"

"Yes. It's important."

He hesitated.

"See you later. About eight?"

"I'll cook," he said, and I reached out and put a hand on his shoulder and kissed him on the lips. He tasted of the smell of grass. But then he always has.

I don't know why I decided to sit on the bench outside the university building. It was sunny, and I had to have my lunch somewhere. I didn't notice him at first. I was concentrating on my prawn cocktail sandwich and the headlines of the newspaper, but I spotted his walk out of the corner of my eye. Alistair walks purposefully. His shoulders back, his arms hanging loose. He strides. I think that's the thing about being with someone so long: your field of vision is adapted to them. They slot into place. There were lots of people walking across the courtyard, but they were background, unimportant detail, noise. Alistair, on the other hand, I noticed, without even looking.

I took a bite of my sandwich and read the headlines. "House Prices Set to Rise," "Killer Jailed for Life," "TV Presenter in Kidnap Drama." And then I saw her next to him. The graduate student. The one with the big tits. They were walking together, stride for stride.

14.16 marry *int* 2 archaic : used to express surprise, asseveration, indignation

WHEN ALICIA woke up, she wasn't sure where she was at first. It was her first morning as a married woman and she stretched out her arms and opened her eyes.

And then she remembered.

She turned her back on the sun pouring through the bedroom window and refused to get out of bed. She curled herself up into a ball, locked her arms around her knees, closed her eyes, pulled the blanket down over her head and tried to will her baby back to life. It was no good though. She couldn't be pregnant. Cecil hadn't done *that* to her.

Part Fifteen

experiment *v* **2** : to try something new, especially in order to
gain experience

15.1 D-Day

I WAS TWITCHING with nerves even though I'd missed hours of the warm-up and a lot of pleasurable speculation about The Dress because the lounge windows had failed a last-minute spot-check and had to be recleaned. Still, I could hear the BBC commentator's voice rising and falling from the TV in the corner of the lounge.

"And so, this is where Lady Diana, soon to be Princess Diana, will leave Clarence House accompanied by her father, Lord Spencer, on what will surely be the most memorable journey of her life."

Tiffany was wearing an expression that I was struggling to pin down until my mother found it for me.

"If you don't take that supercilious look off your face, Tiffany, I'll take it off for you. The bananas for the fruit salad still need chopping."

I had spent days agonizing over what to wear. I'd never been to a wedding before, and in the end I plumped for my red-flowered ra-ra skirt with a white T-shirt, accessorized with my red necklace and matching red bracelets. I combed my fringe down over my forehead, although it kept on kinking upward. My face mooned at me in the mirror. I sighed. Concealing my forehead was a battle that I knew I was forever destined to lose.

Tiffany had put on her all-white sundress and swept her hair up with combs. She'd sprayed it into place and outlined her eyes with blue-frosted liner. I wondered if my mother's blanket ban on the use of cosmetics had been relaxed of late. Or if she was just too busy worrying about her squidgy chocolate log. It had failed to set properly and looked like it might run off the plate. She'd been up since five, chopping and whisking and barking commands at us.

"Finished the windows!" I said.

She didn't look up though, but carried right on beating a bowl of cream with a metal whisk and muttering under her breath. "Don't know where the electric one's got to . . . It's *always* in the box in the cupboard . . . Of all the times to just go *missing* . . ."

She was wearing a new blue and purple Laura Ashley dress that tied in a bow at the back, blue high heels, purple earrings and her gold necklace. Her hair had been blow-dried and then curled with her Carmen heated rollers, and it bounced up and down as she rushed back and forth between the kitchen and the hall and the garden followed by me or Tiffany or my father or a combination of all three of us. Only Damien was exempted, on the grounds that he couldn't walk yet. He jiggled up and down in his baby bouncer and blew kisses at you instead, although at one point I did find him with a duster in his hand.

"He found it on the floor," said my mother defensively. She was preparing cream of mushroom vol-au-vents and carefully scooping the filling into the pastry shells.

"Aunty Suzanne says life's too short to stuff a mushroom."

My mother snorted. "Aunty Suzanne wouldn't know one end of a mushroom from the other."

"Mushrooms don't have ends. They have tops and bottoms."

"*Rebecca!* I can't handle this now. You are either for me or against me. And if you're for me, you can glaze the cheese straws. Get an egg from the fridge."

I got an egg from the fridge and looked at the clock. The first guests would be arriving in an hour, but the buffet plates weren't yet ready and dozens of empty vol-au-vent cases littered the Formica surfaces.

"Mum?"

"NOT NOW, REBECCA!"

Her face was a mask of concentration. Her fingers were working like a concert pianist's. She ping-ponged between the oven and the fridge and the worktop, carrying bowls and plates and paper doilies.

"I'm *for* you!" I said.

And briefly, just for a moment, she stopped and smiled.

I knew that there was something wrong. This wasn't how it was supposed to be. According to the timetable, this should have been the moment that my mother was checking her flower arrangements and retouching her makeup. A light sheen of perspiration shined her face.

"It was that chocolate bleeding log that did it."

I looked up, shocked. My mother never swore. Not even "blimey." I watched as she scooped up a teaspoon of mushroom mix and pressed it into a pastry shell.

"The first one fell to pieces. The second one cracked when I rolled it. And this one!" she spat out the words in disgust. "It looks like dog's doo."

I worried the cuticle on my left thumbnail.

"It's thrown everything out. I still haven't even done the salads or the sausage rolls or . . ."

A vol-au-vent case fell to the floor.

"Bugger!"

I ran across the kitchen to get the dustpan and brush and began to sweep it up, then without awaiting instructions, I went to the fridge and extracted the lettuce and tomatoes and cucumber.

My mother hesitated, her hands hovering.

"No Re . . . ," she began but then changed her mind and started barking rapid commands at me while marshaling the ingredients for a potato salad.

"Okay, you do it. Good. Lettuce. Tomato. Slices not chunks. Cucumber. Slices, a quarter of a centimeter, regular. Lettuce washed. Must be dry. Kitchen towel. Spring onion back of fridge. Washed and trimmed. Large bowl back of saucepan cupboard. And watch the knife, it's sharp."

I fetched a stool and clambered onto it in order to reach the chopping board from the cupboard. My mother grabbed a jar of mayonnaise and gouged great spoonfuls of it into a bowl. Chopping the tomatoes and cucumber was not without its difficulties. I had to reach up to use the work surface, and the knife was long and unwieldy. I tested the edge of it with my finger and looked down to see it had scored a line down the center of my fingertip. Tiny beads of blood emerged, welling like tears, and spilled onto the tomatoes.

"WHERE THE HELL IS THE PASTRY BRUSH?"

My mother was rooting through the utensils drawer. Ladles and mashers and slotted spoons crashed against each other.

"Anything I can do to help?"

My father was standing by the back door. His hands were in his pockets and he shifted nervously from foot to foot.

"IT'S TOO LATE! THERE'S NOT ENOUGH TIME!"

I felt a rising gorge of panic.

"Yes, there is!" I said. "Look, I've almost finished."

Even my father looked as if he was starting to understand the gravity of the situation. "Tell me what I can do."

My mother stopped her hunt for the pastry brush. There was an edge of desperation, of pleading, in her voice.

"James! Please! Hand towels. Bathroom. New soap, pink, top of bathroom cabinet. Check bowl. Bleach. Air freshener. Window open."

Relieved to have a job to do, my father clicked his heels and saluted. "Aye, aye, cap'n."

She turned back to the potato salad. "It is *not* a joke!" she said, and for a moment I thought she was going to cry.

"I know, Mum." My voice carried a quiet assurance that surprised us both.

Tiffany shuttled dishes between the kitchen and the buffet table. I sliced up the tomatoes and the spring onion. My mother slapped the finished vol-au-vents onto a plate.

Ding dong!

We looked at each other in panic, unable to move. Tiffany bounded into the room.

"Doorbell!"

"I CAN'T BELIEVE IT! THEY'RE EARLY!" Her voice was high and ragged at the edges.

She turned to me.

"*Rebecca!* Mayonnaise in. Stir. Spring onions finely chopped. Parsley chopped. Sprig on top."

Then, realizing that she had no choice, she ripped off her apron and patted her hair. She started walking toward the front door then turned back, gathered up the dirty bowls and forks and spoons, looked around the kitchen, suffered a moment's panicked hesitation, then opened the cupboard under the sink and threw them in.

Ding dong!

"Coming!"

She walked out into the hall, stopped in front of the mirror and, in two quick movements, painted her lips a livid red and put on her smile. Pausing to take a deep breath, she flung open the door.

It was Mrs. Ali and Rajiv.

"So pleased you could make it!"

"I hope we're not early."

"Not at all, not at all." Her hostess smile was glued to the corners of her lips.

In the kitchen, I took over the making of the potato salad, cleaned the counter, checked on the sausage rolls in the oven and took the dirty bowls from the cupboard under the sink and began loading the dishwasher. I was chopping the parsley when I became aware that my father was watching me from the doorway.

"Well done, Rebecca. Try and help your mother, if you can, eh? She's under a lot of pressure. There's a good girl."

Mrs. Ali appeared in the kitchen. She had brought a box of brightly colored cakes that looked like no earthly food matter I'd ever seen before. They were bright yellow and appeared to be glowing. I wondered if they might be radioactive. My mother took them gingerly between her thumb and forefinger.

"How delightful! And what an *interesting* outfit."

Mrs. Ali was wearing a long sky blue dress embroidered with hundreds of tiny beads, under which she was wearing matching trousers gathered at the ankle. On her feet were jeweled sandals and around her neck a matching chiffon scarf. I thought she looked like a princess. Although obviously not Diana.

"It's called a salwar kameez."

"Very nice!" said my mother, although it was hard to know from her expression whether she thought Mrs. Ali really *did* look nice, or a complete dog's dinner.

Rajiv's hair had been slicked down and he was wearing a cream Nehru suit.

"Well look at Little Lord Fauntleroy!" my mother said, ushering them through to the lounge.

Ding dong! I left my workstation and headed to the door. A pink acrylic blur passed before my eyes. It was Granny Monroe swooping in for a kiss. *Mwuh!* I dodged but too late. There was an outline in Ruby Rose slap bang in the middle of my cheek.

"Take my coat, Rebecca, there's a good girl. I have to say I'm a bit surprised there isn't any bunting up. For the Coronation, you know, we strung it all the way across our street. It was a wonderful day! My sponge finger mousse was a triumph. The neighbors talked about it for weeks. A cup of tea would be very nice yes, dear . . ."

She had talked her way the full length of the hall and reached the lounge, where, for only the third time in her adult life, she was struck completely dumb.

"Cynthia, this is Meera and Rajiv. They've just moved into Beech Drive." Perhaps Granny Monroe had never seen Pakistani people before. I leaped in to help.

"They're Pakistani!"

"Although British now, of course," said Mrs. Ali. Granny Monroe seemed to recover herself.

"Delighted to meet you," she said. "Of course, my husband had a lot of experience with colonials on account of his work."

"Oh really?" said Mrs. Ali. "Was he in the army?"

"Gas board," Granny Monroe said but didn't elaborate.

I wished they'd shut up. The guests had started to arrive in the cathedral, and according to the BBC commentator, "a shiver of anticipation" was passing through the crowd.

Uncle Kenneth, Aunty Suzanne and Lucy were the next to appear. I looked at Uncle Kenneth with fresh eyes. The cravat was in place alongside the slightly bored expression. Aunty Suzanne was holding a Marks & Spencer quiche and a bottle of white wine. My mother graciously accepted the quiche.

"Shop-bought!" she said. "How very extravagant!"

Aunty Suzanne made a face. But not until my mother had turned the other way.

"It's all monarchist claptrap of course. I don't know what you're making such a fuss about."

But my mother seemed to have decided to ignore her. "It's a good excuse to get all the family together apart from anything else. Now then, who'd like what to drink? I've got red wine, white wine, there's beer for the men. Martini? Dubonnet? Shall I take your jackets?"

Aunty Suzanne took off her coat, to reveal that underneath she was wearing a pair of dungarees. To a wedding! Granny Monroe and my mother exchanged a look. There was no mistaking this one. It was the full dog's dinner. Even Tiffany looked at her doubtfully. She crossed the room to kiss Uncle Kenneth hello.

"Hello, Kenneth!" I watched her look expectantly into his face like the picture of Jesus in my *Tales of the New Testament* picture book when he was awaiting the transfiguration.

"Tiffany," said Uncle Kenneth walking past her into the kitchen. "Anybody seen the corkscrew?"

My mother hovered by his elbow. "Would you like the armchair near the television, Kenneth?"

He rolled his eyes, and disappeared into the garden.

Ding dong! It was the Huxleys from next door. Mrs. H, who normally favored a blue flowered apron and a pair of slippers, was wearing a fawn acrylic trouser suit and had tonged her hair and then pinned it up. Mr. H, on the other hand, was wearing an old pair of jeans and a faded yellow T-shirt, but then none of the men had dressed properly for the occasion. It was as if they didn't care.

"So glad you could make it, Gloria," said my mother. "And at such short notice too! Do go through." They'd been a last-minute addition to the guest list, and my mother seemed keen that Mrs. Huxley should remember this.

Lucy and I positioned ourselves on the hearth rug in front of the television with our noses pressed up against the screen. Damien was in his playpen next to us. He wagged his chubby little fingers and smiled at the TV. We watched the guests pouring into the cathedral, Nancy Reagan in peach, Barbara Cartland in pink, hundreds of women with big hats on their heads. Then again, it could have been a lot of women with big blobs on their heads. The picture quality at this proximity was on the fuzzy side.

Mrs. Huxley had settled herself on the sofa, next to Aunty Suzanne and Granny Monroe, and Mr. Huxley had gone to join the men on the patio, where they'd congregated around the keg of brown ale. Uncle Kenneth was holding a wineglass and swirled it in his hand before bringing it up to his nose. He looked doubtful but took a swig anyway.

"Right! White wine? Red wine? Martini? I've got Dubonnet too."

It had started! There was a shot of Lady Di looking very squashed in a horse-drawn carriage. She was surrounded by what looked like a cloud, and crammed into the corner was her father, Earl Spencer, who always looked like he'd had one too many for the road.

"She's wearing a tiara!"

"Look at those sleeves. They're enormous."

"Is that the state carriage?"

"Well if you'd shut up we'd be able to hear, wouldn't we?"

The crowd was going crazy and the broadcaster was struggling to keep his commentary even.

"There she is, Lady Diana Spencer, just twenty years of age, and about to marry the future king of England. Listen to the roar of the crowd! They're all leaning forward, desperate for a glimpse of the young Diana."

My mother was taking a tray out of the oven. "What's the dress like?"

"You can't really see," said Tiffany. "It looks sort of puffy."

"Right. Who wants a sausage roll? They're homemade. Ah go on, Rajiv. You're a growing lad. Meera? I made them myself, you know."

She was blocking the television. Lucy and I tried to peer through her legs. The carriage had just passed Admiralty Arch.

"No, Tiffany, not you. Now come on, Rajiv, I know you want one."

Rajiv was gazing at the plate. The room was filled with the smell of warm pastry and sausage meat. A dribble of saliva appeared at the corner of his mouth.

"Mum?"

Mrs. Ali was furiously shaking her head at him. "It's pork!"

"Oh!" Our mother looked at her plate of sausage rolls. "I thought it was only the Hebrews who didn't eat pork."

Mrs. Ali shook her head. "We believe the pig is an unclean animal."

Granny Monroe didn't usually leap to her daughter-in-law's defense, but she seemed to decide to make an exception in this instance.

"Doreen keeps a spotless kitchen, I think you'll find."

Ding dong!

"Rebecca! Get the door!"

"Lady Diana is about to step out of the coach, giving the crowd outside the cathedral, and the millions more at home, a chance to have our first glimpse of the dress."

I hesitated but saw my mother's face, her forehead creased in anxiety. Out of the corner of my eye, I caught a glimpse of the squidgy chocolate log. It looked like it had been run over by a carelessly reversing car. I ran down the hall chanting "Whyme? Whyme? Whyme?" and threw the door open. It was Nanna and Grandpa Arnold.

"Oh dear, are we late? We got held up in the traffic."

They shuffled in while I raced back to the TV, arriving just in time to see Lady Diana stepping out onto the red carpet. There was silence while we all surveyed The Dress.

"And there it is!" intoned the commentator. "The dress we've all been waiting to see. It's a magnificent creation!"

"Well that's one word for it," said Granny Monroe. "Could do with a good iron if you ask me."

For once, I was inclined to agree with her. She looked like a mushroom.

"And that hair could do with a brush too." Lady Di's tiara appeared to be on the point of falling off, and although David Emmanuel had rushed forward to fuss with the train, it was a crinkly mass of crushed fabric. It was hard not to think that this was an anticlimax. This was the moment we'd spent *months* waiting for. We all looked at one another doubtfully. Were we missing something? The BBC newscaster, on the other hand, had no such doubts. He sounded as if he was commentating on a football match and it was the final minute and England had just scored.

"It's a truly sumptuous creation!"

My mother put her head through the patio doors. "Don't you want to see The Dress?"

Mr. Huxley and my father were discussing cars because Mr. Huxley's Maestro had recently developed a coolant leak. They looked at her as if she'd gone mad.

The commentator swept on, unperturbed. "And here it is! The best kept secret in Britain. Work on the dress had to be carried out in utmost secrecy. It is made from ivory, pure silk taffeta, spun by the only silk farm in Britain, at Lullingstone. The lace panels were formed from Carrickmacross lace which once belonged to Queen Mary . . ."

"Ooh, look at her," said Mrs. Huxley. "She looks petrified."

"The train is twenty-five feet long, longer than for any previous royal wedding, and it has been hand-embroidered with ten thousand mother-of-pearl sequins."

"Switch to ITV to see if it looks better on there." I obediently leaned forward and changed channels. The shot was a bit closer, but the dress looked even worse.

"A fairy-tale dress for a fairy-tale princess," said the commentator.

"Turn it back to the BBC," said Granny Monroe. "They're the only ones who know how to do royalty properly. Besides it's patriotic."

"Mother! I did ask you to be punctual!" Nanna and Grandpa Arnold had been spotted at last.

"Hello, Mum!" said Suzanne, struggling to her feet. She picked her way across the bodies strewn across the lounge floor and went to hug Nanna. "Come and sit next to me!"

"Dad?" said my mother. "Are you okay there? Or would you prefer the shed?"

Rajiv took advantage of the lull in events to knock over his glass of Coca-Cola.

"Could see that coming a mile off," muttered our mother, dabbing a cloth in time to the trumpet fanfare that had just started up.

There was a close-up of Lady Di and we could see her familiar blush. I sighed. She was impossibly beautiful.

"The eyes of the world are upon her," said the commentator.

"Look at the poor little thing!" said Aunty Suzanne. "Like a lamb to the slaughter."

Shocked, we all turned to face her. She was sitting on the sofa twirling a glass of white wine in her hand.

"Suzanne!"

"Well she is, isn't she? She's only twenty for God's sake; she hasn't got a clue what she's letting herself in for."

There was a pause while Aunty Suzanne took a sip of her wine, an indignant expression on her face (although it wasn't as indignant as Granny Monroe's, who was still rankled by the dungarees).

I couldn't have been more shocked if she'd run naked through the lounge. Or started burning crucifixes. It was tantamount to sacrilege! We might as well have invited Duncan Rogers and his long-haired friends who were having a Stuff the Wedding alternative celebration two doors down, which unlike our own affair involved several flagons of Woodpecker Cider and assorted members of Militant Tendency.

Lucy looked mortified.

"*Mum!*" she said, forgetting for a moment she was supposed to call her Suzanne.

"I was only eighteen when I got married," said my mother but then seemed to decide this wasn't an argument to pursue.

Suzanne waved her wineglass in the air. "The only reason she's standing there now is because she's the last virgin left in England."

"Suzanne!" said my mother and Granny Monroe as one.

"What's a virgin?" said Lucy.

"In our culture, an arranged marriage is not just customary but to be preferred," said Mrs. Ali.

"Yes, well," said Granny Monroe, who seemed to have been waiting for this moment, "you're not living in Bongo-Bongo-land now, you know."

Suzanne looked as if she was about to choke on her wine. "Cynthia!" she said. "I am *so* sorry, Meera." She glared at Granny Monroe. "I'm afraid that our post-imperial legacy has led to certain *outmoded* beliefs persisting in some sections of the population."

"I beg *your* pardon," said Granny Monroe.

"It's not true anyway, Suzanne," said my mother, who refused to allow her Royal Wedding celebration to be sabotaged by a nonbeliever. "She's genuinely in love with him, you can tell. Or maybe *you've* forgotten what that's like."

She spat out the words, enunciating the k in "like" as if it was the k in "killer!" There was a moment's silence while the opposing parties glared at each other, although the BBC commentator hadn't seemed to notice and plowed on regardless.

"It was Charles who chose the Trumpet Voluntary, the 'Prince of

Denmark's March,' by Jeremiah Clarke for the bridal procession. And there he is standing at the altar awaiting his bride, resplendent in his naval commander's uniform."

Aunty Suzanne sighed. "But he's not in love with her. He said as much in that interview. 'Whatever love is,' he said. It won't last, I'm telling you."

She shook her head sadly from side to side. It was too much for my mother. She jumped up and made a grab for a plate of cheese straws. "Just because *you* don't know how to keep your husband happy!"

Nobody said anything. Apart from the BBC commentator, who had moved on to an in-depth analysis of the seating plan and a quick jog through some of the more arcane aspects of royal protocol. I was torn. On the one hand, I was straining to listen to the commentary and to keep the appropriate degree of solemnity that we had just been told the institution of holy matrimony required. On the other hand, it wasn't every day that you heard love being discussed in Beech Drive.

"Inside the cathedral, are the twenty-five hundred invited guests, but of course there are many more people watching at home. An estimated seven hundred and fifty million people around the world will be watching the ceremony."

Aunty Suzanne took a swig of her wine.

"Your trouble, Doreen, is that you're still living in the fifties. Just because you had a shotgun marriage doesn't mean everyone has to. The world's changed. Women are taking control of their destinies. In twenty years' time, there'll be full equality."

"And Archbishop Runcie steps forward to announce the first hymn: 'Christ Is Made the Sure Foundation.'"

"Mum? What's a virgin?"

Granny Monroe, who had been itching to join in the conversation, finally found her moment and turned to Aunty Suzanne. "It wouldn't kill you to put on a dress from time to time, you know. And I'm sure that Kenneth would appreciate it."

My mother looked triumphant.

"Shhhhhh!" commanded Lucy. It was about to happen.

"Do you, Diana Frances, take Charles Philip Arthur George to be your lawfully wedded husband, to have and to hold from this day forth, for better or for worse, for richer or for poorer, in sickness and in health, to love and to cherish, till death do you part?"

We held our breath. Her voice was weak and indistinct.

"I, Diana Frances, take thee, Philip Charles Arthur George."

Philip? We looked at each other in astonishment. She'd botched it! We couldn't believe it! Diana had fluffed the vows.

My mother called out to the men. "She's fluffed the vows!"

Mr. Huxley looked up from his tankard of beer. "Right," he said. "Anyway, they told me it would be £50 for a new starter motor, can you believe it?"

But that was it. They were married, although there was no "you may kiss the bride" like there was whenever somebody got married on television. They launched into another hymn, "I Vow to Thee My Country," which was apparently Diana's favorite, and from now on would be mine too.

There was a sniff from the sofa. It was Nanna. She was crying!

"Nanna?"

"Alicia?"

"Are you all right? What's the matter?" Tears were streaming down her face.

"Oh it's nothing," she said. "It's just so beautiful. They just seem so young and in love."

A box of man-sized Kleenex was passed along the sofa, but the atmosphere in the room had changed. My mother had drawn the curtains on the French windows because of the glare on the screen, and a warm, dark fug had enveloped us. It felt like an illicit pleasure all of a sudden, with the sun shining outside and all of us sitting in an artificial twilight, watching the television. I kept on expecting my mother to burst into the room and say, "WHATAREYOUALLDOINGSIT-TINGINSIDEONADAYLIKETHIS?" but she didn't. She went to fetch a plate of sausage rolls instead.

Charles and Diana were led off to sign the register and Kiri Te Kanawa appeared in a multicolored frock and started singing something high and shrill.

I turned to Nanna. "What was your wedding like?"

She was still sniffing but she smiled when I looked at her. She hesitated, but there was something about the semidarkness and the female company that seemed to take hold of her, although it could have been the Dubonnet.

"It was fine," she said.

She hesitated.

"It was just the wrong man."

We all stared at her.

"*What?*" said my mother.

"Alicia?" said Suzanne.

But Nanna said nothing, and then Archbishop Runcie returned and mounted his pulpit and began to speak in the monotonous drone that all clergymen have to go to a special school to learn. I leaned forward and turned up the volume.

"Here is the stuff of which fairy tales are made: the prince and princess on their wedding day. Those who are married live happily ever after the wedding day if they persevere in the real adventure, which is the royal task of creating each other and creating a more loving world. It must be specially true of this marriage, in which are placed so many hopes."

"Alicia?" said Aunty Suzanne.

But she wouldn't say any more. And anyway, there was something burning.

"Rebecca! Quick! Get the spatula!"

By the time I had regained my position on the hearth rug next to Lucy, they were leaving the cathedral. Happily married, forever and ever.

"This is a day that will resonate in the hearts and minds of all those who have witnessed it," intoned the commentator. "For many years to come."

He was right enough about that. Although I don't think any of us could have realized precisely how.

The food had been laid across the tables outside.

"Well!" said Nanna. "What a spread!"

"Dig in!"

Granny Monroe was examining the ham. "Did you boil it yourself? No, I thought not. I prefer a nice bit of tongue myself."

Mrs. Ali helped herself to a slice of quiche. "It is mushroom?"

"Bacon and mushroom," said my mother. "Oh! I'm sure you can pick the bacon out, if you're going to be *fussy*."

"Did you put mustard in the chicken?" asked Granny Monroe, taking a taste. "No, I thought not. I always put a pinch of mustard in. Gives it flavor."

We loaded our plates. I balanced a piece of (homemade) quiche on the edge of my plate (the M & S one had been banished to the fridge) and made an extra tour of the table to check that I had everything. We all struggled to find a corner of the sitting room in which to sit and eat. The patio doors had been opened, so we were half-in, half-outside. Tiffany balanced on the arm of the sofa. Lucy crouched on the edge of a flowerpot. Uncle Kenneth ignored the food, took a slim panatela out of the breast pocket of his jacket, rolled it around in his hand, smelled it and lit up.

I took a bite of Scotch egg. My mother was talking Mrs. Huxley through her recipe for Chicken Croûtes. Mr. Huxley had progressed to his carburetor. I hesitated then turned to Uncle Kenneth.

"Uncle Kenneth?"

"I looked in Delia for a recipe, but in the end I went with my old Marguerite Patten. She's very good on buffets. You can't fault her on that."

"Uncle Kenneth?"

He crossed his legs and inhaled on his cigar before turning toward me. "Hmm?"

"Is it true that if your mother and father both have blue eyes, you can't have brown eyes?" He was a doctor, after all. He'd know.

"And the fella in the garage, he looked under the hood and started making noises."

"No, Rebecca. If you have a grandparent with brown eyes, you can."

"You have to cook the chicken first. I roasted a whole one yesterday, to make sure that I had enough."

"But if all your grandparents have blue eyes?"

"You have to chop up the chicken very fine. Or you can mince it of course, but I think it's better to have a bit of bite."

"Well, if all the grandparents, then, no you can't."

I looked at Uncle Kenneth. I didn't understand.

"Well, I figured that it couldn't have been the brake disks, because I'd had them replaced a year ago, but I thought 'No, it can't be the carburetor, surely.'"

"So how come Tiffany's got brown eyes?"

"And then you mix it with the mayonnaise and the olives."

"Hmm?"

"But the mechanic, he said, 'Carburetor! Spotted it a mile off.'"

"How come Tiffany's got brown eyes, if all our grandparents have blue eyes?" I couldn't figure it out. It didn't add up.

"Sorry?"

"Then you've got to cut the tomatoes. Thin, mind."

"Is it because Tiffany's your love child?"

My voice must have been louder than I thought. Either that or everyone just happened to have stopped talking at the very moment the words came out of my mouth. My mother froze, in her hand a forkful of Coronation chicken that would never complete the journey to her lips. Everybody turned and looked at me. There was no noise at all, apart from the drone of an airplane overhead and a subdued murmur from the television set.

"Sorry?"

I hesitated. I was suddenly uncomfortably aware that all eyes were upon me. My armpits prickled. My toes felt hot. It was too late to backtrack now though. Wasn't it?

My father's mustache twitched. Granny Monroe opened her mouth to say something but then changed her mind. Why didn't someone tell me to shut up, or go to my room, or that if I said another word I'd feel the back of their hand? Nobody said *anything*.

"What on *earth* gave you that idea?" said Uncle Kenneth eventually, before inhaling deeply on his slim panatela. There was another silence. In for a penny, in for a pound. My mother's sayings had an uncanny knack of coming to me in times of crisis.

"Because Tiffany has brown eyes. She said it was because you'd had an 'affair' with Mum."

The silence deepened.

"Oh for God's sake!" said Uncle Kenneth. "I don't have to listen to this."

His face had turned red. Aunty Suzanne and my father were staring at him. My mother's fork was still poised before her mouth.

"For crying out loud!" he said, turning to Aunty Suzanne. *"No! I bloody well did not!"* He stood up and threw his cigar to the ground. "I wouldn't touch your sister with a barge pole. Jesus! Some of us have got more taste!"

And with that he marched out through the patio doors, down the hall and slammed the front door.

There was more silence. It sounded like it would go on forever. My cheeks throbbed. Granny Monroe's mouth was wide open, displaying an unmasticated Scotch egg. Mrs. Ali had turned her head to the wall. Even Rajiv had shut up.

I stared at the ground, the silence roaring in my head. I didn't even notice the mewling at first. It was deafened by the blood throbbing in my eardrums. And even when I looked up, I couldn't work out where it was coming from. I turned my head. And then I saw: it was my mother. She was making a strange, high-pitched, inhuman noise. A series of pitiful, strangulated yelps. Like the sound the Huxleys' kitten had made the time it got stuck on our roof. Her shoulders were hunched over and she rocked back and forth, back and forth, her newly highlighted and feathered hair trembling.

Everybody had gone, apart from Nanna and Grandpa Arnold. The house had emptied. We were all trying to pretend that it was normal. Except it wasn't. My mother had locked herself in the bathroom and was refusing to come out. My father was sitting in his shed.

I went up and knocked quietly on the bathroom door.

"Mum?"

I could hear the sound of muffled sobbing.

"Mum?"

I waited for a reply, but none came.

"Would you like a nice cup of tea?"

I pressed my ear to the door, but couldn't hear anything.

"Leave her be for a bit," said Nanna. She had appeared behind me, her face taut and anxious. She attempted to cover it with a smile.

"Come on," she said and I followed her back down the stairs. There were half-eaten plates of food on the patio. Forks lay where they'd been dropped. A sausage roll with a bite taken out of it rested on the kitchen work top.

Together we gathered up the dirty plates and cutlery and stacked them by the sink.

"Let's make it nice and tidy for your mum," said Nanna. "She'd appreciate that." I nodded obediently and went to fetch the dishes from the buffet table. I picked up a wooden bowl and looked at the salad I'd made. It had barely been touched, yet it was already spoiled; the leaves lay limp and soggy at the bottom of the bowl.

"What should I do with it?" I asked Nanna.

She peered down at it. "Best throw it away," she said. "It won't keep."

I opened up the bin and scraped it in. The tomatoes I'd so carefully cut, the cucumber, the lettuce leaves I'd washed and shredded. Was it only this morning?

"I didn't realize it was a bad thing to say," I said to Nanna. She was filling the sink, squirting in the Fairy Liquid, and I watched as the bubbles frothed up.

"I know," she said. "It wasn't bad, Rebecca. Your mother's just . . . been under a lot of strain."

Tiffany turned to me and narrowed her eyes. "It's so typical of you, Rebecca. You *ruined* everything."

"Tiffany?" said Nanna. "Would you be a sweetheart and take Suzanne's cutlery back?"

Tiffany, suspicious, was about to object, but remembered just in time that it would give her an excuse to go and visit the Old Parsonage.

"All right," she said to Nanna, a polite smile on her lips. Then she turned to me and hissed, "But don't *think* I'll ever forgive you for this."

When she'd gone, we both relaxed a little. Nanna changed Damien's nappy, and I handed her cotton wool balls and pieces of tissue paper while she took care of the messy bits. He gurgled and waved his legs in the air as if nothing had happened. I looked at him and felt a pang of envy.

"We'll make it all shipshape," she said. She handed me the plates one by one, and I wiped them as carefully as I could, taking pains to remove every last smear. "We'll get this place as clean as a new pin so when your mum's feeling a bit better, she can come down and we can all watch the news together."

She still hadn't emerged though by the time the news began. Grandpa had disappeared. My father was still sitting in his shed. Tiffany hadn't returned from the Old Parsonage, so it was only Nanna and I who sat down on the sofa.

"Emotions and the noise level rose still higher as vast crowds filled the Mall and the royal parks in front of Buckingham Palace," said the reporter.

"Chanted pleadings from the crowd brought extra appearances from the Queen and the Queen Mother, followed again by Charles and Diana. And this time, formal protocol was abandoned, as Prince Charles kissed his bride, causing uproar. Later, the couple rode away in their three-car private train to spend the night secluded from the intense attention that has been focused on them."

"Well," said Nanna. "It's all over now."

"And now for the rest of the day's news," said Trevor McDonald.

"Tensions in Toxteth remain high tonight, after the third straight day of rioting. Police say that they are closely . . ."

But we'd stopped listening.

"Do you think Mum's all right?" I asked.

"She's probably just a bit tired," said Nanna.

I drifted out of the lounge and went and stood at the foot of the stairs. I took each tread of the stair slowly, noticing the air bubbles caught in the white gloss paint on the banisters, the scuff on the carpet where I'd once spilled my cornflakes, the small triangle of wallpaper by the skirting board that had started to come away from the wall. The sound of my mother's crying had stopped. I tried the bathroom door again and this time it gave against my weight.

I don't really remember much of the next bit. Or at least, I've spent the last twenty years trying to forget it. The bathroom looked all wrong. It was the wrong color. No longer avocado, but avocado and red. There was red everywhere. Across the bath, the tiles, the toilet; seeping into a puddle on the floor. And my mother? She didn't look like my mother any longer either. She was on the floor, next to the toilet, slumped forward, her mouth open. A small bubble of red saliva resting on her lips. The last thought I remember having was that she'd go mad when she saw the mess. And then I passed out.

Part Sixteen

afterward *adv* **1** : later, subsequently

16.1   miss *vt* **1** : to fail to perceive or understand

THE ONLY EXACT SCIENCE is hindsight. I'd got the genetics right, though. You can't have brown eyes if all your grandparents have blue eyes. The observations, hypothesis and experimentation were correct. The scientific method does not necessarily work: you never know what piece of information is missing until it's found.

"What color were Grandpa Monroe's eyes?" Tiffany had asked me.

"Blue," I said.

I can still remember what was on the television: *Happy Days*. The Fonz had just walked in.

"Blue," I said.

The Fonz was combing his hair and I was lying across the hearth rug. I even went to check the photo.

"Blue," I said.

They weren't though. They were brown.

It was such a small mistake to make.

16.2   miss *n* **2** : mistake, error, fault

IT WAS SUZANNE who called me. I knew immediately that something was up. It was the tone of her voice; the voice people use when someone has died. Alicia. I waited for the news, my heartbeat accelerating, my body stiffening, preparing for the worst. There was a pause. I listened to my fingers, wrapped around the telephone receiver, pounding with my blood.

"It's your grandfather," she said. "Herbert."

I felt a pang of relief. And then guilt.

"He's had a heart attack."

She hesitated.

"He's dead."

We'd all been looking the wrong way. It was Alicia we thought would go first.

Poor Herbert. He'd been out in the backyard, checking on his ferrets. At least it had been quick, that's what Suzanne said. He'd had a good innings, that's what she said next. Life as a game of cricket. That seems about right to me. Intense periods of boredom. Rules you don't quite understand. And a few, very few, moments of pure unadulterated joy.

Suzanne met me at the train station. I caught sight of her standing on the platform a moment before she saw me. She's changed a bit over the years. The dungarees have gone, although she still keeps up with her reading. It's Naomi Wolf and Susan Faludi these days. She told me off the other week for not wearing lipstick.

She was looking up and down the train searching for my face. And, there, standing next to her was my father.

Suzanne, my aunt? She's also my stepmother. Tiffany and I had been looking the wrong way there too. It wasn't Kenneth and Doreen who were having the affair. It was James and Suzanne.

You can retrofit all you like, but the clues weren't there. I've checked. That's the problem with point-of-view narrative. I thought Doreen and Kenneth were having an affair. You thought Doreen and Kenneth were having an affair. We were both wrong.

It could have been true. I've spent a long time thinking about it. And I suppose there are a few things I missed.

"She's always been one for wild enthusiasms, your Aunty Suzanne . . ." Was that one?

"I don't suppose your father forgets to call, does he, when he's going to be late home from work?" Could that have been another? It doesn't add up to much, though. Believe me. The clues should be there. But I've checked and they weren't.

16.3 miss *v* 3 : to feel the lack of

I SAT WITH Alicia in her little back kitchen. Suzanne and my father were at the undertaker's, so it was just me and her. We sat at the table and she stroked my hand. She looked pale, I thought.

I watched her stand up slowly and fill the kettle from the tap, her hands shaking. We gravitated toward each other when my mother died. I didn't know why at the time, but I can see it now. We were united, I think, not so much by grief, but by guilt. Guilt and sorrow. The twin threads of our DNA. She lost her daughter. I lost my mother. Between us there is a gaping hole.

She flicked on the switch of the kettle and started hunting through cupboards and drawers, assembling the components for one of her elaborate tea ceremonies. She seemed to be much more herself, somehow, humming tunes and looking at old photos.

I watched her spoon out the tea. It's always leaf tea and the milk in first. She swirled the pot expertly, then let it rest on its coaster under its cozy. I think we both found the ritual comforting. I watched her shuffle around the kitchen, searching out proper porcelain cups and a jug for the milk, and for no reason at all, an image of my mother and her favorite sunflower teapot swam into my mind.

"Do you miss your mum?"

I looked up, surprised. Alicia has always had a knack for guessing my thoughts.

"I do."

You can only see the shape of something when it's gone. She should have been there now. Bossing us around. Declaiming at the mess. Although it's true that I've still got Tiffany.

There she was now, striding into Alicia's kitchen, leather boots clacking against the floor tiles.

"You wouldn't believe how cold it is out there!" she said, shaking her head. "There was ice on the road, you know. I think there were even a few flakes of snow when I was on the motorway."

I watched her as she dropped a pair of matching leather bags on the floor. She took off her coat, then her gloves, and put her handbag down on the table, talking all the while. Tiffany has always had this amazing ability to inhabit a room, filling it with her things, her accessories, her perfume, her voice.

She was wearing a crisp black jacket over a pair of smartly ironed beige casual trousers and her hair was tied up in a chignon, but then Tiffany has never looked anything less than polished. "Groomed," the magazines call it, as if she was a racehorse or a prize pony. Her hair has been ironed, her skin peeled.

"Goodness, what a muddle! I can see nobody's been doing much cleaning up around here!"

Alicia and I looked at each other and raised our eyebrows. We'd opened a packet of chocolate-chip cookies and fig rolls and sat munching and staring. Tiffany reached for a dishcloth and started clattering plates and cups.

"I'm so sorry for your loss," she said and bent down and kissed Alicia on the cheek, a perfumed "*mwuh!*" that had been passed directly down the paternal line from Granny Monroe.

"It must be a terrible blow," she said in the voice she uses when she's doing sympathy. "Still, he had a good innings. That must be a comfort." She lingered a moment or two next to Alicia then stood up again. "Now then. Where do you keep your washing-up gloves?"

Alicia and I exchanged a look. I stood up and rummaged beneath the sink to see if there were any. My mother always said there were two types of women: those with Marigold washing-up gloves and those without. Alicia was without. The same as me. We both have careworn hands.

"Oh well," said Tiffany, removing her jewelry, taking a pot of moisturizer from her handbag and rubbing the cream into her palms. "A bit of spit and polish should sort it out. I'll just start on the oven, I think."

I watched her as she filled the sink with water and frowned at my grandmother's antiquated selection of cleaning products. I still have Tiffany, so Doreen and Doreenisms live on. She inherited half my mother's DNA and all of her sayings.

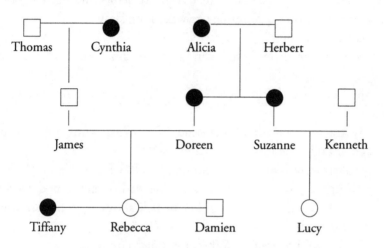

Figure 15. **Inheritance of "Doreenism" gene**

I've shown myself as a non-inheritor but I'm probably just kidding myself. I've always known that Tiffany was a chip off the old block. Although, of course, I must be too. That's the part I have problems with. You don't have to be a geneticist to work out that it's not just door slamming that runs in my family.

16.4   miss *n* **2** : mistake, error, fault

SUZANNE ARRIVED back at the house. She was carrying a bunch of gladioli and started hunting through the cupboards to find a vase. I caught a waft of them, a sweet, heavy scent, and felt suddenly queasy.

"Suzanne?"

I finally had to give up calling her Aunty Suzanne when she became my stepmother.

"Uh-huh?" She turned to me and smiled. Her hair is short and graying these days, and there are crow's-feet around her eyes, but she's still attractive. I looked at her and thought, That's what Lucy will look like when she gets older. And I felt a long-buried pang of something. Genes fall the way they fall, but I couldn't help thinking that out of Suzanne and Doreen, Suzanne drew the long straw.

"Is Lucy coming?"

"Not till tomorrow. She's catching the same train as Damien, I think."

She looked at Alicia then. "Mum? Are you going to have something to eat?"

My grandmother shook her head. "Later," she said, and hummed a fragment of some forgotten melody.

Suzanne looked at me and mouthed, "How is she?"

I shrugged my shoulders at her. She hadn't mentioned Herbert once yet. I'd tried to encourage her to talk about him, but she'd just changed the subject.

"Right," said Suzanne. "Who's for a nice cup of tea?"

Alicia and I turned and looked at her, nodding our heads as one.

We sat around the table together.

"Suzanne?"

"Hmm?" She took a sip of her tea.

I hesitated but then said, "How did Mum end up with Dad, and you with Kenneth?"

I'd never actually come right out and asked her before. She had been my father's first love. I knew that much. Suzanne was the mystery girlfriend with whom my father had caught the ferry to Crete. It's where her muddy-cup-of-coffee-in-the-morning routine dates from. That was a clue, I suppose, although I don't think I could have been expected to spot it.

My father had been Suzanne's boyfriend. And Kenneth had been my mother's.

She hesitated, trying to be diplomatic, I think.

"Kenneth became a hippie . . . and your mother didn't . . . well, that wasn't really her cup of tea."

"And?"

"And, I don't know." Her forehead creased as if she was trying to remember. "Kenneth and I, we both liked the same music. And your father, bless him, wasn't the most liberated of men."

"I thought my mother stole him off you."

Suzanne looked at me sharply. "Nobody stole anyone. We were all adults."

She hesitated.

"Just about."

We sat in silence for a little while. Eventually she said, "Your mother started seeing your father and then she got pregnant. And that was that."

She sighed.

"And then me and Kenneth, well we hooked up."

Hooked up. Suzanne has never quite lost the argot of her youth. Next, she'd be telling me it was because they had a good vibe.

She took off her glasses and polished them with her T-shirt.

"We had, well I suppose what you'd call a good vibe."

I smiled and shook my head at her.

"Right," I said. "Good *karma*?"

"No," she said, ignoring my sarcasm. She put her glasses back on and shrugged her shoulders. "I think you can safely say that none of us had good karma."

We went together—Alicia, Tiffany, me—to put flowers on our mother's grave.

Tiffany drove, and I sat in the back with Alicia and held her hand while she gazed out of the window. What was she thinking? I wondered. Since her illness, her mind had become opaque to me. We stopped at a florist's on the way, and Alicia and I hesitated outside the doorway while Tiffany bounded in and started asking complicated questions about eucalyptus leaves. I examined the buckets outside and picked out a bunch of pink carnations, my mother's favorite flower.

"She'd have liked those," said Alicia. "Why don't we get a nice bit of fern to go with it?"

We stood and waited for Tiffany. I went into the shop to find her and watched her lingering over the bouquets of lilies, red-hot pokers, gerberas, sweet William, ornamental cabbages. She refuses to believe that our mother's favorite flowers were pink carnations. Actually, that's not right. It's not that she refuses to believe, she simply doesn't believe.

She turned to me.

"What about oxeye daisies? She grew them once in the garden." She does this every time we go to visit our mother's grave. I make noncommittal noises and let her buy what she wants. Whatever is most in fashion. Whatever flowers we're supposed to currently like. If my mother was still alive, after all, she'd have a flower bed full of ornamental cabbages.

We parked outside the graveyard and I helped Alicia from the car. She's so frail these days. So old. When I was growing up, I thought she was ancient then. But she wasn't, not really. It was a trick of the light.

We walked across the graveyard together, Alicia taking small, uncertain steps; Tiffany carrying a carelessly artful arrangement of pinks and lupins.

"He was such a beautiful little baby boy." I looked at Alicia, confused until I realized she wasn't with me in the graveyard, she was years back, miles away. But then I felt as if I was drifting off from my moorings too. I caught a whiff of a newly dug grave and it took me back further than I wanted to go. I turned and looked at it, a mound of fresh earth, covered with the decaying blooms of dozens of flowers. I turned quickly and walked up the graveled path.

There were flowers everywhere when my mother died. "With Sympathies On Your Loss," they said. They filled dozens of vases, milk bottles, jugs. I've never been able to abide them since. It's the smell that gets me. Alistair buys bunches from the supermarket that have almost no scent at all. He likes yellow chrysanthemums that never die, that never smell. But occasionally, I'll walk past them and catch the faintest of wafts and remember what it was like sitting there alive, while my mother lay dead.

"I'm very glad that vicar's gone," said Tiffany. "He's much better, the new one. High church. None of that happy, clappy nonsense. What was his name, the old one?"

I didn't bother to answer. But then Tiffany rarely asked questions that required a response. I let her talk on, finding it vaguely comforting; her ability to latch onto the banal and simply to chatter, to fill the empty space.

"It's shocking the state of this place. Somebody should get onto the council. Right, where's the pot? I'll go and find some water."

I stood by my mother's grave and stared at the patch of ground where she lay. Alicia knelt down by the edge to clear away the weeds. I watched her for a minute or two before I realized that she was crying.

"Alicia?"

She didn't say anything, just buried her face in her hands. She was sobbing freely now. I knelt down beside her. The soil was damp against my knees. I was awkward against her. I put my arm around her shoulder and could feel the bones beneath her skin. I could feel her whole body shaking against mine.

"There was nothing you could have done. There was nothing anybody could have done," I said, although I don't think that either of us believed me.

16.5   miss *n* 5 : a young woman

SUZANNE AND MY FATHER had gone to see to the arrangements. And Tiffany had checked into a hotel. A dust allergy, she claimed. There was only Alicia and me left in her house, and she was holed up in the kitchen making a fruit tart for our dinner. She was still refusing to talk about Herbert, but Suzanne said it was most likely the shock and that we shouldn't try to force it.

I went upstairs and sat down on the edge of the bed that used to be my mother's. The pictures of Richard Chamberlain, tattered at the edges now, yellowed with age, stared at me from the walls. A heart-throb still, after all these years. I sat on the pink candlewick bedspread and looked around me. I've never quite been able to picture her as a person in her own right, as a teenager in this room, with a life that had yet to include me. I turned over an ornament of a white china swan in my hands and tried to imagine the girl who had chosen it, the girl who had bought it and placed it carefully there, on the bedside table, next to her lamp. The first thing she'd see in the morning; the last thing at night.

She was a manic-depressive. Bipolar disorder, they call it these days. There was an inquest, although I didn't know about it until years later. I've made a point, subsequently, of reading all the court documents. She'd been on lithium, but Dr. Richards, a new, young GP at our local hospital, said that drugs only treated the symptoms not the cause and sent her off to see a psychiatrist instead. The coroner recommended that a medical inquiry should be carried out and questions asked about Dr. Richards's competence. But I don't think it ever happened. He moved on to another practice, although I'm not sure where, and my mother's demise was recorded as "death by misadventure." (**misadventure** *n* **1** : [law] an accident without concomitant crime or negligence **2** : bad luck **3** : a misfortune)

But then, we all have our own theories.

I put the swan back down and picked up a ceramic hedgehog. She'd always liked her knickknacks. Our house had been full of them. Shepherdess figurines, porcelain urchins, swooping dolphins. What had happened to them? I suffered a sudden, painful pang as I pictured them in my mind's eye: a wandering tribe of unwanted ornaments doomed to walk the earth forever.

I stared at the dressing table, with its mirror and mother-of-pearl brush set. The perfume atomizer. The drawers that had once held my mother's clothes and that now gave off that ubiquitous stale, musty, sour smell of old people's furniture, of forgotten blouses and long-discarded cardigans. Of other people's lives. Downstairs I heard Alicia shuffling back and forth in the kitchen.

There's a suspected link between bipolar disease and Alzheimer's. They're working on a theory that it's caused by abnormalities in mitochondrial DNA. It's what the study was about. My grandmother, my mother, and me; fruit flies all.

"What's mitochondrial DNA?" I asked Alistair, my face a picture of perfect inquiring innocence. Although I already knew. We were in the bathroom. He was brushing his teeth and I was sitting on the edge of the bath.

"It's the powerhouse of the cells," he said and hesitated, pulling up his lips to stare at his teeth. He's always been very particular about his teeth. I saw him looking obliquely at me via the reflection in the mirror. I sat and pretended I hadn't noticed. He took back up his brush and talked and brushed simultaneously.

"It's transmitted down the maternal line. Mothers give it to both their sons and their daughters."

He rinsed the brush under the tap then took a mouthful of water, swilled it around his mouth and spat it out.

"But only daughters can pass it on," I supplied.

He paused for a fraction of a second.

"That's right," he said and dabbed his mouth delicately on a towel before walking out of the room. He had the decency, at least, not to look at me. His little carrier monkey.

I stood up and systematically opened each drawer in the chest. Searching for something, I wasn't sure what. There was nothing. No forgotten sweater or skirt. Nothing left of her. Apart from us, of course—Tiffany, Damien, me. I picked up the ornament of the white china swan again. It had a winsome half-human face. I wondered if I'd have ever chosen it. If I'd been me in a different place, a different time. I put it back down on the bedside table and sat and stared into space. I have half my mother's genes. I listened to Alicia rattling a saucepan and muttering to herself. I spread my hands out in front of me and looked at them.

Which half, I wondered. Which half.

16.6   miss *v* 6 : to fail to experience

ALICIA WAS WEARING a plain black dress, and her white, almost silvery, hair was piled on top of her head. She looked sad and tired. I wanted to put my arm around her, but she was trying to keep busy making pots of tea and burning toast.

The others had gone ahead to the chapel. We sat around the kitchen table in our funeral clothes listening to the clock ticking.

"We deserved each other."

I looked at her.

"Me and Herbert. We deserved each other," she said. "That was the thing about us. It's what kept us together. He knew of course. Herbert always knew everything."

"Knew what?"

But she wouldn't say. We sat in silence, listening to the clock ticking. Alicia turned to me.

"You're going to keep it, aren't you? This time?"

"Keep what?"

She didn't answer. She just looked at me and brushed the hair away from my face.

I didn't say anything, but let her take my hand in hers and stared at the photo of my mother on the kitchen wall. She stared steadfastly back at me. With a half, lopsided, bittersweet smile imperfectly reflecting my own.

A car tooted its horn.

"Come on," said Alicia eventually. "That's us."

16.7   miss *v* 7 : to be absent from

THEY WERE ALL there waiting outside the chapel: Tiffany and her husband, Charles, Suzanne and my father, and standing slightly apart, Damien.

"Rebecca!" said Tiffany and gave me a scented kiss. She was wearing a wide-brimmed black hat, a tailored black suit and sharp, pointy heels. Designer Mourner, I think, was the look she was going for. She cast her eyes behind me. "Where's Alistair?" she said.

"He's busy." I turned to Charles, who was shuffling awkwardly next to her.

"Rebecca!" he said and gave me a tweed-covered hug. I thought I caught a faint hint of whiskey on his breath.

Damien walked toward me. He was smiling but sadly. It pained me; he looked all wrong. Damien's natural state is happiness. It's his default mode.

"Hello, Damien."

His dark curly hair flopped around his face. Everybody falls for Damien, in the way that you fall for puppy dogs. You can't help yourself. He walked up to me and wagged his tail.

"Ah, Rebecca," he said and reached out a hand and stroked my hair. A camp puppy, that is. A Pekinese, perhaps. Or an Afghan hound.

Was Damien simply born happy? Or is he just too young to remember any of it? Although I don't suppose it matters in the end. He just is.

The sound of organ music floated through the door of the chapel, and we stood and watched the mourners troop past. Lucy arrived in a taxi. She came and stood next to me and we both stared at Tiffany. She was commanding the steps and extending an elegantly gloved hand to the arriving guests.

"Do you think she's modeling herself on the Duchess of Kent these days?" said Lucy.

I shrugged my shoulders and together we watched a stream of elderly people filing into the pews. It was a good turnout. That's what people say, don't they, of funerals, as if it was a football match or an Alan Ayckbourn play. A man with a crombie hat and liver spots stopped in front of me.

"Hello, crumpet!" I looked at him confused. I had no idea who he was until I felt his hand on my bottom.

"Uncle Reginald!" I hadn't recognized him. But then, I had no idea he was still alive. He's in his nineties now, but still as straight as a rod and dressed immaculately in a tweed suit.

"You get more gorgeous every time I see you." Good old Uncle Reginald. The perfect gent, although according to Lucy he's been shacked up with someone called Harold since 1962.

Granny Monroe appeared, bent over at the shoulders but still punctilious with her appearance: lipstick in place, hair dyed, curled and sprayed upward.

She stood on the steps and looked around her. "I have to say I've never been keen on these chapel dos. You only get a really good funeral with the Church of England."

"Hello, Mum," said my father and went to give her a hug.

She sniffed. "You never even know what the hymns are going to be."

Lucy turned to me. "You're as related to her as you are to Alicia, you know."

I looked at Granny Monroe, her hair sprayed into a tungsten helmet, her eyes sweeping critically across the steps, but I don't think I am. Family trees don't work like that; you know which branches lie where; how they connect; which ones will bear your weight.

It was almost time to go in. We looked at our watches and scanned the street. A taxi pulled up and two women stepped out. They climbed up the steps toward us.

"Hi!" The woman was in her mid-fifties and had a nasal twang and long vowels. "Susan Norton," she said, shaking my hand. "Herbert's niece? I'm his sister's, Elizabeth's, daughter. And this is my daughter, Celine."

It was the Americans. Finally! They'd arrived. Celine, my shadow cousin once removed. She was in her thirties and was wearing a sharply tailored business suit that even Tiffany looked at sideways. I wondered if she still drew hearts over the i in her name.

"Hi," she said. "It's so nice to meet you at last."

All it needed was Elizabeth, the family beauty, to roll up and the line would be complete. It would be like uncovering the missing link.

"It's a shame your grandmother couldn't make it," I said to Celine. She grimaced.

"She's under the knife."

"Sorry?"

"She's having a face-lift. Courtesy of husband number four."

I don't know why this news should have pleased me so much.

"We'd better go in, I suppose," said my father, looking at his watch.

The minister gave the eulogy. Even though he'd never met Herbert. A family man with varied interests, he said. It didn't sound like the Herbert I knew, somehow. He'd been cleaned up, sanitized. "His butterfly collection was a source of great joy and he was a lifelong collector of military paraphernalia."

I thought of Herbert lying in the pink satin-lined coffin. We'd gone to see him at the funeral parlor. I'd taken Alicia, who'd wanted to look at him one last time. He was wearing his best black suit and a burgundy tie. "That was his funeral suit," said Alicia. I wondered if he'd known he'd wear it to his own.

"Probably," she said, sensing my thoughts. "You know Herbert."

After the service, we left the chapel and went outside. The sun was struggling to come out from the clouds.

"Ashes to ashes, and dust to dust," the minister said, and threw the first clod of earth onto the coffin. Alicia threw the next, and then the rest of us filed past, taking a handful of damp soil and scattering it over the remains of our grandfather. I said a prayer for him. Suzanne cried. Alicia remained composed. But then I think she'd made her peace with him a long time ago.

The minister gave the final blessing. And that was it.

It was strangely unmoving. This Herbert, this family man with varied interests. It felt as if we were burying another man. One I didn't know. And Herbert, my grandfather, Herbert, my mother's father, Alicia's husband, had managed to elude us; to be absent right up to the last; to be missing from his own funeral.

Part Seventeen

memory *n* **7** *biol.* : persistent modification of behavior resulting from an animal's experience

17.1 relative *adj* 3 : dependent on or interconnected with something else

"I THINK SUZANNE could at least have run to a few more interesting canapés," said Tiffany, inspecting the contents of the buffet table. "I mean egg sandwiches? How terribly retro."

"Herbert liked them," I said.

She hesitated but then said, "Well, I mean, really? He's dead for God's sake. I don't think you can use that as an excuse."

The funeral tea was being held back in the Old Parsonage. I wandered through the rooms, staring intently at the places that once held the macramé pot holders and Kenwood Sodastreams of my memories.

Granny Monroe grasped my elbow and peered up into my face. "When Frank O'Brien, who lived next door, died, there was an all-day wake with outside caterers in. They were Papists, of course. But even so. Everyone agreed that it was a lovely do."

She wielded a plate at me as if to underline her point. I stared at a half-eaten chicken drumstick, a cheese sandwich and a pile of crisps.

"Really?" I said eventually.

She looked at me. "You were never the sharpest knife in the box, were you, Rebecca? Where's Tiffany gone?"

I went to help Suzanne. She was bustling around, filling glasses, replenishing the buffet counter, and Damien was at her side.

"It's such a comfort having a gay man around," she said. I raised my eyebrows at him. Suzanne has always been terribly proud of Damien's sexual orientation. She views it as one of her life achievements.

My father appeared, and I watched as he went up behind her and squeezed her waist.

"Sukes," he said. "Are you okay?"

She turned round and hugged him. "Jimbo!"

I watched them together. She dabbed something away from his upper lip. They're happy together; you can't deny it. She even sews his buttons on for him, although he's had to become quite busy in the kitchen. He enjoys it; wears an apron, bakes cakes, the works. My mother would have a fit.

Lucy came and stood next to me. "Makes you want to throw up, doesn't it?" she said. Suzanne and my father have been together longer than he was with my mother, or Suzanne was with Kenneth, but Lucy and I, products of the ancien régime, still find it hard to take seriously. She calls them Charles and Camilla.

We watched her kiss him on the cheek and begin shepherding ancient relatives into armchairs and sofas. Lucy wandered off and I was left alone, until Kenneth came up and stood next to me.

"Hello, Rebecca," he said, looking at me expectantly.

"Kenneth," I said. My mind went blank. Even now, I don't know what to say to him. But then, I still don't play bridge. Or golf. He was with Penelope.

"Hello, Penelope," I said. She's one of those women who like to be appreciated for the special effort they've made with their appearance, and I'll willingly oblige. It seems to make her happy. "You look very nice."

She has that expensively highlighted, blow-dried, high-maintenance, fiftysomething-year-old hair that I know that however hard I tried I'd never be able to achieve.

"Oh, thank you. It's Max Mara actually."

"What is?"

"The suit."

"Oh."

She used to be Kenneth's secretary but promptly transformed herself into his "personal assistant" as soon as she got a ring on her finger. He ran off with her a few months after Doreen died. And a few months after that, we moved into the Old Parsonage. But then Tiffany always gets her way in the end.

"Don't think much of what she's done to the drawing room," I heard her say as I turned the other way.

I scanned the room for Alicia, but couldn't see her.

Lucy appeared at my side. She looked pointedly at Penelope and said, "What did the witch have to say for herself? No, let me guess. 'Do you like it? I get it done at a salon in London, *actually*.' Or, 'Oh thank you. *Actually* I picked it up at Harvey Nicks.' She's very big on actually."

"Anger is a negative emotion, Lucy."

"Is that a Suzanne mot juste?"

"I read it in one of Tiffany's columns."

"Ha!" she said.

We stood together watching the parade of relatives, half-relatives and step-relatives as they moved awkwardly among the furniture swapping their anecdotes of death. Kenneth was attempting small talk with the minister, but they kept on looking at their teacups and shuffling their feet.

"No wonder your mother dumped him," said Lucy, shaking her head at her own father.

"What?"

"Kenneth. When your mother stole James off Suzanne."

I turned to look at her.

"Suzanne tells it differently," I said.

"Right. And when your mother got pregnant, she was the first to offer her congratulations? I don't think so somehow. She was jealous of your mother for years."

I felt as if the room had just shifted, and a doorway I hadn't spotted before had opened.

"Jealous?"

"She just covered it with all that yin, yang, I'm-too-centered-to-be-angry stuff. It's why she feels so guilty."

Suzanne too, I thought. Sometimes I think my mother's death is like *Murder on the Orient Express*; we all had a hand on the knife.

Aunty Margaret waved at me from the other side of the room. Step-Aunty Margaret. I inherited a whole new subset of relatives when the families merged. We went on holiday with them the summer after my mother died.

I waved back at her, although the holiday hadn't been much of a success. I wasn't speaking to Suzanne at the time, Tiffany wasn't speaking to my father, and Lucy developed an allergy to shellfish. I found that I didn't much care for abroad after that. But perhaps I'm just trying to protect my mother's memory. I still feel a pang that she never lived to experience the era of the low-cost airline and the no-frills flight. Although I'm probably being maudlin. My mother, in all likelihood, would have thought they were common.

Lucy came back and stood next to me.

"Do people use 'common' as a pejorative these days?" I asked her. We've kept up our dictionary studies, although I suspect she trumped me on *Joy of Sex* positions long ago. She shrugged her shoulders. "Maybe they never did. Maybe it was only ever Doreen."

She teases me sometimes about my mother. But it's not like talking ill of the dead, it's like talking ill of Tiffany, which is sport, not bad manners.

She turned then and looked at me.

"So?" she said. "Have you made up your mind?"

17.2   **deus ex machina** *n* : an improbable solution, artificially introduced to resolve a difficulty or untangle a dramatic plot; *Latin* the God from the machine

I FOUND ALICIA eventually. She was sitting outside on a bench. I sat down next to her and took her hand in mine.

"Alicia?"

But she didn't answer. We sat in silence, watching the trees in the back garden swaying in the wind.

"Do you miss him?" I said and she looked at me, her eyes confused.

"I don't know," she said.

"Herbert was Herbert," she added eventually.

We sat together until the cold started to creep through our clothes and Alicia began to shake.

"Come on," I said and helped her to her feet. I took her hand and held it tight, feeling the weak winter sun warming my back.

"Al-eesha?"

The voice came from the other side of the terrace. Alicia clenched my hand and we turned round slowly, taking tiny, hesitant old-lady footsteps. I could feel the pulse in her thumb beating against my palm.

There was a figure. Standing at the end of the terrace. It was a tall, thin, elderly man. A tall, thin, elderly man whose skin was the color of a Callard & Bowser toffee. Or light tan shoe polish.

"Al-eesha," he said.

I looked from him to Alicia and then back to him again and shook my head slowly from side to side. *Cecil?* It was like the kind of scene you get at the end of a Thomas Hardy novel, not in a back garden in the middle of suburbia in the early years of the twenty-first century. I couldn't believe it. Even after all the stories Alicia had told me, I had never quite imagined him as real flesh, real blood.

"What on earth . . . ?" I began to say, but didn't know how to finish the sentence.

He hung back, nervously wringing his hands, waiting. And then, finally, he walked forward, over the paving stones, over the years. He lunged toward Alicia.

"Al-eesha?"

His face was expectant, his eyes shining.

She looked at him, confused. "I thought you were dead."

"I was waiting."

She turned toward me. "Rebecca? I think I'm having one of my turns." But I just shook my head.

She stared at him, then seemed to make up her mind.

"You're fifty-two years too late, Cecil Johnston. Look at me!" And she flapped her liver-spotted hands at her shrunken body. "I'm no use to man nor beast!"

His face sank. "I thought about you every day."

She stood shaking her head from side to side. Then she broke free from my hand and started walking off toward the house before turning around again.

"When did you get so *old*?" she said.

I just stood and stared at him. I had so many questions, but in the end, I couldn't think of anything to say.

17.3 **family** *n* **5** *biol.*: a taxonomic group containing one or more genera

I COULDN'T FIND HER. I looked everywhere, but she'd disappeared. I searched the kitchen, the hall, the conservatory. I went and checked the bathroom. In the lounge, I found Tiffany picking up objects on the sideboard and examining them.

"Lalique, if I'm not very much mistaken," she said, turning over a vase in her hands. "Very nice too. I wonder how much that set them back."

"Have you seen Alicia?"

"No."

"Have you seen the Eames chair? I think it's original."

I walked out into the hallway, where Lucy was saying good-bye to some neighbors.

"Have you seen Alicia?"

"No."

"I can't find her."

"She probably wants some peace and quiet."

I hesitated, unsure whether to tell her . . . but she caught me by the elbow and said, "Come on. We need alcohol."

She glanced quickly at my stomach. "Unless . . ."

But I just shook my head.

We sat around the kitchen table and Suzanne opened a bottle of wine. Lucy went to get three glasses from the cupboard and filled them to the brim. There were only the three of us. People had started to head home, and there was a dispiriting sense of the house emptying. Tiffany was making calls on her phone. My father had gone to the bottle dump. Damien and Charles had both headed back to London. And Alicia was still missing.

Suzanne took a sip of her wine and embarked on an extended monologue about anti-globalization. I slumped in my chair wanting to tell them about Cecil; not knowing how. My head throbbed.

Lucy slapped her wineglass down on the table. "Don't you get fed up with being so fashionable in your views?"

"It's not a question of fashion," said Suzanne.

"Oh come on. You've always liked to be ahead of the game."

"It's principles."

"Yeah, but your generation just had the principles, you didn't have to live with them."

"What do you mean?"

"We just got your crappy leftovers. You had free love. We got divorced parents. You made us think we would be treated equally, that we just had to work hard, and it's all one big fat lie. It's all very well being an armchair feminist, but you never had to put any of it into practice."

"I marched! I went to Greenham!"

"Greenham!"

They were glaring at each other. Lucy and Suzanne have always enjoyed a good row.

"Well what have you ever done?"

"I work. I have to prove myself equal every single day."

"I worked."

"*Before* you got married."

"It was just what you did in those days. You gave up working when you got married." Suzanne sighed and took a swig of her wine. "I wish I could have had a proper career."

"No, you don't."

"I do!"

"No, you don't; you'd have hated it. You sat around espousing equal rights while running off and buying flouncy soft furnishings on the joint account."

My father walked in through the back door. Suzanne looked up.

"Oh there you are James. We're discussing the role of the penis in the workplace. What's your opinion?"

He shifted uncomfortably on his feet. "I think I'll just go and check on the greenhouse," he said and walked straight out the back door again.

"Anyway," said Suzanne. "You never know. Maybe you'll meet a nice man and start a family instead."

Lucy sat in silence for a moment and then erupted with laughter.

"I can't believe you just said that."

Suzanne had the grace to look shamefaced, and stared at her glass.
"No, well, neither can I."

I started to clear my throat, to make a space in which I could
speak. But Suzanne beat me to it.

"To Herbert," she said, raising her glass sadly in one of those sudden changes of register that you only get at funerals. "My father. God
rest his soul."

Lucy and I raised our glasses too and we all chinked them together.

"Herbert," we said and felt instantly sobered.

We sat in silence for a moment or two, the kitchen light bright
overhead, my eyes hurting. I stood up from the table then and went
back through to the lounge. It was almost dark now. Tiffany had
turned on the lamps and was giving Charles detailed instructions on
her mobile phone.

I walked across the room and looked out into the twilight. It took
a moment or two for my eyes to adjust. And then I saw him. Cecil. He
looked awkward and thin, standing there all alone. He'd taken off his
hat and was twisting it around in his hands, staring out into the garden. I watched him and wondered if I should go out and talk to him.
I hesitated, and as I did so, he turned toward me. And it was then that
I saw it.

There, at the top of his face, beneath his hair, above his eyes, was
my forehead. My high, hairless forehead.

I splashed cold water over my face and stared in the bathroom mirror.
I pulled the hair back from my face and gazed at my reflection, looking for other signs; an explanation; something; anything. I felt dizzy
then. Dizzy and faint. The past was spinning back through my head.
I sat down on the edge of the bath and closed my eyes.

When I eventually stood up, the house was quiet. I walked slowly
back through to the lounge. Tiffany was still there, talking into her
phone. I saw her mouth moving but her words drifted over me.

I stood at the window and looked out, hardly breathing. He was
still there. I stared at him, at his eyes, *Damien's* eyes, enmeshed in a
tangle of fine lines.

He was sitting on the bench twisting his hat in his hands. Damn
Alicia and her stories. Did Herbert know? I wondered. Did my mother?

I felt a sudden, intense pang that she wasn't there now. Although I know what she would have said. "You couldn't make it up!" Or "Well! That takes the biscuit!"

I'm wrong though. Because there's Tiffany. She joined me at the window and stared out, confused.

"Who's he? The cleaner?"

"No," I said, turning toward her, taking in her gently sheened tights, her carefully ironed hair, her quizzical-but-loftily-amused expression. "He's your grandfather."

Later, we both stood and watched as Alicia walked out into the garden. She hesitated and then hugged him, her body trembling.

"She's crying," I said. It was only when she turned around that we realized that she wasn't. She was laughing.

Part Eighteen

end *n* : extreme limit, point beyond which a thing does not continue

I

It would be comforting to think of this as a happy ending. Cecil and Alicia, refound. But it isn't. He's too late. We're all too late.

The doctor comes and shakes his head. She's entered the last stage of the disease. Some days she recognizes me. And some days she doesn't. I make cups of tea for her. We both do. Cecil and I. He comes to visit all the time now. He'd lived just fifty miles away all his life, although she never knew.

I've learned only tiny fragments about him, about his life. He's never married, I know that much. He has that gaunt, uncared-for look that comes from a lifetime of wifelessness. I'm filled with the urge to cook him big, heavy meals—Irish stews and lamb hot pots—but he doesn't eat them. He just sits and strokes her hand and says, "I'm here."

Tiffany has taken his reappearance in her stride. "Marvelous material," she says. She's started writing articles about her Afro-Caribbean "heritage" and has bought a book on soul food. I went round to her house the other day and she served Jamaican patties as a starter.

It's Suzanne who goes and spoils it. She comes to visit bearing vegetable soup in a Thermos flask and some homeopathic tablets that look like horse pills. Cecil shuffles into the room then promptly shuffles out again.

"What's he doing here?" she says.

"What?"

"Him."

"You know about Cecil," I say.

"Oh yes, I know about Cecil."

"Suzanne!"

"What? He's supposed to get some sort of medal because he shows up half a century late?"

I hesitate, unsure how much she really knows. How much I should tell her.

"Suzanne?" I finger the edge of my teacup nervously. "There's something I think you should know."

I choose my words carefully, anxious for her feelings. "Cecil . . . ," I say, "is actually my grandfather."

She looks at me bemused. "What makes you think he's your grandfather?"

"He's got my forehead. You can *tell*."

And she shakes her head at me. "Sometimes you're more like your sister than you think you are, you know."

It's Suzanne who knows the full story, not me, not Cecil, not even Alicia anymore.

"Herbert was your grandfather," she says.

"But my *forehead* . . ."

"Haven't we been here before?" she says. And a twenty-year-old shiver runs through me. "Herbert was your grandfather."

I slump into my chair. I can't admit how disappointed I am.

"You don't always get the ending you want, you know," she says.

This isn't the ending I want either. I refuse to believe that Alicia is dying, but the doctor is adamant. It feels like I'm being burgled. I want to make her young again. Make Cecil young again. Put them back together, wipe out the rest of it.

I'm infuriated by it, infuriated by him.

"Why the bloody hell didn't you marry her?" I say to him.

And he just smiles and shakes his head. "She was already married."

"She'd have left Herbert like a shot."

"We believe in families. 'Families Forever,' that is what we say." He refound his faith in prison. Not Adventism; he broke his mother's heart with that. He became a Mormon.

"Out of the frying pan into the fat, if you ask me," I say. And walk out of the room, furious. I can't believe that I've started quoting proverbs.

.   .   .

I sit by Alicia's bed and say, "I'm here." And sometimes she looks up and sees me and smiles. And sometimes she doesn't. I eat chocolate-chip cookies and it works for a bit, but as soon as my mouth is empty, I feel hollow again.

II

ALICIA DRIFTS in and out of time. She wakes up and it's 1948, goes to sleep and it's 1963. She's reeling back through the years.

"I've got papaya for you," I tell her, holding up a fruit.

"Mummy'll tell us off," she says. "You'd better put it back."

Tiffany researches neurologists on the Internet. She comes down in her car to pick Alicia up and take her off to appointments. London, Oxford, Birmingham. I do nothing but sit around and feel helpless. I go out and stand in the driveway and see Alicia's face in the passenger window. She looks at me confused.

"Are we going on a picnic?"

I take her hand through the open window.

"Because I've made some potted shrimp sandwiches. They're in the fridge."

"I've packed them," I lie. "They're in the back."

And she folds her hands across her lap, ready for a treat.

Later, I wonder if Tiffany perhaps *was* taking her on a picnic. And I'm the one who's confused.

"I'm sorry about the sandwiches," I say when she returns.

"Sandwiches?" she says.

III

Suzanne sends me two yellowed pieces of paper in the post. A birth certificate and a death certificate. Cecil Bernard Monroe. Born July 4, 1949; died July 4, 1949.

She picks up the phone on the second ring.

"I don't understand."

"He died," says Suzanne.

"Who died?"

"Alicia's baby."

She pauses.

"I wasn't sure whether to tell you or not. She's blanked it, blocked it out. I thought maybe it should stay that way."

"What baby?"

"Cecil's. The one she was pregnant with when she got married."

"But I thought that was a mistake. That she wasn't . . . That her and Cecil, they never actually . . ."

"For Christ's sake Rebecca, it was 1948, not 1498. People did have sex, you know."

I can hear her breathing down the line.

"So . . . what happened to him?"

"The umbilical cord wrapped itself around his neck. He was alive. But only for a minute or two. A blue baby."

We hang up, but later there's something bothering me and I ring her back.

"So, how did you find out?"

"She had a breakdown. When we were children. And it all came out. Your mother took it very badly."

"Took what very badly?"

"The breakdown."

She hesitates. There's a radio on in the background and I can hear a distant traffic report.

"It affected her, I think," says Suzanne eventually. "She never really trusted Alicia after that. She wouldn't let her mother her. She was . . . less stable somehow, afterward."

The line hummed. There was something bothering me.

"So Alistair's wrong then," I say. "It's nurture. Not nature."

She pauses and then sighs.

"You know Rebecca. I don't really think it's a question of right or wrong. Life happens. And you get on and deal with it."

IV

I'M SITTING at the kitchen table in the dark when Alistair arrives home. I hear him turn the key in the lock, and then his footsteps in the hall. I sit and wait and then say, "What would you say if I told you I was pregnant?"

He jumps, startled.

"I didn't see you there," he says and looks down at the envelopes in his hands.

"What would you say if I told you I was pregnant?"

"Hmm?" He flicks through the stack of letters.

"What would you say if I told you I was pregnant?"

He looks up then and studies me.

"I'd say 'You know my views on the subject.'"

"Okay, bye then," I say and pick up my bag.

He hesitates. "Where are you going?"

But I don't bother to answer. I just carry on walking toward the door.

"Rebecca?"

I stop and turn toward him.

"I know about your graduate student."

I watch him as he opens his mouth and then closes it again. He taps the envelopes against his hands, as if he's weighing something up in his mind.

"Oh," he says finally.

I gaze at him, uncomprehending. I can't understand why he's not denying it. I never thought for a moment that he wouldn't deny it.

I slump into a chair.

"Shouldn't we talk about this?" he says eventually.

I shake my head. He's about to say something but seems to have trouble forming the words.

"So? Are you . . . ?"

His lips open but he stutters invisibly. I watch him until, finally, the word falls off his tongue.

"Pregnant?"

I nod my head slowly up and down.

"Christ!" he says and sits down heavily in the chair opposite. After a minute or two, he looks up at me. His eyes are pleading.

"Rebecca?"

And suddenly I know that it's all going to be okay. I feel weak with relief. He wants it. He wants *me*. I wait for him to form the words. He opens his mouth and I see his lips move, but I can't hear what he's saying.

"What?" I say.

"I said, I've fallen in love with somebody else."

He hesitates.

"I'll pay, of course, if you want to get rid of it."

V

My skin is puffy and inflamed, and when I scratch my elbows, dry scales fall like snowflakes to the floor. My cuticles bleed.

I go to see a rented flat in East London with damp walls and a broken fridge, and take it on the spot. I buy a car, paying in cash, although the clutch rattles and there is moss growing between the windows and the rubber seals.

"Nice little motor that," says the salesman. "Handy being able to go as you please."

"Fuck off," I say and hold out my hand for the keys. I drive away at speed, the road ahead blurred and fuzzy.

I go to Safeway, but when I reach the frozen food section, I rest my head against the cool of the freezer cabinets and my tears drip onto a box of fish fingers. I watch translucent trails slide across Captain Birdseye's face. When I finally look up, the shoppers are still shopping around me. Nobody has noticed. I slam my trolley into a promotional stand of shampoo and walk out of the shop with a tin of sweetcorn under my coat.

VI

THE SPECIALIST says it's just a matter of time. That the synapses of her brain are becoming choked and tangled. That they're dying from within. That soon she will forget everything: names, faces, dates, a whole life.

She's already forgotten how to eat. A nurse comes in, three times a day, and lifts her, and chivies her, and spoons vegetables into her mouth as if she's a doll and it's time to play. I watch her as she chats to Alicia, not noticing that she receives no reply. She keeps her running. When all I can do is sit and watch and wonder when she'll forget me. When her heart will forget how to pump blood around her body. When her lungs will forget how to breathe.

She is sitting propped up in her armchair, a rug across her knees. It's one of those rare days when she seems to emerge from behind a thick cloud of unknowing. Her voice is unsteady.

"I woke up that first morning after the wedding, and I knew I wasn't pregnant."

"Alicia?"

"Cecil had never done *that* to me."

Gently, I turn to her and say, "You slept with Cecil, remember. In Filey."

"I tried to will my baby back to life, but it was no good."

I hesitate.

"You slept with Cecil. In Filey."

She drifts off for a moment or two, her eyes fixing upon a point in the ceiling, and then she returns.

"Did I?" she says and looks at me, frightened. Her face contorts and then she clenches her fists and starts pummeling her lap with her hands.

The doctor says it's the Alzheimer's. She can't distinguish between what's real and what she's chosen to believe is real. I sit and stroke her hand and wish I could perform the same trick. For five minutes I'm still with Alistair, my mother is alive and Alicia is well. We're all living happily together on Walton Mountain running around in patchwork dungarees and eating homegrown vegetables.

"Time to change her catheter," says Cecil, walking into the room. I watch a thin line of dribble escape from her mouth. When I arrive home, the flat is empty and the milk has gone off. I throw it in the sink and watch it go down the drain in thick, viscous clumps. Later, I walk into the kitchen and it's still there: the smell of death.

VII

"Cecil. He was called Cecil."

She's in her bed, the sheets pulled up around her, only her withered neck and her head in view. Her hair has thinned. Almost like baby hair now, fine and downy. I can see her scalp.

"I know," I say.

"My baby. He was called Cecil."

I hold her body as it shakes and trembles, fifty years of forgetting rising like fat to the surface.

Everyone says that I'm overreacting. My father is forced into action. He comes down to London to take me out for lunch.

"There's nothing you can do," he says.

I'm unclear how this is supposed to make me feel better.

Alicia rings me and I drive two hours to go and see her.

"What's Rebecca doing here?" she asks Cecil.

I stay an hour then drive home playing the radio at full volume, stopping only to buy three packets of fig rolls at the service station. When I look at Alicia's face, my mother's stares back at me.

VIII

I'M KEEPING the baby. And everyone's thrilled. *Thrilled.* My family fusses over me. I've become one of them. A breeder. It feels as if I'm being overtaken by something else. As if I'm part of a single mononuclear organism that wants its own kind to propagate, no matter what.

Everyone keeps congratulating me. "You must be so happy," they say. I nod at them. I must be. I just don't understand how.

IX

ALICIA TURNS to me in the middle of her dinner.

"You've left Alistair."

I nod my head at her and feel my eyes filling up, the sphincter of my stomach contracting. I have yet to master my self-pity.

She looks at me for a moment and then says, "Good."

I arrest my face mid-sob and look at her. "I didn't know you didn't like Alistair."

She is staring at the wall; I can see the milky cataracts of her eyes. She looks at me steadily, and then says, "He didn't make you happy, did he?"

It's as if I've received an oracle. I sit and stare at the bars of the electric fire. He didn't make me happy. I listen to the clock ticking and wonder why I hadn't realized that years ago. I blow my nose noisily on a piece of old tissue I find in my pocket. He didn't make me happy. And I loved him anyway.

She turns toward me again. My grandmother, the soothsayer.

"I've got enough starch to see me through the winter," she says confidentially.

I spend the evening watching Cecil watching Alicia. When he lifts a hankie to wipe away the spittle from her lips, I find it unbearably tender and turn on the news. I need to see people starving and being blown up by bombs. I am desperate for other people's unhappinesses.

X

I'VE BECOME OBESE. I lollop around inside vast rolls of fat. I can't control my own body. Alicia is wasting away. Her skin hangs empty off her frame, while mine fills and plumps. Everything about me is growing and swelling. Not just my belly, but my hips, my bottom, my ankles. I have fat hands. My baby is growing inside me, unaware that I'm surrounded by death. My daughter. I saw her picture on the screen at the hospital. A kidney bean that made me weep.

XI

I AM CULTIVATING my anger, nurturing it. I stomp through the London streets, furious that everyone else is living. I join the Anti-Racism League, a radical women's group, the Socialist Worker's Party—anywhere people will get cross and swear at things. I go to a meeting in an unheated north London hall. I have no idea what anyone is talking about. At the end, I'm given a cup of lukewarm tea with too much milk and a Bourbon biscuit.

"Is it a boy or a girl?" asks a woman standing next to me. She's in her early sixties and has the sort of no-nonsense haircut and plain face that makes me want to bury myself in her bosom and beg for maternal love.

"A girl."

She shakes her head and says, "There'll be troubles ahead for her, then."

XII

ALICIA CALLS ME in the middle of the night.

"You've got it all, haven't you?"

"Got what?"

"Everything. Cecil. All that."

"I've got it."

"Good," she says. Satisfied.

I hesitate.

"Why does it matter so much?"

I can hear the static buzzing on the line.

"It's all that matters."

"Alicia?" I say, but she doesn't answer. Eventually, I realize that she must have put down the receiver on the table.

"Where's Victor?" I hear her say in the background. "I wanted to tell him that we're out of soap powder."

XIII

Dear Sir,

It has recently come to my attention that one of your employees, a park warden with a dog called Duke, is a racist who believes, and furthermore, acts on the belief, that the "blacks are the ones who make all the trouble."

It is people like him, and organizations like yours, where SOME-ONE, in all likelihood, knows that this man holds such views, that have led to my present situation, namely that my grand-mother married the wrong man and is now dying.

To continue to pay my council tax would be tantamount to con-doning this man's behavior, and your irresponsibility as an organ-ization in continuing to employ him.

I am therefore canceling my standing order and enclose an invoice for £6,742, namely the monies paid to you in the last seven years, in which I have been resident in the borough.

Yours sincerely,
Rebecca Monroe.

Tiffany says I'm being childish, and I hesitate for half a day, but then go and see Alicia again, and sour-tasting bile rises up into my throat. I send it by registered post.

XIV

I FORCE MYSELF to go to a prenatal class, but I can't stand the sight of so much happiness. The room is overheated and feels stuffy with emotion. I sit on my yoga mat and fail to reach my toes.

"You have to have a partner," says the instructor. "Otherwise you won't be able to do the exercises."

"My grandmother's dying," I say, desperate for sympathy. I've started confiding in total strangers. Yesterday I told the assistant in the newsagent's and she gave me a free packet of Tic Tacs.

The instructor looks at me for a moment. She has fashionably cut hair, colored at the ends, and superior posture.

"You poor thing," she says and I snivel in agreement. "You still have to have a partner, though. Otherwise you won't be able to do the exercises."

The rest of the class stop exchanging notes about their midwives and listen attentively.

"He was having an *affair*."

The instructor is on the verge of saying something but walks over to the CD player and puts on some whale music instead.

The next week Lucy insists on coming with me.

"Are you the birth partner?" asks the instructor.

"I'm *the* partner," says Lucy. "Post-op transsexual. We're hoping for a hermaphrodite."

Afterward we go for a cup of tea.

"I never liked him anyway," she says, and then sees my face.

I concentrate on eating my custard tart. I lick the spoon then lift the cup to my face so she can't see my tears. I don't know how you're supposed to stop loving someone.

"It's easy," says Lucy. "You just have to imagine him in bed with Miss Big Tits."

XV

A WOMAN ON THE BUS turns to me and says, "Pregnant women are so beautiful." And I'm filled with a desire to smash her face against the window.

I get off at the next stop and waddle through the streets until I develop a blister on my heel and my legs start throbbing. My daughter kicks me in the stomach. I sit down on a bench, winded by guilt.

Later that day, I read an article Tiffany has written about teenage single mothers.

"They're just looking for something to love," she claims. I don't understand when this became such a crime.

I ring up Tiffany to tell her that I've written a letter of complaint to her editor. Although it won't do any good. She encourages hate mail. It makes her look "controversial" and is worth another ten grand a year.

"Alicia's looking worse," I say.

I hear her hesitate at the other end of the line.

"She's had good innings, Rebecca. Maybe she wants to die."

"Nobody *wants* to die," I hiss. Then hang up quickly before either of us can realize what I've said.

The next week, Tiffany writes about the modern inability to come to terms with death, and I get into my car to drive over to her house. I want to rip her arms out of their sockets but am diverted by an all-night bakery. I fill my mouth with warm bagels and fall asleep on the backseat curled up in a ball. During the night, I lie and listen to the sound of drunks peeing against my car tires.

XVI

My father comes to visit me again. I suspect that Suzanne has sent him. He sits at my new kitchen table, and when he tries to move his elbows, they stick to the surface of the wipe-clean tablecloth.

He brought me a self-assembly cot and the new family tree he's drawn up.

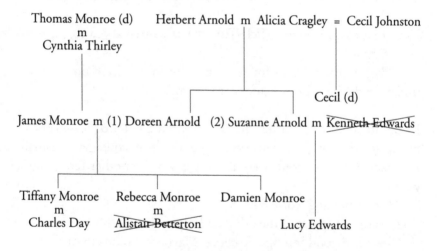

Figure 16. **The Monroe Family Tree (Revised)**

There's special software apparently that enables you to build family trees for families like mine. It has symbols for the divorced branches and the step-branches and the half-branches; dotted lines for unmarried alliances and estranged spouses.

"You can even create 'family orchards,'" he says, "with peripheral trees budding off in divergent directions."

I look at it, then say, "I'm still married to Alistair."

He shifts uncomfortably in his seat. "I know," he says. "I was just trying to be realistic."

We sit in silence for a moment and then I turn and look my father in the eye.

"He cheated on me."

He hesitates for a moment.

"I'll get Suzanne to ring you," he says and moves off quickly toward the car.

XVII

IT'S THE FIRST TIME I've been single in a decade, and no man will come near me. I am desperate for sex but have become Untouchable. I start taking the Tube, pointless journeys to Willesden Green and Clapham South, just to be able to look at men, to make them aware of my presence. I heave myself onto the train and throw them meaningful looks.

It's usually the women, though. Who stand up. The men read their newspapers and pretend not to see me.

I am desperate to feel alive. I want to feel dead. I ring Alistair to see if he'll sleep with me.

"You're the only person I can ask."

He doesn't answer immediately.

"I don't think that would be a very good idea," he says eventually.

"Who ith it?" says a voice in the background.

Later, I picture them having sex. Then, more cheerfully, being consumed by twenty-foot flames.

"It's a natural part of the splitting up process," says Suzanne on the phone. "You're bound to feel anger."

I think about it for a moment.

"But I really *do* want them to be consumed by twenty-foot flames," I say.

XVIII

Snapshot 1

Sitting by my grandmother's bed watching her sleep. She opens her eyes suddenly and looks at me.

"Doreen? I told you to tidy your room."

I look over my shoulder. But there's only me in the room.

"I did," I say.

"Good." And she closes her eyes again.

In the bathroom, I stand and stare at myself in the mirror. When Tiffany arrives, she says, "You look like you've seen a ghost."

I say, "I think I just have."

Later we sit together and watch television mindlessly. It's a quiz show with two families competing against each other.

"I was always jealous of you," says Tiffany.

I try to turn to look at her, but my body has been cemented to the armchair. My neck swivels, owl-like.

"What?"

"You never felt the need to pretend to be anyone else."

We sit in front of the TV set and watch the news and the weather and a nature program about orangutans and I realize that I don't know anything at all.

Snapshot 2

There's an empty seat in the middle of the Tube carriage and I heave myself toward it, slumping gratefully down. I've got three shopping bags and my toes have swollen inside my shoes, fat little tubes of flesh that rub sweatily against my socks. I haven't washed my hair in three days. It sticks to the sides of my head in lank tendrils.

The man sitting next to me says, "There's something very sexy about pregnant women."

I turn to look at him. He's in his forties, with a cheap executive briefcase at his feet and a soiled newspaper in his hands. There's a small fleck of spittle on his lower lip. I stare at his five o'clock shadow, the large black pores on the side of his nose, his gray polyester stay-pressed trousers, slightly bobbled. He wears his tie loose at the neck.

We get off at the next stop together and take a taxi to my flat. He tries to be tender at first, but I grab him impatiently. I don't want his tenderness. I want to feel alive. I want to be split in two and left in pieces on the bed.

He reaches down and opens me like I'm a brown manilla envelope.

Afterward, he flops on the mound of my belly as if he's been beached by the tide.

"I wouldn't let my wife have sex like that if she was pregnant," he says.

XIX

A HEADLINE in the newspaper: "Woman, 38, Struck Twice by Lightning." Any time now I'm expecting them to find the devil in the detail.

I phone Peter, my supervisor, to tell him that I finished my thesis. It's hard to say which of us is the more surprised by this development. He talks on and on, and I stare at the typescript out of the corner of my eye. It's about the discourses of post–sexual revolution Britain; the impact of Americanization from 1945 to the present day; the interplay between private lives and the dominant culture. Mostly though it's about *Dallas*.

I hear Peter distantly at the other end of the line. "So, what have you decided to call it?"

I hesitate.

"The Family Tree."

"It's not very . . . academic," he says eventually. "It sounds like one of those novels. You know, three generations of women blah blah blah. Triumph over adversity. After many trials, it all turns out okay in the end."

"Soap opera and its associated literary forms, family-based dramas, etc., are often denigrated or overlooked by critics," I say. "This is, in part, due to the fact that they attract a predominantly female audience."

I can hear Peter breathing at the other end of the line. We both know I never answer him back.

"Whatever," he says eventually.

"Anyway," I say. "I don't think it does."

"Does what?"

"Turn out okay in the end."

XX

I PHONE ALISTAIR in the middle of the night.

"Why did you marry me?"

"What time is it?"

His voice is blurred, confused. It's 2:30 A.M. I listen to him thinking at the end of the line.

"Because I loved you."

I wait. For the catch. But none comes. He's silent.

"Is that it?"

"Yes," he says.

I replace the receiver. My tears fall onto the polypropylene tablecloth, lying in pools next to the crumbs and coffee stains and grains of salt. I dial the number again. My number.

"He'd be eleven now," I say.

I wait for Alistair to answer. I can hear him breathing. The line clicks.

"There's nobody at home to take your call," says the voice. "So pleathe leave your methage after the tone."

I hang up and kick the fridge until my toes start to bleed.

XXI

ALICIA'S CHEEKS have sunk in on themselves. Her eyes are hollow sockets. When I pick up her wrist, it's as frail as a sparrow's claw.

I sit for hours with her in near-silence. Sometimes, still, she surfaces.

I watch her rising from the depths, her eyes turning toward mine, her pupils shrinking into focus. "Will you promise me one thing?"

I look at her in astonishment. She has never asked anything of me, ever.

"What? Anything. Of course."

She hesitates.

"That you'll call her Doreen."

My heart stops beating.

"Isn't there *anything* else?" It's as if Fate has come knocking.

"Little Doreen," she says.

I feel like I'm being suffocated by my own body.

XXII

When the moment comes of course, I'm not there. Tiffany phones me.

"She's on her way out."

I stagger down the stairs and hoist myself into the driver's seat. My stomach presses against the steering wheel.

I drive across London, crossing red lights, swearing at motorists, beeping my horn.

But I'm too late. I'm on the motorway when my cell phone rings.

I pull over onto the hard shoulder and watch car after car speed past. Mine shakes in their wake.

"She's dead," says Suzanne.

I put down the phone and try to slump forward, to rest my head on the steering wheel, but my belly's too big. I have to lean back in my seat in the end, wedged into position. I watch the cars pass until they blur. Streams of snot run down my face. I want to stay on the hard shoulder forever. I can't see. I can't move. I'm trapped. The trucks scream past the car. I open the window and howl at the traffic. My grandmother forgot how to breathe.

XXIII

LATER, it starts raining. I sit and listen to the metallic clatter of the drops striking the car's roof. I don't know why but it calms me. I turn on the ignition and indicate right. I have to go back into the stream of traffic. I sit and wait for a gap. The fluttering in my stomach finally stops. I feel like I'm back in the dual-control car in which I learned to drive. My hands are on the wheel. But Little Doreen is manning the controls.

XXIV

I DON'T COPE so well with the second funeral. When Alicia's casket is lowered into the ground, I want to throw myself on top of it.

It's not a pretty sight. An eight-months pregnant woman wailing uncontrollably. Tiffany and my father try to restrain me, but my layers of fat get in the way. My triple chin wobbles with emotion. The only person I can bear near me is Cecil. He touches the inside of my elbow and it soothes me instantly. He stands by the side of the grave, his hat in his hand, his expression unreadable.

My face is red and blotchy, my eyes swollen. I can hardly see the grave. We throw earth onto the coffin and my daughter kicks me in the abdomen with no sense of the attendant cliché.

I don't even keep my promise. When she slithers into the world in a puddle of blood and mucus and pain, the nurses lay her on my belly. Her eyes, huge, blue, otherworldly, stare at me. Her lips are pursed in fury. I suspect she knows that I almost consigned her to a hospital waste incinerator.

"Alicia," I say finally.

Later, she starts crying and I feel the first hot rush of love and guilt and fear.

Acknowledgments

Special thanks to my three best readers: Isabel Henton, Louise Crowe, and Anna Sutton.

To David Mossman.

To all my family but especially my mum, Pat Cadwalladr, and my sister, Sian Cadwalladr.

To Nicky Beaumont, Max Davidson, Mark Espiner, Mark and Maggie Martin, Ricardo Pollack, Zoe Waldie, Peter and Mary Wood, and Steven Pinker.

To Jonny Geller at Curtis Brown and Deborah Schneider at Gelfman-Schneider; and, last but certainly not least, to Jane Lawson at Doubleday and Laurie Chittenden at Dutton.

Nominated for the Specialist Writer of the Year in the British Press Awards, Carole Cadwalladr is a journalist and lives in the UK. *The Family Tree* is her first novel.

Select Bibliography

During the course of writing this novel, I found the following books particularly illuminating and would like to gratefully acknowledge the authors.

Jennifer Ackerman, *Fate in the House of Chance: A Natural History of Heredity* (2001)

Alex Comfort, *The Joy of Sex* (1971)

Jilly Cooper, *Class* (new edition, 1999)

Richard Dawkins, *The Selfish Gene* (revised edition, 1989)

Richard Dawkins, *The Extended Phenotype: The Long Reach of the Gene* (revised edition, 1989)

Jared Diamond, *Why Is Sex Fun?: The Evolution of Human Sexuality* (1997)

Gerd Gigerenzer, *Reckoning with Risk: Learning to Live with Uncertainty* (2002)

Frances Hodgson Burnett, *A Little Princess, The Story of Sara Crewe,* (new edition, 1996)

Nancy Mitford, *Noblesse Oblige* (1956, new edition, 2002)

Steve Jones, *In the Blood: God, Genes and Destiny* (1966)

Steve Jones, Y: *The Descent of Man* (2003)

John Ratey, *A User's Guide to the Brain,* (2001)

Matt Ridley, *Genome: The Autobiography of a Species in 23 Chapters* (2000)

Steven Rose, *The Making of Memory: From Molecules to Mind* (new edition, 2003)

Marguerite Patten, *Cookery in Colour* (1972)

Trevor Phillips and Mike Phillips, *Windrush: The Irresistible Rise of Multi-Racial Britain* (1998)

Steven Pinker, *The Language Instinct* (1994)

Steven Pinker, *How the Mind Works* (1998)

Steven Pinker, *The Blank Slate: The Modern Denial of Human Nature* (2002)

David Shenk, *The Forgetting: Alzheimer's: Portrait of an Epidemic* (2001)

Delia Smith, *Complete Cookery Course* (revised edition, 1992)

Oneykachi Wambu, *Empire Windrush: Fifty Years of Writing About Black Britain*